Where is Creativity?

T0362216

Where is Creativity? A Multi-disciplinary Approach goes beyond the orthodox image of creativity as laying inside the brain-mind, to explore how and why it also emerges from relationships between people, from physical spaces such as workplaces and cities, as a result of new media technology and the Web, and due to the effects of broad contexts of the economy and industry. It explores contemporary psychological, sociological, anthropological, economic and philosophical debates concerning creativity in an accessible way, which non-specialist and creative practitioners can appreciate, culminating in a picture of the anatomy of creativity which seeks to provide a concrete guide to the 'doing' of creativity to complement a deeper understanding of its nature and origins.

The book will be useful for teaching staff and students; businesses and practitioners; and professionals and policy-makers working within a wide range of creative and innovation-based industries.

Jim Shorthose works across the different aspects of the creative ecology – in higher education, advising creative businesses and working with cultural organizations. He is the author of several books which traverse the spaces between theoretical debates about creativity and concrete artistic practice.

Neil Maycroft is Reader in Art and Design at the University of Lincoln, UK, and is the author of several books and numerous articles on material culture, as well as broader discussions of the nature and origins of creativity, especially as applied to design.

Where is Creativity?

A Multi-disciplinary Approach

Jim Shorthose and Neil Maycroft

Routledge
Taylor & Francis Group

LONDON AND NEW YORK

First published 2017 by Routledge

2 Park Square, Milton Park, Abingdon, Oxfordshire OX14 4RN

52 Vanderbilt Avenue, New York, NY 10017

Routledge is an imprint of the Taylor & Francis Group, an informa business

First issued in paperback 2020

British Library Cataloguing-in-Publication Data
A catalogue record for this book is available from the British Library

Library of Congress Cataloging-in-Publication Data
Names: Shorthose, Jim, 1959– author. | Maycroft, Neil, 1963– author.
Title: Where is creativity? : a multi-disciplinary approach / Jim Shorthose and Neil Maycroft.
Description: 1 Edition. | New York : Routledge, 2017. | Includes bibliographical references and index.
Identifiers: LCCN 2016055876 | ISBN 9781472437266 (hardback) | ISBN 9781315547466 (ebook)
Subjects: LCSH: Creative ability. | Creative ability in business.
Classification: LCC BF408 .S4496 2017 | DDC 153.3/5—dc23
LC record available at https://lccn.loc.gov/2016055876

ISBN: 978-1-4724-3726-6 (hbk)
ISBN: 978-0-367-60595-7 (pbk)

Typeset in Bembo
by Apex CoVantage, LLC

As always, we dedicated this book to our kids, George, Raya and Rose.

Contents

Tables

Preface

Truth to tell, the study of creativity remains a marginal topic in psychology and related fields, and quantum advances are few and far between. So far as I have been able to ascertain, in the past two decades no powerful new approaches have threatened dominant concepts, frameworks, or paradigms. . . . That said, we may be on the cusp of important breakthroughs in two areas. Turning first to the realm of computers, intelligent systems have advanced enormously in recent decades. . . . The other realm poised for breakthrough is that of the biological understanding of creativity.

(Gardner 2011. p. xx [Preface])

We tend to agree with Howard Gardner that the dominant approach to the study of creativity does appear to be predominantly psychological, and that the growth of research within neuroscience and the related fields of artificial intelligence are indeed feeding into that picture. However, whilst neuroscience is developing apace, we are sceptical as to the degree to which this field of study will lead to great breakthroughs in the understanding of creativity. We are even more sceptical about the rather florid claims that are made about artificial intelligence. It seems that neuroscience wants to become the once and for all answer to the question of creativity. But this assumes that creativity is a 'thing' to be uncovered. It is our view that the thing we call creativity is a large number of different things, which we sometimes experience as flashes of inspiration, but sometimes come from a long, drawn-out process of hard work and boring detail. Which sometimes is the result of individual creative thinking, and sometimes the result of collaborative teamwork. The idea of a 'breakthrough' to uncover some secret, so far undiscovered centre to this is to misunderstand the nature of creativity as a varied, multi-faceted, sometimes planned, sometimes haphazard series of interlocking processes. And to see neuroscience as the best route to a future mapping of this is questionable to say the least. Neuroscience is the current fashion, but we would do well to remember that only twenty years or so ago it would have been genetics, claims of the 'creativity gene', which would have been the flavour of the month. I suspect that eventually neuroscience will come up with the idea that creativity is an 'all brain experience'. That is, we will be told that creativity is 'somewhere in the brain', and that will not really tell us anything much other than what we already know. And then someone from way back in history will remember that creativity also resides in the body, the hand and the fingers too! Neuroscience has a role in understanding creativity, but so do many other perspectives. It is not a special, scientific and therefore privileged insight. As for the idea of the next ratchet up, artificial intelligence, this will require us to accept that 'one day' we will be able to create creativity. Well, firstly, we can already do creativity. Secondly, to create artificial creativity we will need to be able to get down to the core of what human consciousness is. Not only can we not conceive of how we can uncover the answers, we cannot conceive of how to approach the questions. Can we really ever be able to 'prove' what human consciousness is for everyone, for all time, for all experiences? No. We will presumably one day end up having smart machines, but will this really be human intelligence? And will this really be creativity? No. Creativity is at one and the same time vastly more complex than that, but also much, much more simple than that. Creativity is at one and the same time born of such far sighted and imaginative thinking, but also contradictory, accidental, irrational and just plain crazy at the same time. Pursuing such a 'scientific' approach is, let us be clear, to involve rationally planned research agendas, unified research methods, reproducible research, testable truth claims and objectively demonstrable outcomes. And such an approach to something so multi-faceted as creativity is so far wide of any credible mark of all the things it encompasses, that we can say that it is simply to ask the wrong types of questions. There is a very big, possibly insurmountable, epistemological and perhaps ontological gulf here between what neuroscience and AI proponents claim, and what will ever be feasible. It is not so much that not enough progress has so far been made, it is more that an inappropriate stance is being adopted and hyped.

But there is a cultural corollary to all this noise about scientific breakthroughs about creativity. As we will discuss at greater length in Chapter 1, this triad of 'scientific' psychology, neuroscience and AI stuff both flows from and reproduces, is both driver of and consequence of, a predominant cultural myth. That creativity is best studied as individual phenomenon flowing from isolated 'mental units' is questionable. Much of what we want to say throughout our book takes this myth to task, and suggests that creativity lies as much within many spaces and relationships – between people, the relationships people have with their places and with the contexts in which creative things happen. In terms of jargon, we might say that creativity is highly over-determined. A scientific approach would need to tease out these over-determined 'causes' to lay out specific effects thereof, a difficult task given that each time creativity happens it includes accidental, haphazard and under-experienced factors. We are sceptical as to the possibilities of this, largely because we see such an approach as epistemologically questionable and limited.

We tend to take a more social view of things. As Chapter 1 of our argument will make clear, we do not buy into the basic notion of the isolated individual as a psychological 'unit' acting or reacting in isolation from the relationships and cultural situations which shape and order our creative lives. The laboratory of cognitive psychology, neuroscience and AI was never very convincing to us. But there are more positive reasons to take a more social view of creativity. As we hope to show after Chapter 1, there are many, much more convincing arguments stemming from various relationship-based orientations which situate creativity in far more likely settings. Our more aggregated social view comes from a reading of these debates, but also from our own personal experiences as creative people. We have experienced first-hand the collaborative nature of creativity, its link to city life, the differences which the Web has brought and, inevitably, how the broad context of work, a capitalist economy and broad cultural aspects have impacted upon it. It seems facile to us to try to understand something so inherently social and cultural as the act of creation in any other way. Science is an insightful and far reaching tool of enquiry when used in the right place, for understanding the right target. But it is not always thus. The over application of a scientific bent, especially as it has been driven through the 'social sciences' in the past two hundred years, has had many less than positive consequences, such that it has been used where it is not appropriate, and has developed its own kind of arrogance. Certain aspects of the creative brain-mind are perhaps amenable to a certain degree of scientific study and can add to a broader debate, but our view is that the vast majority of the terrain to be studied for a holistic account is better covered using other vehicles – other less scientific branches of psychology, sociology and anthropology, the testimonies and experiences of creative people themselves, the histories of our places and technologies, and the dull compulsion of the economic. There are many narratives which are germane to a broader study of creativity, which have the added bonus of not implicitly sponsoring the myth of the lone creative person. To use a cliché, we are all in this together.

But we also take a more social view for political reasons. The myth of the lone creative person is but a short cultural step from the view that only some people have it and, more worryingly, others do not. As we will argue in several contexts throughout the book, this seems a rather absurd argument, which denies, or at least limits, the possibility that all humans can flourish through their creativity. It seems part of the cultural underpinning which separates and divides some people from others, 'professionals' from 'amateurs', 'celebrities' who are idolized for their often rather dubious creative credentials from 'others' of lesser talents. If 'pop will (eventually) eat itself', so will creativity if it continues along such a path. But of course it never will because we all know only too well that we are in touch with our own creative experiences. Even if it brings us no celebrity, we all know that our inherent human capabilities to cook a meal for our loved ones, make our children laugh, to choose the right dress for the right occasion are all highly creative acts born of skill and insight. Whilst the elitist protestation implicit in the cultural myth of the lone creative person will no doubt continue, it is facile for more serious studies of creativity to ignore this wider panoply of activities. But it is also damaging to continue this denial if it prevents our society and culture, our education system and other cultural institutions from developing more open conversations about how we can all be, indeed become, more through our mutual capacities for joint creativity. To put it bluntly, creativity will be more creative if it is enabled to become more democratic. And this is the reason why our book has ended up rather critical, indeed more critical than even we expected when we set out. The polemical attitude runs throughout, but the particularly polemical points are clearly marked. As we have said, we take a more social view.

But all this is not to say that we have a definitive account of creativity. As can perhaps be appreciated from what we have said so far, we do not really think such an account is ever truly possible. And this is one of the main reasons we changed tack from our initial task. When we first proposed writing this book, we were asked by the publishers for a one sentence description of the kind of book we had in mind. We replied with the idea of 'offering both a multi-disciplinary over-view of current conceptual insights into the nature of creativity, and applied research ideas germane to its concrete practice'. Later in the proposal, we also said, 'The proposed book will be useful for teaching staff and students; businesses and practitioners; professionals and policy-makers working within a wide range of creative and innovation-based industries'.

A big topic. Maybe we are taking on too much? Which is one reason we are starting with our disclaimer about avoiding anything which sounds like a definitive account of creativity. That certainly would be too much. As we have said, we are convinced that creativity comes in many different shapes and sizes, and that the creative processes of any one individual will differ each time they do it. We are also convinced that different people will have their own idiosyncratic ways of doing their creativity. So each instance of creativity will have many different ways in and out for each person, and will involve myriad components which the person in question may or may not be fully aware of. And then we must multiply that by the number of creative people. Which is everyone. So instead of a futile attempt at defining what creativity 'is', we will try to offer some useful insights by approaching things more obliquely. Because of our social view, and our belief that creativity resides within myriad relationships, we have focused upon the question of 'where' it resides. We think this enables us to explore a broad, multi-disciplinary sweep of arguments and debates so as to pursue a more holistic account. This wider net seems to offer a better way of accounting for its multi-faceted and aggregated nature.

And in pursuit of this we have constructed an argument, a critical narrative designed to deal with the question of the different relationships and spaces in which creativity might reside. We have not been concerned too much with quoting every commentary, citing every biographical statement, recognizing every theory or experience of creativity. We hope that we successfully constructed an insightful and interesting account which does its job of presenting some key contours of germane debates. We have not been concerned to show our erudition just for the sake of it. If we have failed to mention something or someone you feel was necessary, or have not laid out a particular argument sufficiently fully, then we ask for your patience.

We have tried to make our critical account of the complex concepts and debates as easily digestible as possible. This is not always easy, but it is an approach which fits into a larger series of books which have been the centre of our attention for several years now. The fulcrum of this is a kind of a 'translation' service. After many years of teaching in higher education, allied with taking an active role within our local creative network to offer advice, both creative and business, one overriding thing has become very clear. There is a wealth of ideas, concepts and debates which offer great impetus to creative practitioners of all kinds. But not many creative practitioners have the time or inclination to become expert enough in those academic debates to become sufficiently aware of, or able to extract, the valuable lessons within them. They have their studio practices, and do not want to become experts in philosophy, or economics, or psychology in order to develop that practice. That is where the translation service we offer comes in.

We have published several such books within this spirit, and this is the latest one. It tries to do the same job. But this brings certain requirements. To make the translation effective, a mixing of theoretical points and practical applications is necessary if is to become useful within concrete creative practitioners. So whilst we have started our account of the creative person, and have gradually worked out to ever broader scales – towards relationships between people, to places such as cities, to the new media of the Web, and out to the broad social and economic contexts by referring to current academic debates, we end with something which tries to be of a more practical nature, an anatomy of creativity. We should say however that we offer this anatomy and account of the 'stages' of creativity with a certain hesitancy. We see it as a useful part of our account, but at the same time as often too mechanical. And this is why we end on what is perhaps our central point.

Because we take our social view, because we see creativity as residing in many relationships, because we see it as over-determined and an ever moveable feast, and because we see the talk of a linear anatomy of creativity as too mechanical – for all these intertwined reasons we ultimately take a dialectical view of creativity. Such an approach seems to us a better way to see the contradictory nature of creativity, born of ever interpenetrating opposites, semi-, under- or un-experienced facets, tentative explorations and imaginative leaps that seem to come from nowhere as well as the clear-sighted plans and rational ways forward.

But this is now starting to pre-empt the substance of the book itself, so let's stop with these preliminary statements and get on with things.

Jim Shorthose
Nottingham
October 2016

Chapter 1

Situating creativity

In his book *On Creativity: Interviews Explaining the Process* (2003), John Tusa writes the following:

> 'Creative', 'creation', 'creativity' are some of the most overused and ultimately debased words in the language. Stripped of any special significance by a generation of bureaucrats, civil servants, managers and politicians, lazily used as political margarine to spread approvingly and inclusively over any activity with a non-material element to it. 'Creative' has become almost unuseable.
>
> (Tusa 2003. p. 6)

Well, Mr. Tusa seems to be able to use it OK, but his ideas represent far more troubling problems than this small piece of self-contradiction. He seems to believe that an 'ideology' is at work here, one which has been responsible for this relegation of the idea of creativity to such worthlessness. And he seems to believe that Primary Schools are the leading edge of this ideology!

> If the origins of this ideology can be traced anywhere, they surely lie in a generation of primary schools where anyone's PlayDo model, anyone's finger painting, anyone's clay bowl was deemed as praiseworthy as anyone else's.
>
> (Tusa 2003. p. 6)

Maybe Mr. Tusa is just a grumpy old man whom we can afford to just ignore. But behind his grumpiness there are some deeper and more pervasive problems. Although he uses the phrase *creative process* within the title of his book, his rejection of the 'ideology' he identifies rejects the *creative outcomes* of primary school children. This is a confused position. He should perhaps recognize that the primary school kids are being encouraged to take part in the very creative process which he seems to value. That they are being encouraged to view the possibility of creativity being a part of their lives. Could Mr. Tusa give the primary school kids perhaps a little more time to become another Anthony Caro, Lucian Freud or Grayson Perry?

But there are even deeper problems with the view which Mr. Tusa seems to represent. He goes on:

> The trouble (*with the ideology of primary schools*) was that a laudable recognition of worthiness . . . sidled evasively into the proposition that everyone's faltering acts of creation were as 'good' as anyone else's. This is manifest nonsense.
>
> (Tusa 2003. p. 6)

Firstly, as many, many interviews and biographies of creative people have shown, over and over again, acts of creation are always 'faltering'. Secondly, creativity always takes time, and we are talking about primary school kids! Mr. Tusa's views are also manifest nonsense. But most profoundly of all, he represents a self-avowedly elitist view of creativity. Creativity, as he sees it, seems to be associated with a 'special achievement', which presumably he feels he is best placed to make judgements about. And this is presumably why he has chosen such 'special' people for his interviews – which are in fact some of the usual suspects. Mr. Tusa should recognize that this 'specialness' is not a result of the mysterious 'genius' like qualities within the artwork of his selected few, but is instead the result of a much broader cultural-institutional-market selection process far beyond what resides within the internal qualities of his friends. Others have decided what is 'special' about their work, and also why the work of others is not 'special'. This is how elitism works. Mr. Tusa is conflating fame and celebrity with the 'specialness' of a particular piece of work. He is mistaking creativity in its fullest sense with success on the art market in a very restricted sense, and only then art which he values. Creativity is something inherent to the human condition, whether Mr. Tusa likes the particular outcome of it or not. Creativity is part of our evolution, part of the way our brains and minds work, part the way we all interact with the world. Creativity is not the same as the art, but is found in many, many fields of human endeavour. Creativity is as much in the processes of thinking, planning and innovating before any actual outcome appears. That is a lot for Mr. Tusa to sit judgement on, and he is insufficiently qualified for the job! In confusing the idea of creativity with an assessment of the art objects produced by 'special' people, it is Mr. Tusa himself who is in fact reducing the scope of creativity; restricting the debate about 'what' and 'where' it resides; and peddling the view that only 'special' people can be creative. It is indeed an elitist view. But it is also a reductionist view which restricts considerations of creativity to a very small portion of what needs to be considered.

The *elitist-reductionist conception* of creativity represented by people like Mr. Tusa is what we challenge throughout this book. It is his conflation of creativity with the art object which we argue against. It is his acquiescence to the notion of a 'special' genius-like figure as the locus of creativity which we reject. It is the focus upon the isolated individual as the source of creativity which we find facile. And finally, it is the idea of an 'ideology' at work within primary school which we quite frankly find silly (Mr. Tusa really ought not use big words such as 'ideology' without finding out what they really mean). In contrast to this elitist-reductionist view of creativity, Howard Gardner (2011) writes:

> . . . a study (*of creativity*) will need to examine individuals vs group creativity; revolutionary creativity vs evolutionary creativity; creativity in new as opposed to standard domains; and the way in which societal fields (institutions, gatekeepers, teachers) steer the promotion and evaluation of creative efforts. . . . A single variety of creativity is a myth. . . . I argue, further, that each creative breakthrough entails an intersection of the childlike and the mature; the peculiar genius of the modern in the twentieth century has been its incorporation of the sensibilities of the very young child.
>
> (Gardner 2011. p. 6)

But as Karl Marx once said, we should replace our easy assumptions with explanations. And so with the idea of creativity. Instead of simply assuming that we know (kind of) what creativity 'is', we should do more to actually explain it. Our contribution is to try to gather together various discrete ideas from various discrete disciplines so as to add to this explanation, and try to situate creativity. Mr. Tusa's thinking represents a common cultural assumption which over-emphasizes the idea that creativity comes from a mysterious touch of genius that only some individual people (i.e. not you) have. This comes wrapped in the idea that creativity is a *deus ex machina* (descending from God) thing, and so this already militates against the idea of discussing and sharing ways to be more creative. Too many people are encouraged to believe that creativity is something that stands over them in a way that declares other people, the genius-like people, are the ones who can succeed at that kind of work. We lowly mortals can only stand in awe and passively consume what Mr. Tusa and his friends create in, through and for the Official Cultural world.

This view comes with ready-made, but false, distinctions between certain predesignated creative endeavors – the Arts-with-a-capital A, the Sciences and its related professions on the one hand, and endeavors such as cookery, educating your children, gardening and making each other laugh on the other, which are deemed to somehow belong to another, lesser type of human activity. The whole notion of creativity as residing 'out there' is unhelpful for an active cultural community and the educational future of our children, which is the future of our whole society.

But there is also the view that creativity is 'in here'. Psychological theories of creativity and the biographies of creative lives tend to discuss how and why specific 'bits' of creativity come about due to inner personal dynamics – inspiration, memory, perceptions and even madness. This view continues the problems associated with the aforementioned over-emphasis upon the single, isolated individual as the locus of creativity. Whilst this is obviously a factor, as we will discuss below, this comes with an under-emphasis on the collective, collaborative, social nature of creativity, developed in the relationships between people.

But recognizing the importance of the collaborative spaces between creative individuals, and the interrelationships between that and broader social and economic settings, begs some rather complicated questions. Does your creativity come from the 'hard wiring' that makes up our personality, or from our lifetime of experiences of other people and the world? Does creativity come from within our own mind, or from the people we have been talking to? Does creativity come from our understanding of how things are supposed to look at this particular point in cultural history, or from what our memories of being a child are saying to us?

We do not pretend we have any conclusive answers to these questions. Our tour of ideas about where creativity resides will not arrive at any final destination. Instead, we will propose that the different ideas about creativity expressed by practitioners, philosophers, scientists and social scientists suggest that it probably resides within many complicated, moving relationships between lots of interconnected factors. For instance, when it comes to the motivation to be creative, it is likely that there are many complicated and multifaceted aspects involved. Creative motivation probably comes from the interrelationship between the time we spend thinking and planning, and the time when we are not consciously trying to be creative. It probably comes from the interrelationship between playing, and being urgent and serious. It is likely that these processes need to be repeated, and that all sorts of iterative routines and rituals are necessary to get into the right motivational mind-set to follow things through. This probably involves an interplay between being logical on the one hand, and emotional or intuitive on the other. It is likely that creative motivation comes not just from thought and action, but also from emotion. Not just from the brain or mind, but from the hand and body too. Creativity is too multi-faceted and over-determined for us, or anyone else, to claim a conclusive definition.

Because it is such a common experience that creativity just 'comes', some may not want to analyse it too much. Because then it might not come any more. Is creativity best left at the visceral, emotional, intuitive level so that we can simply respond to our experiences? Perhaps we should not look too closely at creativity, because that runs the risk of routinizing it, making it too 'rational' and systematized, sanitizing it in such a way that the 'magic' goes out of it. So maybe we need some caution, and again avoid anything which sounds and feels like definitive conclusions. We still need to think about and discuss creativity for clear, discernible reasons:

- talking more clearly about the specifics of creativity to others enables us to talk about these specifics to ourselves, and so get a better sense of it.
- generating greater self-reflexivity about our creative selves enables us to understand ourselves, what we want and where we are going with our creativity in a more fully rounded way.
- developing professional strategies to stimulate creativity and hold onto it when it does arrive means that we are not left at the whim of creative inspirations 'just coming'.
- exploring the myriad ways in which creativity can come from collaborative relationships means that we need not simply rely upon our creative self, and we can explore ways to grow such relationships into sustained professional creative spaces.
- being able to pass on ideas about what creativity is and where it comes from more effectively is necessary for improving the educational capacities we provide for our children, which is the future of our society.

The various conceptual discussions of creativity which we will discuss, like the creative practice itself, are situated against various cultural contexts. Perhaps the most ubiquitous is the cultural assumption that creativity is something that some people just 'have', and that others do not. A corollary of this tends towards the assumption that creativity comes from some kind of 'spark of genius', implying that it is therefore too mysterious to talk about. This in turn brings us to the strange, aforementioned adjunct which implies that all we can do is wait for creativity to come. We can think of no other realm of human activity in which so many people seem so sanguine about such a passive stance towards something so fundamental to our existence. We seem to currently believe that we can fully analyse and 'know' the unpredictability of the weather, the workings of the human body, the machinations of the macro-economy and the nature of the cosmos. But at the same time we can only passively wait for something so innate to our character as creativity. These assumptions in turn elevate the view that creativity can only be understood through the characteristics of those people whom Official Culture has deemed to be the successful. This view downplays the broader selection and validation processes presided over by 'cultural experts' and re-validates the initial assumption distinguishing between the 'creative' person and the majority. Unspoken assumptions about creativity form an internally self-validating one-dimensional (Marcuse 1964) discourse which perpetuates the myth that truly creative people are those geniuses held up to us by the Cultural Institutions which select and validate, and their selections and validations must be right, because look how creative the people are whom we have selected for you! Despite what he may believe about himself, Kanye West is only 'Kanye West' because of this selection and validation process. The badge of success conferred upon him by the 'cultural experts' is the summation of a cultural process which lies beyond his own creative action. He is therefore emphatically not the genius he believes himself to be, and his existence is not anything like a useful touchstone for understanding the nature of creativity.

In contrast, we argue that each and every individual has great potential for creativity, and the distinctions between the 'creative person' and the 'rest' are facile, because this would imply the existence of 'non-creative' human beings, something we reject. Second, creativity is as much about relationships as it is about individuals, and these relationships can take many forms and flow from many sources – the social and cultural groups we find ourselves in; the broader social and cultural environments we live in; the ways we now form many of our relationships on-line. So third, we must set the question of creativity against broad historical contexts which form the field which decides what 'counts' as creativity right now, as well as the economy which often dictates who gets selected and validated, and why, and institutions which wield the power to open gates to some and not others. Any account of creativity which does not situate its discussion against these contextual features can only ever be a very limited account.

Too often during our research we have heard people declare themselves to be 'not really creative'. Ideally we would, as a culture, challenge this by paying more respect to the creativity of bringing up one's kids, gardening, arranging one's living space, being good at love, getting dressed in the morning, cooking a meal, running the cafe bar in which I sit whilst I write these words, packing for a trip and riding a bike. Whilst we do not have the space in this book for this fuller account of everyday life creativity, we can declare our belief that whether it is for thinking about creativity for our own purposes, sharing ideas about it with others for collaboration, or for passing ideas on to the next generation, we can and should do better in exploring creativity.

We should try to do this if for no other reason than that creativity is one of those things which both defines us and unites us. For even one person to have learned so much self-alienation as to genuinely believe that they are 'not creative' is a waste of human talent and an indictment of the unexamined assumptions we have alluded to which always situate creativity somewhere other than with these people. As we will argue below, whether for our own creative practices or for more public cultural reasons, creativity is a wellspring for our common human lives, and as such it is too important to be left so unexamined. As many involved in creative work know, the mysteries are not as great as some would have us believe, and the undemocratic tenor of Mr. Tusa's argument are deeply unhelpful. There is a creative person inside us all. Which brings us to the question of motivation as a key factor in situating creativity.

We all tend to be very good at devising a sense of personal and social identity for ourselves. It is probable that we devise such an identity because having a clear idea of where our self starts and ends is necessary for dealing with the things which make us capable of social and cultural survival. However, we tend not to be quite so good at devising and sustaining a deep sense of purpose for our lives. The 'meaning of life' is a question humans have been struggling with since whenever, but we still have no definitive answer. And things certainly do not get any easier when we try to consider a sense of creative purpose. We kind of know we have one, or at least sometimes have one. But we also know it would be good if it were clearer, and that after years of toil, it often gets forgotten, compromised or left behind in the pursuit of enough money to pay the rent and feed the kids. A sense of creative purpose, and the concomitant motivations behind/within creativity are often as slippery as the creativity itself. These 'why' and 'if' questions are sometimes as hard as the 'what' and 'how' questions which face creative people every day. Our on-going ethnographic 'research', which has been trundling along for around twenty-five years now (asking creative people what their motivations are at the end of workshops, lectures, networking events and other drinking occasions) keeps suggesting that there is a complex spectrum of reasons why someone might want to engage in creativity. It is sometimes not that clear to them. But it seems to involve the following features, or at least complex mixtures of these features. Creativity might be:

* for its own sake guided by intrinsic meanings, or stem from a clear and well-defined industrial orientation guided by extrinsic motivations
* about autonomy and self-definition, or the 'rules' of professional membership and institutional spaces
* a proactive sense of new issues to be communicate to the world, or a reactive response which seeks to supply an existing outside demand
* about thoroughly personal questions, or about an audience orientation which seeks to speak to others
* a risk orientation offering deliberately difficult and challenging work, or a viability orientation offering something more 'appealing'
* subversive of mainstream cultural values, or reproductive of the mainstream

Central to this mixture of motivations, and an important element in situating creativity, is a distinction between a concentration on processes on the one hand, and a focus upon outcomes on the other. Obviously a concentration upon outcomes – what gets exhibited beyond the studio, editing room or rehearsal space – comes with most creative territories. We all want/need to show our work eventually. But for some, most obviously those with an entrepreneurial bent, the outcomes taken to market is pretty much the sole motivation. But another source of creative motivation are that which is much more rooted in the enjoyment, obsession, meaning within the processes of creativity itself. The musician, the painter, the crafts-person who might work on the same project for years with little interest in showing the world what they are doing. And so much the better for that because, no matter how much success and public acclaim one might get, a continued concentration upon the processes which happen inside the rehearsal space, the studio or the workshop is going to be necessary if that creativity is going to be long-term.

Within their 'social construction of reality' thesis, Berger and Luckmann (1967) suggest that modern life bombards us with such a scope and pace of experiences, images, changes and emotions that it is increasingly common that we experience a 'cognitive nervousness' – a shakiness within our sense of self and how we fit into the world. Whilst most people will experience this as a less-than-comfortable background feeling within their everyday lives, perhaps creativity sometimes stems from the motivation to 'do something' about it – to grasp ourselves and our nervousness by seeking ways to more fully 'be' in the strange, ever changing place that the world has become. This disorienting 'nervousness' might be something creativity accepts and embraces on both a personal and intellectual level to fuel creative motivation. Perhaps this alludes to a *creative nervousness* whereby we are not sure where we are going and why, or even how we are trying to get there, just as we realize that we must set out in that direction.

It is likely that the motivations which underlie and drive a creative life are as multi-faceted and ever shifting as the various processes and outcomes involved. It is likely that many creative people struggle to articulate their creative purpose precisely because it is so central to their identity and sense of self. But these motivations, purposes and senses of self, complex and shifting though they are, are clearly central to any discussion of situating creativity. At the end of the day, each reader will have to have their own discussion, with themselves or others, about their creative motivations and purposes. It would be silly for us to try to tell you what they are or could be. But it is not so silly for us to suggest that becoming more self-aware and clear about one's motivations and purposes is a very, very useful aspect if we are to try to situate creativity.

And to do that question any kind of justice, we are going to need a broad approach.

A broad approach

There are many, many books which discuss what creativity is and how to do it. Many of these books are rather pop-psychology oriented, and border on being self-help manuals. Whilst his work is more developed than some, Edward de Bono has for many years been the market leader of this kind of position. But it is a rather self-referential position. De Bono only ever really refers to himself, and much of it is a little outdated now. But a more serious problem is the fact that this kind of approach is almost devoid of anything that situates creativity in a wider social and economic context. De Bono appears happy to consider creativity as a purely internal process, something he feels he can unpack with discussions of lateral thinking alone. Whilst such an orientation can offer useful additions, thinking techniques and lateral thinking games alone cannot account for the myriad interpersonal relationships, emotional tussles and broader socio-cultural contexts which shape and situate creativity.

At the other end of the spectrum, there are many business-oriented books which locate creativity as one of the key drivers of success in the contemporary economy. Such orientations tend to discuss ways of organizing and managing business so as to encourage creativity. But these orientations tend to take creativity as a given. They therefore tend to pay insufficient attention to the nature, character and deep understanding of creativity itself. The burgeoning debates concerning the creative industries, which has emerged over the past twenty years, has been part of this. Whilst focusing upon creative business, and the consequent debates surrounding the new economy, cultural policy, organizational innovation and other related issues, most of these books still have to really get to grips with the nature of creativity itself. For instance, David Hesmondhalgh and Sarah Baker's book *Creative Labour* (2010) approaches the creative industries from a labour process perspective. Whilst we are admirers of their work, they write the following about creativity: 'To create is simply to bring something into being', they bemoan the 'recent fetishization of creativity in policy', and ask 'How did the concept of creativity come to be the object of such reverence?'.

The processes of creativity – the individual iterations, the emotional ups and downs, the relationships of all kinds, the compromises needed to bring it to fruition, the other compromises needed to situate it in the world somehow – all suggest, very immediately and very loudly, that this rather dismissive notion of creativity is insufficient. And this strange neglect of deeper and broader understandings of creativity is shared by many others:

- individual artistic practitioners seem to readily accept the self-mystifying sense of creativity as something which just comes 'from nowhere' – overly obscure.

- economists focus almost solely upon the economic impact of the creative industries and often neglect the real nature of the creative processes which underpin that arena of productivity – overly macro and structural.
- business leaders speak from a particularly market orientation and usually prefer to speak of 'innovation' in a way which holds up market success as the locus of their definition of creativity. As such, they pay insufficient attention to the other powerful cultural impacts which creativity not geared towards market success has – overly market-oriented.
- cultural policy-makers develop broad cultural plans and systems of governance that often under-represents the fine details of creative communities and the relationships that make them up – overly institutional.
- leaders of cultural organizations talk about strategy, growth and management and neglect alternative cultural meanings held by independent creative practitioners – overly managerial and programmatic.

Clearly there are numerous languages at work here, and because all approaches must adopt a particular perspective there is an inevitable opportunity cost of being relatively blind to other ways of thinking. This is the logic behind the ubiquitous silo-istic thinking one must contend with when trying to adopt a broader approach towards situating creativity. In pursuit of that, a wide-ranging yet still coherent debate about multiple, intertwined strands is needed to allow for a deep account of individual creativity which stays cognisant of broad interrelationships and contexts. In comparison to silo-istic orientations, such an approach has various beneficial trajectories:

- to translate debates developed within the sciences on the one hand, the humanities on the other, and the arts on yet another for a *cross-disciplinary conception* of creativity, such that lessons can be learned and applied beyond the realm in which they were first discovered
- to combine research from multiple fields – neuroscience, psychology, philosophy, sociology, anthropology, new media, economics, business, organizational studies and creative biographies – in pursuit of aggregated knowledge for a *multi-disciplinary conception* of creativity aiming at a more holistic understanding of creativity
- to seek cross/multi-disciplinary so it might get us a little closer, albeit in a partial and contingent way, to an 'anatomy of creativity' which might help in taking us from the conceptual to the concrete, from the theoretical to the applied and the practical

It is these concerns with cross/multi-disciplinary which underpin our particular approach. But in seeking to situate creativity and set out the benefits of this broader multi-disciplinary approach, it is necessary to give it some detailed contours around which the various debates are organized. It seems apposite to start with the creative person, which is still the orthodox starting point for most debates about creativity. But everything we have so far said shows that debates about the creative person can only be a starting point.

Evolutionary theory situates human creativity as the outcome of our bigger brains, which gave us greater capacities for both creatively adapting to and shaping our environment. So creativity is partly the driver and the partly the outcome of this evolutionary process, which was subsequently passed on through natural selection such that our greater capacity for creativity is now part of our human nature (although we use that term with a high degree of circumspection). As we explore in fine detail in the next chapter, these greater creative capacities hinge upon our more developed abilities in self-reflection and self-awareness, which enable a greater capacity for abstract and conceptual thinking, and thus imaginative projection applied within forward planning. We know that many animals use tools, so the idea of humans as tool makers – *Homo faber* – is only part of the qualitative evolutionary leap which humans made in pre-history. It seems that the creative person's greater ability for creativity stems as much from conceptual thinking skills as using tools. And this conceptual thinking has meant a qualitative leap in our given capacity to think about the way we think, which has meant we are better at both generating, but equally importantly, at sharing and co-developing abstract ideas and plans before we decide upon concrete actions. This unique level of self-reflexivity has given the creative person what Harth (1995) has called the 'creative loop' – a multi-faceted and intricately over-lapping series of feedback loops with which we creatively think about our creativity, and abstractly plan our plans.

> What distinguishes us more than anything else . . . is our acute awareness of a self, and a mental preoccupation with our own being that goes far beyond the kind of self-preserving behavior that all animals exhibit.
>
> (Harth 1995. p. 27)

In common with evolutionary theory, modern neuroscience is also brain-centred, and is the current leading edge of scientific accounts of what it is to be human. The ever more detailed description of what specific regions of the brain are responsible for what are being increasingly held up as the route to understanding the fundamental nature of the human condition. But we should remember that only thirty years ago genetics saw itself in this way, but now genetic determinism has been largely rejected in favour of a more holistic account flowing from disciplines such as epigenetics. Maybe the current hype about neuroscience will eventually give way to another, equally holistic account of the human condition and its innate creativity, as either a 'whole brain' phenomenon, or maybe even a 'whole body' thing. This starts to get us into the very, very deep waters of debating human consciousness itself, which are beyond us here.

Evolutionary theory, often in cahoots with neuroscience, currently has a lot to say about the 'hardware' of the creative person – the way the brain has evolved and how it is 'wired up' (Begley 2009; D'Amasio 2012). But the different branches of psychology have had just as much to say about the 'software' of the creative person – how inner perceptions, expectations and memories enable and shape human creativity. Although the brain is a necessary precondition for the mind, it is not an equivalent thing. The conscious mind is a complex series of ever present, ever shifting processes which select, shape, confirm, ignore, remember, forget, re-remember, judge and re-assess what the brain (and the rest of the body) is doing. Although the vast majority of this mind-processing stuff is unconscious, it seems probable that it is intimately connected, in complex ways, to the information processing which forms part of the foundations of creativity. And it gets even more complex when we note that the creative mind, because it is so adept at self-consciousness, is also capable of being mindful of its own mind-ness, capable of thinking about the way it does its thinking. As we become aware of ourselves as selves, we develop greater capacity for generating new combinations of old ideas, which is the basis of the *combinatorial conception* of creativity which cognitive psychology puts at the centre of considerations of the creative person (Boden 1990; Sternberg 1999).

Here the stress is upon our cognitive abilities to actively shape and change our minds, to actively choose the way we process information in relation to our perceptions and expectations. Information coming from the external world is not fixed or objective, but rather bent and shaped into a personal 'reality'. Most psychological perspectives put this process of active mental selection and shaping at the heart of creativity, and suggest that the creative person is someone with a heightened ability to do this, or with heightened motivations to reject the old combinations of ideas and seek new ones. As we will see in the next chapter, there are many psychological perspectives within this overall endeavour, each with their different starting points and trajectories with which they understand creativity.

But a common problem with being concerned only with genetic make-up, neurological brain wiring or the interior psychological dynamics of individual people is the inevitable consequence of falsely isolating lives from the relationships which shape them. It is pretty obvious to anyone who has engaged in active creative work in the real world for any length of time, that it flows as much from relationships as much as internal biological, neurological or psychological processes. As we noted above, the idea of creativity is still often clothed in its own cultural myth of the 'lone genius'. This myth sponsors the general belief that creativity is the output of the people who have toiled in glorious isolation from us mere mortals. And this myth is itself the emanation of another connected myth noted above – that only officially sanctioned cultural objects are the true repositories of creativity. The cumulative effect of these two intertwined pieces of cultural myth give us our currently *individualized conception* of creativity. Whilst it is obvious that internal, highly personal factors are often the wellspring of creativity, it is equally clear that any debate about creativity worth its salt must take into account lots of other relational factors for an account of creativity to have sufficient breadth.

Sustained enquiries into the nature and impact of relationships upon creativity come from many different traditions – from social psychology, sociology and anthropology. The Humanist tradition of social psychology places a more fully rounded human being at the centre of its thinking. For such Humanistic thinking, personality is *over-determined*. This is jargon for saying that people are not the result of one cause – genetics, nature, nurture, brain wiring – which leads to one effect – the personality. Rather, any effect, including the creative person, is a result of multiple, combined and mutually interpenetrating causes. Such a view situates creativity as the consequence of myriad interrelationships between the creative person and other people, places, technological facilities and broad social, cultural and economic contexts. Rather than a purely psychological view of creativity, such a view takes us towards a more *social conception* of creativity premised upon all the relationships which our social being implies.

So in Chapter 3 we develop this more social view by exploring various perspectives which relate creativity to social and cultural interaction. It continues to unpack anthropological accounts of how human groups form social bonds fostered by the 'making special' ceremonies of creativity and culture. It also looks at research from social psychology which locates creativity within group processes, as well as the sociology of creative groups and networks. This social conception of creativity is given added texture by the reflections of creative collaborations and other relationship-based processes within specific communal locations of co-creativity, which in turn signals the importance of a *geographical conception* of creativity, intertwined as it often is with place.

Whether it is for their physical beauty, the ready access they give us to other people and creative conversations, or the fact that they represent something we dream of belonging to or something to escape from, physical places and their concomitant meanings have always been a key factor within creativity. There are all sorts of different levels and facets to the affinity between creativity and places. When Karl Marx referred to city life as the 'end of the idiocy of rural life', he was not being unkind to rural people, but rather he saw the developing cultural places within growing industrial cities as allowing people to come together more effectively to do politics and culture. Cosmopolitan urban centres have always been key stimuli for creativity. Florence was the cradle of the Renaissance; Victorian London brought us an explosion of scientific and technological development; Paris between 1905 and 1939 was where the key movements within Modern Art were born; Los Angles created 'Hollywood'; Detroit and Manchester gave us in turn Motown and The Smiths; Silicon Valley is the place of current technological development. There are many various ideas which seek to explain why this affinity between places and creativity is a key one, which we will explore in Chapter 4. All these places can be seen as examples of what Hall (1991) has called the 'creative milieu' of certain places, which is in turn both the driver and the consequence of interrelationships between place and creativity.

But as well as physical places, much has been made in recent years of the consequences of new media as new kinds of non-places (Augé 2008). The new media landscape, which includes but is bigger than the social media of Facebook and Twitter, has developed over the past twenty years or so to change creative processes in some fundamental ways. The hype around new media means that it is easy to overstate these changes, but nonetheless they are there. Perhaps the most significant of these is the altered relationships between the once all-powerful Institutional Centres of creativity – record labels, TV stations, film companies and publishers – on the one hand, and the independent 'edge' of creative practitioners and the communities they often form into on the other. Those who were previously marginalized by the Institutional Gatekeepers are using new media to circumvent the Institutional Centres such that edge-to-edge, peer-to-peer and Open Source collaborative sensibilities for creativity now by-pass the centre and often animate, and are animated by, a much more vital creativity. New media are allowing new forms of creative production and dissemination to develop in ways which can by-pass hierarchy, ego-centric management and overly competitive commercialism. The edge can ignore the Centre and can speak directly to other members of itself.

But as well as new media facilitating new independent 'structures' of creative production and dissemination, they also offer new ways of finding collaborative, relationship-based processes. For Clay Shirky (2010), this new media landscape offers a 'cognitive surplus' which facilitates greater access to the creativity of other cognitive minds across the world which everyone can now draw upon and share. For him, this has led to 'collaborative spirals' of creativity. We will explore this debate and its implications for situating creativity in Chapter 5.

Professional creative practice is a response to, and simultaneously the creation of, broader cultural and economic contexts. We are in the midst of a shift from an old economy of 'heavy' industry towards a new economy of 'weightless' production – of ideas, images, meanings and experiences. So the stress within business is upon creativity and innovation as never before, because speed and flexibility of response to emergent markets becomes more key to commercial success. This means that creativity is a necessary constant within many business strategies, and organizing for constant change a necessary aspect of management. And this has had many implications for the shape of creative contexts. It may be too much to suggest that we can identify a discrete *business conception* of creativity, but it is clear that business and economics is having an increasingly loud voice in thinking about creativity in some quarters. And thinking about the creative industries is having an impact upon traditional business thinking. For instance, whilst traditional businesses have historically benefited from economies of scale – where being large led to commercial success because marginal costs were reduced – now many creativity-centred businesses benefit more from economies of speed – being able to move, change and respond rapidly and flexibly. Given this, there are now often business advantages in staying small.

And because creativity is often so situated, collaboration is becoming as necessary for creativity as winning competitions was within the previous, more traditional forms of industrial production. Henry Chesborough (2008) has made a distinction between 'closed' and 'open' approaches to business innovation. In a 'closed' approach, management tends to draw tight boundaries around company creativity to protect confidentiality; assume that all the creative skills needed are already within those tight company boundaries; and focus upon overt competition geared towards getting to market first.

In an 'open' approach, business success tends to be predicated more upon collaborative interconnections between companies as beneficial for company creativity and innovation; recognizing that creative skills are often outside of the company and need to be brought in for co-creativity; and focusing upon getting to market most creatively and best, rather than first. The adoption of such open approaches perhaps in part explain the current vitality of network-orientations within creative business sectors. The aforementioned Open Source sharing, peer-to-peer collaborations and myriad other creative micro-experiments are becoming an increasingly common adjunct to orthodox business plans and models. The entrepreneurial spirit is being complemented by alternative approaches, forged by an *alt-trepreneurial spirit* behind the business contexts of creativity. This is but another way of saying that relationships within and for creativity are becoming increasingly significant in real-world economic settings.

But beyond the economic, all human activity exists within even broader socio-cultural and historical contexts. It would be strange to suggest that creativity was any different. So it is beholden on any sufficiently broad account seeking to situate creativity to discuss the interplays between these socio-cultural and historical aspects which shape and select what is to 'count' as creativity. The most fully developed account which sets the acts of personal creativity within a broader *contextual conception* of creativity is that offered by the 'systems perspective' of Howard Gardner (2011) and Mihaly Csíkszentmihályi (1996). For instance:

> . . . creativity results from the interaction of a system comprised of three elements: a culture that contains symbolic rules, a person who brings novelty into the symbolic domain, and a field of experts who recognise and validate the innovation. . . . (*Therefore*), creativity does not happen inside people's heads, but in the interaction between a person's thoughts and a socio-cultural context. It is a systemic rather than an individual phenomenon.
>
> (Csíkszentmihályi 1996. p. 84)

In the systems theory of creativity, the individual talent of the creative person – their personality, experiences, motivations, etc. – is firmly situated within two broader contexts. Firstly *the field* – the Institutional 'expert systems' of judges, critics, curators, buyers which form the professionalized selection process which creativity must speak to, convince, deal with in some way. And secondly *the domain* – the broader and deeper 'symbolic systems' which form and shape each creative discipline and the broader culture it sits within, which is what creativity refers to, reproduces, challenges, rejects and/or uses as its sounding board. We will explore these contextual features of the location of creativity in more detail in Chapter 6.

But the systems theory of creativity is perhaps a little too neutral about these broader contexts, a little too sanguine about how they work, a little too accepting about their democratic and meritocratic pretensions. Many of the Institutions which have large amounts of power within the various real-world fields and domains of creativity tend to use their power to reproduce and enhance their power. This takes us right back to the one-dimensionality of Mr. Tusa's elitist-reductionist account of creativity with which we started this chapter. The field in particular tends to reproduce hierarchies which all too often damage creativity rather than foster it. So, as well as providing an account of their significance, Chapter 6 will also include a detailed critique of the contextual features of creativity. And this brings us to the broad question of the way all our various accounts of creativity impact upon the public realm and the question of the public understanding of creativity as a largely missing part of its location, which we will discuss in the polemic at the end of this chapter. But before that, lets continue to try to situate creativity in a broader sense. Specifically, can we situate creativity as a particular kind of 'logic'?

The 'logic' of creativity

Policastro and Gardner's (1999) 'robust generalization' of creativity might be a good place to start such a consideration. They suggest that creativity sometimes entails a focus upon theory building which seeks to explicate a novel way of thinking and seeing; that it sometimes entails a practical problem-solving orientation geared towards a specific concrete issue; that it sometimes seeks to develop symbolic systems to express deeper meanings about the world, back to the world. And these various orientations in turn lead to different *trajectories of creativity*.

As we started to discuss above when we briefly considered creative motivations, sometimes creative practitioners accept and work within the pre-established traditions of their chosen field or paradigm. Others challenge such parameters *as* their creative work. Sometimes practitioners are concerned with commercial considerations, whilst others are not. Increasingly creative businesses seek to combine the two in new ways. Many of this new breed of creative entrepreneurs navigate between and across these orientations within their working week. It is probably true that different people go through different creative processes, and that this happens in different ways each time they do it. Sometimes creativity will be an iterative process tried over and over again until the practitioner is happy with the results. At other times it comes from a flash of inspiration which occurs all at once, almost fully formed. These points are but different ways of suggesting there are multiple, multi-faceted logic(s) at work within any creative endeavour. So perhaps creativity is located within a certain 'logic', but it is a very disparate 'logic'.

But the very idea of a 'logic' behind creativity goes very deep into our cultural roots, and indeed discussions of logic are part of the very foundations of the discipline of philosophy itself. Central to the very roots of a lot of Western thinking is the notion of *formal logic* – the kind of thinking which Western culture tends to value the most due to its internal consistency, logical coherence, clear definitions and fixed meanings which support propositions and plans. On the whole, Western culture tends to favour this kind of logical thinking because it helps us to avoid contradictions, emotional responses and the 'woolly' thinking that confuses one thing with another. And this kind of logical thinking often gets played out within goal-oriented rational behaviour, or what Max Weber has called *instrumental rationality*:

> . . . instrumental rationality . . . (*is*) determined by expectations as to the behaviour of objects in the environment and of other human beings; these expectations are used as 'conditions' or 'means' for the attainment of the actor's own rationally pursued and calculated ends.
>
> (Weber 1975. p. 120)

The idea of creativity as puzzle-solving behaviour, a version of creativity popular within science and industry, is usually underpinned by this idea of goal-oriented, purposive, instrumental rationality as the best, that is, most 'logical' way forward, because it is the source of 'calculated action' to get towards specific 'ends'. But instrumental rationality is not the only kind of 'logic'. Weber also outlines

> . . . value-rationality (wertrational), that is, determined by a conscious belief in the value for its own sake of some ethical, aesthetic, religious, or other form of behaviour, independently of its prospect of success . . .

But he also refers to

> . . . affectual (*especially emotional*) rationality, that is, determined by the actor's spe-cific affects and feeling states, (*and*) . . . traditional, that is determined by ingrained habituation.
>
> (Weber 1975. p. 121)

So, as well as the 'logic' of instrumental rationality, we also have value-based rationality, affectual or emotion-based rationality, and tradition-based rationality. Weber's distinction is useful because it points to the basic hallmarks of other types of rationality that are equally prevalent within creativity. As well as being underpinned by instrumentally considered interrelationships between causes and effects, actions and consequences, it is likely that creativity also involves:

- expressions of aesthetic or ethical value within a particular creative act as *an end in itself*, as opposed to a calculation geared towards pursuing an instrumental end which is 'outside' of that act and extrinsic
- motivations which are resistant to definitive explanation and meaning, and which is more akin to an ineffable feeling, as part of one's *emotional state* which spark strange reactions rather than clearly stated purposes
- actions which happens out of a *sense of tradition*, or responsibility to that tradition as an expression to a particular public culture writ large

Clearly creativity does not always flow from clear, instrumental purposes that are amenable to clear, rational action. Sometimes, all we can say is that creative ideas are things-in-themselves that grow and develop according to what creative practitioners experience as 'their own' agenda, pace and trajectory. It is probable that creativity involves non-rational factors such as vagueness, wanderings, visceral reactions, non-goal-oriented play and other experiences which propel creativity within a cognitive, intellectual space that is between different kinds of logic. This starts to take us back to the individualistic conception of creativity to some extent, but it also encapsulates activities which are the more social aspects of creativity. For instance, David Bohm's (1998) discussion of creativity echoes this idea of a multi-faceted 'logic' at work within creativity. For him, it seems we all

- get a 'kick' out of solving a puzzle, playing with sometimes arcane ideas, connections and details until we 'come up with something'
- enjoy the feeling of discovering something new, even if it is only new to us, and stepping into the unknown
- value demonstrating a feeling of 'oneness' and connection between our self and the 'implicate order' of the world when do this kind of stuff
- experience our selves more fully when we demonstrate this 'oneness' because it involves an inevitable self-reflection and therefore greater personal and communal self-awareness

As Bohm puts it,

> . . . real originality and creativity imply that one does not work only in the fields that are recognised . . . but that one is ready in each case to inquire for oneself as to whether there is or is not a fundamentally significant difference between the actual facts and one's perceived notions that opens up the possibility of creative and original work . . . it is always founded on the sensitive perception of what is new and different from what is inferred from previous knowledge.
>
> (Bohm 1998. p. 31)

According to Bohm, creative practitioners often articulate these different, multi-stranded 'logics' at work through features such as:

- exploring tenuous paths, hidden circles, hints at routes to unknown destinations
- cherishing the sometimes arcane details they contain and lessons they promise for the future
- finding a way to express the poetics within these tenuous paths and arcane details
- experiencing a sense of wonder in the ineffable meaning they represent
- broadening this sense of meaning and purpose out as this process becomes clarified and new connections are made
- developing a sense of location for one's relationship with the wider world
- distilling this meaning into increasingly clear statements to the rest of the world
- offering this self-finding for other people's appreciation
- folding these reactions into further circles of development and connecting to new branch lines within the general path
- repeating new versions of the process

Instrumental rationality may play a part in each of these aspects, as particular, concrete bits of action are made. But it would be superficial to suggest that the whole creative process can be incorporated within instrumental logic. Clearly creativity does not always reside in the arrival at a destination, and often lies within a sense of journey that has no ultimate purpose, aim or objective other than that. As we will see in the next chapter, creativity often resides within a multi-faceted attitude involving idiosyncratic mixtures that move between contradictory aspects such as:

- idle playfulness and seriousness
- a visceral need for self-expression and open experimentation
- clear motivation and disorientation
- continuous involvement and accident
- regular momentum and a concern to 'break the rules'
- a regular creative style and a need for creative release
- developing daily routines and embracing chance, luck or accident
- working according to one's experience and enjoying one's innocence
- operating with audacity and embracing one's ignorance
- bearing the tensions within creative work and finding the great happiness which it also offers

These are just some of the contradictory facets which seem to appear regularly within the experiences of creativity. They defy any notion of a constant 'logic' at play, but nonetheless, they do start to signal something of the internal dynamics within the processes themselves.

In his book *Play Ethic*, Pat Kane (2005) sees the freedom we all have to engage in open exploration as another component of a creative 'logic', which differs markedly from the more 'puritan' view of life enshrined within what Weber has called the 'Protestant work ethic'. Part of the 'logic' of creativity seems to be a resistance to 'getting a proper job', 'growing up', and 'being responsible', which this work ethic asks of us.

> The modern version sees players as the ultimate embodiment of human freedom. They move through the world with imagination, passion and confidence. Players are constantly dreaming of new possibilities, in the midst of constraint and routine, and they have the energy to make some of them, at least, a reality. . . . To be a player is to try and live and thrive between freedom and determinism, chance and necessity. It is this seeming paradox that the player needs to embrace. It is pointless to ignore a rhetoric of play, or to promote one set of rhetorics above another, for the sake of an easier intellectual life. . . . Players need to be energetic, imaginative and confident in the face of an unpredictable contestive, emergent world. Players also need to accept the complex relationship between all forms of play whether ancient or modern.
>
> (Kane 2005. p. 47)

On the other hand, it is clear that creativity often comes from a serious felt need to express something which holds deep meaning. A sense of seriousness and urgency is often vital if creative work is to be taken through to fruition. In dealing with the contradictions between idle playfulness and seriousness, along with many other felt aspects, creative people often exhibit *divergent thinking* or *ideational fluency*. Whilst convergent thinking tends to be about working along set trams lines to arrive as efficiently as possible at instrumental solutions, divergent thinking puts more value in imaginative wanderings and other playful explorations to take thinking beyond instrumental rationality. Divergent thinking starts with 'what if' types of questions, and a 'let's see what happens' outlook. It is more about enjoying the journey than seeking efficient arrival. This is another way of saying that creativity is often as much about the process as the outcome.

And divergent thinking has its own specific characteristics. Rather than going in a straight line, such creative 'logic' is usually more circular, taking in influences from many strands as it goes along. It often grows out of itself, as feedback loops from mid-points in the project send one back to new beginnings and fresh outlooks. That is, the 'logic' of creativity is often *emergent* (Johnson 2002), and as such, it needs to be gone over again and again. That is, it is *recursive*. A creative practice (understood as career or business) usually requires 'practice' (doing it again and again until it gets good). That is, it is *iterative*. Creativity often comes from aimless wanderings which generate ideas that one was not actually searching for. That is, it is *serendipitous* (Johnson 2010). Creativity is often achieved by taking various circuitous routes rather than trying to bash away at things head-on. That is, it comes from *obliquity* (Kay 2011).

This 'logic' of divergent thinking, emergence and recursivity based upon multiple iterations is ultimately an expression of a creativity which seeks new relationships between what one is trying to do on the one hand, and (re)seeing the tools one has to hand on the other. This entails putting the means (the plans, tools, concepts, etc.) and the ends (the ultimate objective) in a different order. Bringing us back to Max Weber, the aforementioned instrumental rationality tends to focus only upon the means, and it proceeds by then trying to apply these pre-established means to all ends in a consistent and routine way. In contrast, Weber's idea of *substantive rationality* starts with a more open and relaxed idea of the ends, and only then decides upon the means which are relevant and useful for that specific job. This is the fundamental difference between the bureaucrat and the artist. Hacking is a modern name we have given to this process of getting something done with ideas and tools that were originally intended for other tasks.

And when such interrelationships between means and ends, objectives and tools have been (re)seen, many creative people report the experience of being 'in the zone', or what Csíkszentmihályi (1990) has called experiencing *creative flow*. Flow is experienced when:

- there are clear goals every step of the way.
- there is immediate feedback to one's actions.
- there is a good balance between challenges and skills.
- action and awareness merge.
- distractions are excluded from consciousness.
- there is no worry of failure.
- self-consciousness disappears.
- the sense of time becomes distorted.
- the activity becomes *autotelic* – whereby the creative act is experienced as being 'its own thing'.

With the experience of flow, creativity becomes *autotelic*, such that it takes on a 'logic' of its own, and is propelled forward by its own inner meaning and dynamics alone. It is experienced as its own pleasure. Particularly when things are going well, creativity becomes its own reason and its own reward. Process and outcome become wrapped up together. 'Being in' the creativity becomes more immediate and meaningful than 'having it' for the pursuit of an external need or demand. With an autotelic creative 'logic' everything is already and always 'there' within it.

In Chapter 7, we bring our attention back to the possibility of making useful comments about this 'logic' by offering something of an anatomy of creativity. We will explore some established schemas and typologies concerning 'stages of creativity'. We do this not as some kind of conclusion or definitive account. We have already said we would avoid that. Rather we offer this anatomy as merely as a loose synthesis which draws together some applied lessons for concrete practice which can be gleaned from the preceding chapters. We approach this anatomy of creativity with a degree of trepidation, given our previous comments about its highly over-determined, idiosyncratic and ever moving nature. As Krishnamurti has put it:

> . . . creative thinking is the infinite movement of thought, emotion and action. That is, when thought . . . is unimpeded in its movement, is not compelled or influenced or bound by an idea and does not proceed from the background of tradition or habit, then that movement is creative . . .
>
> (Krishnamurti 1996. p. 68)

And so, in attempting to situate creativity as part of the broader, multi-disciplinary account to come, we have argued that there are many strands and features which come together to mutually inform each other to drive creativity forward. But as our broad account will show, many of these strands and features are contradictory, and this, along with the notion of constant movement, already starts to hint at the necessity of a *dialectical conception* of creativity for a fuller appreciation of its 'logic' of creativity, and for situating it as the emanation of a process of flux and change which is born of an interpenetration between and across many contradictory facets.

A dialectical conception of creativity

Given what we have already said, dialectical thinking promises a fruitful addition to our considerations. The notion of dialectics is not always an easy idea to grasp for the non-specialist, especially within Western cultures which tend to operate with a particularly formal logical tradition. But we suggest that the linear, rather mechanical nature of formal logic is perhaps not best suited to grasping the ever changing, ever moving nature of creativity and the inner contradictions which seems to drive it.

So it may be worthwhile saying some initial words about dialectics as a way of thinking before we apply it to our unpacking of some of the features of the dialectical conception of creativity itself. To fully grasp the notion of dialectics, it is good to start with the often unspoken nature of formal logic. Since the ancient Greeks, the very idea of logic has been codified into three 'laws'. Firstly, the *law of identity* – which holds that all things must have a formal definition to allow us to clearly identify their nature. Things – ideas, propositions, entities – must be clearly allocated a 'thing-ness'. Secondly, the *law of non-contradiction* holds that each 'thing' must be itself, and thus cannot be seen as something else. The identity of an idea, proposition or entity cannot be confused with something which it is not. And thirdly, the *law of the excluded middle* holds that 'things' cannot be identified as laying between one thing and another. All very sensible. But such formal logic encourages binary thinking – is it 'this' or 'that'? Is it 'here' or 'there'?

So whilst these laws of formal logic enable us to fix and keep hold of formal definitions and the identity of things to enable clear, rational and logical thinking, they are not so useful when it comes to appreciating the moving nature of things – the way ideas, propositions and entities develop, change, merge, re-emerge and grow out of themselves, as things often do in the real world. Dialectics is a form of logic which is better able to understand phenomena as *processes of change* as a result of interactions which happen either within themselves or as a result of interactions with other things. The basic premise of dialectics is the idea that these processes of change are the true essence of things in the world. Change happens as a result of the inevitable inner nature of the things themselves, because all things have within them their own relationship to their opposite, their own inner contradiction.

Take something quite simple, such as the colour red. Formal logic would argue that once we have defined what 'red' is, then we can have a clear and shared idea of what 'red' means as a concept. Red is 'red' given its identity. It cannot be confused as another colour. And it is necessary for a logical consideration of 'red' to exclude any middle ground between it and something else. Dialectics, on the other hand, would argue that we can only really appreciate red and its defining 'red-ness' because of its opposite. It is only when we appreciate all that is not red – blue, green and yellow – that we can fully understand the 'red-ness' of red. It is only by having non-red that we get 'red' as an idea. If the world did not have blue, green and yellow, then 'red' would not be able to exist. So it is the *interpenetration of opposites*, the mutual interplay between red and non-red, which allows red to be 'red'. Dialectical thinking suggests that things are best understood in terms of their opposites.

But 'red-ness' is a rather mundane example. If we now consider something more complex and moving, something like history, we get to the real point of dialectical thinking. For dialectical thinking, history, or at least specific historical periods, are defined by this interpenetration of opposites and the contradictory forces which each historical period encapsulates. So, for instance, feudalism had within it social, political and economic forces which were contradictory to that 'stage' of history – the weakening of the power of the church and a gradual secularization of society; the growing political power of the merchant classes which was beginning to challenge the absolute power of the monarch; and the gradual transformation of the economy towards a more capitalist organization. So dialectical thinking, rather than understanding history as a 'still image' by defining the fixed features of feudalism, argues that feudalism is best understood in terms of its inner dynamic of change driven by its inner contradictions. With this we get a more 'moving picture' of the process of change and flux from one 'thing' to another. So, as well as locating its understanding in terms of the interpenetration of opposites, dialectical thinking puts the idea of flux and change centre stage.

Given all this, we argue that dialectical thinking offers a more profound way of understanding the 'logic' of creativity. A fairly standard way of summing up dialectics is the notion of the interrelationships between a *thesis* – an original idea on the one hand – and its *antithesis* – an idea which offers alternative, contradictory views on the other hand. And from the interplays between a thesis and its antithesis, a *synthesis* emerges – a wholly new idea flowing from within those very interplays. Thus, it is these internal contradictions which lead to movement, change and constant flux. It is important for dialectical thinking, and very apposite for understanding the 'logic' of creativity, that such change and flux come from *within* the interplays rather than as a result of some outside force of change.

So, applied to the 'logic' of creativity, we might put this as follows:

- **Thesis** – the basic idea, proposition or plan one might be thinking about within one's creative work – 'I am going to do this thing, this way . . .'
- **Antithesis** – within that very way of seeing and thinking there are other contradictory possibilities which have arisen precisely due to the initial work leading to the

original thesis – 'I am going to do this thing, but because of that initial work I now realize that I could do it a different way . . .', or 'I have become interested in doing this other thing, and can now see how my original idea can be applied to a new end'.

- **Synthesis** – the interplay between the original thesis and its antithesis can now lead to a changed view of things. The new creative trajectories and outcomes have grown out of the interplay between contradictions and opposites – 'I was planning to do this, in this way, but then I explored a little more, and new ideas came up, and so I am now planning to do that, in that way . . .'

And then this new synthesis becomes a new thesis, which inevitably has within it its own antithesis, and the process of creativity starts another cycle of flux towards a new synthesis. This view enables us to understand the ever moving and dynamic processes within creativity and helps to draw out a fuller picture of its 'logic'. And we can apply such dialectical thinking to the inner details of creativity when we delve into some of its particular features. We can see myriad dialectical relationships between the internal aspects of the creative person, and between the creative person and the rest of the world, as, similarly, interpenetration between various opposites, such as:

- **Your brain and you** – the way your brain functions to take in information whilst simultaneously reflecting back upon its own brain-ness. This process selects certain ideas and information in terms of what is important to this thing you call 'You'. Being aware of this selection process is a good way of getting better at doing it. Being good at creativity entails being good at self-awareness.
- **You and others** – the way this thing called 'You' – your personality, experiences, motivations and skills – are shaped by the relationships you have with everything that is 'Not-You', that is everyone else. And then the way this 'Not-You' of everyone you meet is shaped in turn by their experiences of you. 'You' *are* 'Not-You', and 'Not-You' *is* 'You'. Being good at creativity often entails being good at relationships.
- **Now and the past** – the way that you are working on 'Now' is the culmination of a long series of 'Not-Now' events from your past, which have formed your current perceptions of 'Now'. The present is a culmination of the past, and your sense of creativity for the future is made from the idea you have of the present. Being good at future creativity entails being good at the history of you and your creativity.
- **What you do and what you don't do** – the way you define what your creativity 'does' against ideas of what you 'don't do'. The 'presence' of your creativity is made up partly from what you have decided should be 'absent'. Connecting the interplays between these 'presences' to 'absences' is what sometimes makes new bits of creativity move. Being good at creativity sometimes entails knowing about what you 'don't do', so that you can then 'do it'.
- **Your imagination and the real world** – the way your inner, subjective experiences are shaped by the objective social, political and economic realities of the World, which you then in turn shape to imagine other possible Worlds, and so seek to change things. The 'outer' shapes the 'inner', so that the 'inner' can then seek to re-shape the 'outer'. Being good at creativity often entails being good at thinking about 'what is' so you can think about 'what ought to be'.
- **Working and not-working** – the way creativity involves researching, thinking and planning something so that you can forget about it, go for a walk, do something else,

get drunk, so that you can arrive at a solution without appearing to have thought about it. Many creative people report that the flash of inspiration comes when they are relaxed, comfortable, taking time away from work. Being good at creative work often entails taking a bath.

- **Person and city** – the way that creative people and groups have shaped cities, and indeed for some, have actually created city life, just as the greater social contact offered by cities have shaped the work of creative people and groups. Being good at creativity often entails going 'into town'.
- **Person and culture** – the way the creative individual generates new ideas which impact upon the broader culture, just as the broader culture shapes what 'counts' as creativity, selects which bits are to be celebrated and decides how the creative individual is doing in terms of 'success'. Being good at creativity often entails finding happy compromises between what you want and what they want.
- **Focused action and relaxed semi-action** – the way in which creative focus often comes from a period of relaxed semi-action, just as the relaxed semi-action stimulates the creative person into focused action. Being good at creativity often entails knowing when it is 'not working' and when to do something else. It is important that this is actually 'something' else, to keep your mind active but not too focused. Doing nothing at all doesn't seem to work so well.
- **Worldliness and naivety** – the way a smart creative interaction with the world often stems from asking fairly naïve and childlike questions, just as that very naivety spurs the creative person to develop more insightful questions. Being good at creativity often entails choosing the right question at the right time within the lifetime of the project as it emerges out of itself.
- **Complexity and simplicity** – the way creativity requires drawing together multiple, often competing, sometimes contradictory ideas so they can be corralled into more simple statements, just as blindingly simple statements, images and designs can then sometimes convey a whole world of complexity and nuance. Being good at creativity often entails being good at navigation between 'levels' of meaning.
- **Deliberate and non-deliberate** – the way that deliberately 'paying attention' is often supplemented by more unconscious or playful spheres of non-attention, just as these attentions can then become re-forgotten and 'embodied' parts of creative flow. Being good at creativity often entails skilful navigation between non-deliberate remembering and deliberate forgetting.
- **Continuous and discontinuous** – the way that creative processes carried out in continuous ways are often refreshed by a break, just as the break carries within it the new creative insights developed through our daily concerted efforts. Being good at creativity often entails mixing a holiday from work with a working holiday.
- **Goal-defined and non-goal-defined** – the way that the attention paid to specific things for specific reasons to achieve a specific goal is sometimes informed by those more open-ended activities we engage in for no specific thing, reason or goal. Non-goal oriented thoughts can be given a creative 'home' by goal-specific needs. Being good at creativity often entails not trying too hard, so that we can try hard.
- **Discipline and playfulness** – the way creative processes require the shelving of play if it is to come to full fruition, just as that very playfulness is the wellspring of the fruitful thing to be disciplined about. Being good at creativity often entails being a grown-up child, or a childlike adult.

- **Extroversion and introversion** – the way many creative people exhibit an extrovert eagerness to engage with the world by overcoming a nervous shyness about their work, just as that shy introversion gives them time and space to develop better articulations of their creative self to the outside world. Being good at creativity often entails choosing the right identity for the right occasion.

- **Pride and humility** – the way creative people exhibit a proud declaration about their achievements, which itself emanates from a humble recognition that they are building upon the work of others and can never really fulfil their dreams or their ambitions. Being good at creativity often entails knowing when to shout and when to be quiet.

- **Tradition and rebellion** – the way that creative traditions can give location to work and educate us into themes and techniques, just as we challenge and push these 'locations' to shine light on new directions and possibilities. Being good at creativity often entails finding a good balance between learning one's craft from previous masters and challenging their authority.

- **Objectivity and passion** – the way that one's creativity requires an objective sense of what will and will not work, just as that very work flows from an innate passion for something that you put your heart and soul into, and will defend to the end come what may. Being good at creativity often entails working to create your 'baby' so as to let it die away, to be reborn at another time.

- **Difficult tensions and great pleasures** – the way that grappling with the tensions, sufferings and difficulties of creativity gives us great pleasure, just as those pleasures remind us of the great tensions to come. Being good at creativity often entails accepting the pain because we know of the joy to come.

But all this tends to reside within the dialectical interplays of the creative person themselves, what Gardner (2011) calls the *asynchronous dynamics* within an individual person. But he also goes on to identify a dialectical interplay between the individual and the broader context within which they exist. We will look at these contextual features in much more depth within Chapter 6. For now, it is useful to note that Gardner sees a similar dialectical interplay at work between the *creative person* on the one hand; *the field* – the system of cultural institutions, gatekeepers, critics and opinion makers on the other; and *the domain* – the current state of play within particular creative disciplines, traditions of work or paradigms on another. As he puts it:

> . . . creativity does not inhere in any single node, nor, indeed, in any pair of nodes. Rather, creativity is best viewed as a dialectical or interactive process in which all three of these elements participate.
>
> (Gardner 2011. p. 14)

The point is creativity does not come from 'things' – ideas, propensities, universal mindsets, single attitudes, linear plans, one-way logics – but from the various interplays, differences and contradictions between such 'things' as they mutually inform each other, be that within the asynchronicities *within* the person, or those which persist *across* different contextual locations of creativity. We feel that this more dialectical conception of creativity adds immeasurably to an understanding of it as a series of moving processes and helps to situate it against a particular 'logic'. This is why the dialectical motif runs through the rest of this book. By applying this kind of dialectical thinking, we are better able to situate creativity as the emergent emanation of multiple interplays between things. If creativity resides anywhere, and has anything we could tentatively call a 'logic', it is this space of interplay between opposites leading to change, flux and eventually new ideas. As Henri Matisse once said, 'I don't paint things. I only paint the difference between things'.

The public understanding of creativity: a polemic

Looking at things in terms of dynamic interplays between the creative person on the one hand, creative relationships on the other, and creative places and media on yet another, implies some fundamental tensions.

Insufficient conscious self-reflection upon one's creativity can be a bad thing if it simply leaves us passively hoping that creative inspiration will arrive the next time when we need it. But too much theoretical reflection upon one's creativity might lead to a clumsy, awkward self-consciousness. Too much focus upon the broad contexts of creativity runs the risk of under-valuing the inner wellspring of individual creative imagination. Too much 'hard edged' analysis of creativity risks sanitizing it. But equally, too much celebratory, self-indulgent navel gazing upon individual pieces of 'extraordinariness' only takes us back to the false dichotomies and nascent cultural hierarchies we touched upon above. These kind of implicit tensions underlay two common reactions whenever you tell anyone you are trying to write a book about creativity – 'Wow, that's a big subject. You will never be able to pull it off', and, just as common, 'I'm not sure I would even want to know. It feels like that would kill it somehow'.

So a delicate balance is needed. In seeking to strike our balance and preserve a dignified degree of hopeful humility, we have listened to Henry Moore. In 1937 he wrote an article entitled 'The Sculptor Speaks' for *The Listener Magazine*, in which he expressed the potential dangers of saying too much in public about creative practice, but also of the benefits of saying something.

> It is a mistake for a sculptor or a painter to speak or write very often about his job. It releases tension needed for his work. By trying to express his aims with rounded-off logical exactness, he can easily become a theorist whose actual work is only a caged-in exposition of conceptions evolved in terms of logic and words.
>
> But though the nonlogical, instinctive, subconscious part of the mind must play its part in his work, he also has a conscious mind which is not inactive. The artist works with a concentration of his whole personality, and the conscious part of it resolves conflicts, organizes memories, and prevents him from trying to walk in two directions at the same time.
>
> It is likely, then, that a sculptor can give, from his own conscious experience, clues which will help others in their approach to sculpture, and this article tries to do this, and no more. It is not a general survey of sculpture, or of my development, but a few words on some of the problems that have concerned me from time to time.
>
> (Moore 1937)

We would like to claim a similarly contingent place for ourselves with regard to this piece of writing, but similarly share a few words about debates that have interested us along the way. And not least of the reasons is our belief that a greater *public understanding* of creativity is needed if the false dichotomies and hierarchies discussed above are to be overcome.

In recent years, much progress has been made in improving the public understanding of science. But the arts have done much less well. Indeed some proponents of the arts seem to have deliberately gone in the other direction, to become increasingly arcane and obscurantist about their creativity. Science has presented a relatively coherent 'story' about what it is for, how it works and how people can become engaged in scientific creativity. Science, including the creativity it rests upon, has also been proactive in highlighting its two underlying features – the scientific method and the history of how science has contributed to solving human and social needs.

In contrast, the public understanding of artistic creativity is in a fairly parlous state. The public 'story' of art is rather under-explored and incoherent, except within the enclaves of the experts. The processes and methods of creative origination, the nature of artistic work and its contribution to human and social needs is chronically under-discussed. Celebrations of the sterile art object have displaced public debates about the creative process, as well as, one suspects, many aspects of self-reflection on the part of individual artists concerning where their artistic creativity comes from. Increasingly, it seems, success on the art market is what defines an artist and gives them their artist-ness. Public narratives concerning artistic creativity still seems to be locked into the rather ridiculous, tautological definition of art as 'something that artists do'. And who are these artists you may well ask? Well, they are the people who do the art. The public understanding of artistic creativity seems to have settled for this opaque, self-reverential position first set out by Arthur Danto, and has ignored critiques of it set out by writers such as John Carey (2006). As a result, being an 'artist' remains a relatively closed process which many people find more difficult to join. Discussion of the contribution of artistic creativity to public cultural life is too often restricted to quasi-religious celebrations of art objects, to dusty cultural policy reports which no one reads, or to evaluations of community arts projects, which even fewer people read. The economists restrict public discussions of creativity to the economic impact of the creative industries in terms of business growth, job creation generating inward investment, encouraging cultural tourism and all the rest. The facet which each of these failures of public understanding share is their tendency to always discuss the nature of creativity by discussing something else! As a result, the contribution of 'artistic' creativity to public quality of life, personal well-being, effective cultural communication, education and the rest is too often left implicit.

In short, improving the public understanding of scientific creativity has been about explaining what science has done, and can continue to do for a collective 'us' in terms of addressing broad human problems. It could perhaps be summarized by a sentiment which says – 'we know science is complicated, but we will pay particular attention to explaining it to everyone, because it is important to us all'. Too much about artistic creativity has been about what the arts can do for an individualistic 'me', in terms of exploring the self and identity. It could perhaps be summarized by a sentiment that says, 'I know my work is quite complicated, but it is about me and if you don't understand it, then that is a problem with you the viewer'. And because this is a closed, opaque discussion, public understandings of creativity are too often focused upon the identity of the artist themselves, which damages the idea that creativity is something potentially open to all people. It is no coincidence that people are so often heard to say, 'I don't really understand art'. And it is but a short step from there for them to believe that they cannot therefore do it themselves because they lack some mysterious creativity component to their personality.

Of course, artistic creativity can be about an unexplainable inner dialogue focused solely upon self-identity. This is part of the grandeur of artistic creativity, and can be an interesting and worthwhile experience for others. But it can also be about more than this. If it neglects clear and effective public communication about its processes in favour of celebrations of its object outcomes, then its own artistic pretensions will only damage the idea that all people can consider artistic creativity as part of their life. Such approaches to creativity are undemocratic in a deep and fundamental sense, and our current age is characterized by too large a democratic deficit that goes under-challenged in the cultural sphere. Neglecting to explain or, more strongly worded, deliberately mystifying the processes of creativity leads too many people to the idea that they can only engage as passive consumers of the creativity of other, more professional practitioners. In his book *Art and Agency*, Alfred Gell (1998) suggests the alternative view. Rather than an emphasis upon the inherent aesthetic qualities of the art object itself, his view is that the creative process is best perceived in terms of the agency it allows for – what motivates the production, what the circulation of creativity means for a broader social collective, and what the various receptions of creativity might tell us about our society. He suggests that creativity, and its outcomes, is a 'social fact', which needs to be considered as a process that goes far beyond isolated individual art acts. Creativity is a social fact because it is the underpinning of kinship, political culture, economic exchange and social histories just as much as it is the wellspring of individual identity and meaning.

No matter how personal and 'separated off' artistic creativity may feel for the individual creator, sustaining the creative process, getting it circulated and received are social and economic procedures. There is a 'politics' to creativity, because what gets selected as worthy of our attention is never a neutral process. By adhering to a less than developed public understanding of creativity which reproduces the elitism of Mr. Tusa, this 'politics' is inherently, chronically and unjustifiably undemocratic. Mr. Tusa's elitism and Mr. Danto's tautologies are shot through with problems, most of which are laid out very cogently, as we have already noted, by Carey (2006) in his book *What Good Are the Arts?* There are quite a few of them, but perhaps the one that concerns us most here is the problem associated with the self-selecting and internally self-validating nature of the public discourse offered by the 'experts' and 'cultural leaders' of artistic creativity. Their pronouncements too often culminate in statements which, explicitly or implicitly, say to the public that you are only really involved as customers or consumers. And this culminates in a very superficial, very exclusive, very judgemental and very negative public understanding of artistic creativity. It conceives of creativity as an act which is *a priori* denied to the vast majority of people. So we see a crisis of legitimacy which corresponds to the aforementioned democratic deficit, which is increasingly similar to that affecting professionalized politics and their associated technocrats. In contrast to the 'art is what artists say it is' notion of creativity, Gell (1998) suggests that we situate artistic creativity more against criteria of how communities of people use it to speak to each other, what they use it to speak about, indeed, the extent to which it does actually speak to people in the context of their everyday lives.

Rather than the reverential placing of the art object in the gallery or museum, the blockbuster movie in the cinema or the factory-made music track in the shop as the locus for a public understanding of artistic creativity, the fundamental question of situating creativity for a broad public understanding is perhaps best approached by asking what it is for. This starts to raise all sorts of questions about creativity and communal life within the public realm, which we will touch on at various points below. But already it signals the view that rather than situating creativity within the exhibition catalogue or the price list, we should renew interest in situating it within an *ethical conception* of creativity (see Shorthose 2011;

Shorthose and Maycroft 2011) concerning how we are to live together. Gell's (1998) view emphases the agency and intentions of individual people, along with the artistic causations, results and transformations this leads to for the culture of the broader community. Rather than viewing artistic creativity as being located within the aesthetic qualities of individually considered pieces of work, he views art as a system of creative action which resonates with, and indeed changes the world of, those communities. Thus his notion of creativity is a much more social conception.

This is the basis of an *anthropological conception of creativity* which contrasts markedly from the rather insipid object-based view of artistic endeavour. Creativity is too fundamental to the everyday lives of people and the public realm to be left so designated by a small, self-selected cultural elite who have little or no public mandate, and left so mystified. A renewed public realm that simultaneously stimulates and is stimulated by our joint creativity needs to become more of our joint co-creative capacities as a regular aspect of our everyday lives. And one of those aspects is discussing and sharing ideas about creativity itself.

For example, important representatives of the anthropological conception of creativity are Ellen Dissanayake (1995), Lewis Hyde (2006) and Marcel Mauss (2002). For instance, in her book *Homo Aestheticus: Where Art Comes From and Why* (1995) Dissanayake argues that it was only from the 18th Century onwards that the specific experience that we now regard as 'aesthetic' became separated from other human experiences. For Dissanayake, it was this which underpinned the questionable assertion that artistic creativity exists only as a specific aspect of taste for a limited number of people. The separation of the aesthetic from broader human and social dimensions has given us subsequent Institutionally-located production-distribution-validation-production circles of the gallery-critic-auction-room-museum industry, which has come to be held up as the arbiter and repository of our greatest acts of creativity.

> Looking at the plural and radical nature of the arts in our time, aware of the economic ramifications where canvases may be 'worth' millions of dollars and where critics, dealers and museum directors, rather than artists or publics, largely decide this value, philosophers concerned with art have concluded that art no longer exists (if it ever did) in a vacuum or ideal realm for its own sake, with its sacred essence waiting to be discovered, but must be considered as it appears in and is dependent on a particular social context. . . . It exists, if at all, only as a socially and historically conditioned label.
>
> (Dissanayake 1995. p. 41)

In contrast to this view, Dissanayake is animated by what she calls a *species-centric view*, which sees creativity as residing within articulations of something much more social and practical, in ways which bring people together in communities of mutual interest and action.

> The species-centric view of art recognises and proclaims as valid and intrinsic the association between what humans have always found to be important and certain ways – called 'the arts' – that they have found to grasp, manifest and reinforce this importance. That the arts in postmodern society do not perform these functions . . . is not because of deficiency or insubstantiality of an abstract concept but because their maker inhabit a world – unprecedented in human history – in which these abiding concerns are artificially disguised, denied, trivialised, ignored or banished.
>
> (Dissanayake 1995. p. 41)

Dissanayake situates artistic creativity as central to the articulation of cultural meanings which 'make special' the necessary common actions around which communal social bonds are formed and sustained. She situates creativity at the very centre of the potential for play, ceremony, symbolism, festivity and other rituals within a public realm, which enable 'ways of making important things and activities special'. A conscious and concerted return to something like Dissanayake's anthropological conception of creativity is an antidote to the object-based conceptions of creativity which lift it out of social relationships and cultural contexts and situate it in the mystique of purely internal insights and notions of individual 'genius'. When it comes to our initial question of situating creativity we could do worse than make the following connections between creativity and its 'making special' functions. Building upon Dissanayake (1995) we might suggest that creativity could be situated within:

- **Making human** – the human impetus to articulate something between creativity and 'making special' has, it appears, existed throughout history and is geographically widespread. It appears that creativity has always been linked to growing and sustaining common and mutual bonds of sociality.
- **Making democratic** – artistic creativity can be anything and can come from any-where. The interminable self-selections of the elitist conception, which seeks to define what art 'is', should be given up on, and all forms of creativity be made more radically open to all. Institutions of creativity which do so much to distinguish 'insiders' or 'professionals' from 'outsiders' or 'amateurs' operate from an *a priori* democratic deficit, and they should therefore stop with such demarcations.
- **Making de-Institutionalized** – trying to assess the relative merits of isolated acts of artistic creativity separate from their broader 'making special' functions is ultimately regressive. The Institutions which house the self-elected elitists, the cultural 'experts' and 'leaders' are only really operating within their own internally self-validating ana-lytical propositions. As such, they are inherently 'one dimensional' (Marcuse 1964) in much the same way as Mr. Tusa. As we will argue in Chapter 6, cultural dialogue which is more radically open to public discourses about creativity, as well as the devel-opment of spaces for active public creation, offer much more, both for the public who are meant to be served by the Institutions, and for the Institutions themselves.
- **Making critical** – 'making special' through public artistic creativity is behaviour which is potentially common to us all, and a thoroughgoing recognition of such shows in sharp relief the paucity of this internally self-validating Institutional view. The 'making special' nature of creativity could be linked to an inevitably critical pro-cess of multiple voices entering the public realm through their creativity to challenge the rather smug view of the Institutional 'insiders'. Just as in other realms of cultural politics, creativity is always already connected to critique as much as to success within the current market paradigm.
- **Making public** – ultimately, the centrality of the 'making special' function within creat-ivity helps us to remember the mutual interplay between human and social evolution. It helps to highlight the links between the passionate and the intellectual, the emotional and the practical. This is, in short, the interplay between an interior individual life and the public realm. 'Making special' hints at the dialectical relationship between the subjective and the objective, and proclaims the special function of artistic creativity for articulating within and across these broader elements of social and cultural life.

So, if all these elements are necessary for a consideration of creativity – the internal in relation to the external, the subjective in relation to the objective, the passionate in relation to the concrete, the Institutional in relation to the critical – our approach to creativity must indeed have many contours – the creative person; the creative group and its social nature; the public nature of creative spaces and places; the de-Institutionalizing nature of the new media landscape which is offering a more publicly open notion of creativity; the broader contexts of creativity. All need to have their place in a cross-fertilizing multi-disciplinary debate about the location of creativity. These are the broad contours of our book, and the chapters which follow will explore these aspects in turn.

Let's now turn to more detailed explorations of the more specific sites of creativity by, firstly, looking at a broad range of ideas concerning the creative person. This will then enable us in subsequent chapters to explore how the creative person interacts with other sites of creativity such as their relationships with other people, with particular places, with the new media landscape and with the broader contexts they must operate in.

Chapter 2

The creative person

It is probably true to say that the most common idea concerning the location of creativity is the one which situates it within the creative person – its brain or mind, in the personality or personal attitudes, in the memories or aptitudes of the individual. The *combinatorial conception* of creativity is perhaps the most commonly expressed facet of this, and lies at the centre of various branches of psychology. It suggests that creativity is in essence 'new combinations of old ideas' which flow from the way the individual processes information on the basis of these personal propensities.

But as we will see in some detail below, the psychology of creativity comes from many different perspectives. According to behaviourist psychology, the most basic and perhaps now rather outmoded of these perspectives, we think and act according to *reinforcements* which establish common responses to certain stimuli. For this view creativity is the behaviour of certain individuals which is deemed to be the more unusual or unexpected combinations of stimuli and response. But as we will see in detail below, the combinatorial conception of creativity (Boden 1990; Smith et al. 1995) is more strongly associated with cognitive psychology, a perspective which emphasizes our innate human abilities to actively shape our responses to the world on the basis of a repertoire of personal perceptions, memories and expectations. For cognitive psychology, we are not simply passive receptors of external stimuli, nor are we fixed into making reinforced responses on the basis of those external stimuli. Rather, we actively choose the way we process information, and it is this which is the fundamental basis for making new combinations of old ideas.

> . . . as far as cognitive theorists are concerned, creativity represents . . . differing ways of getting and handling information, and different ways of combining data in seeking effective solutions. . . . Hence, the cognitive approach to creativity asks about the extent to which highly creative people are prepared to take risks in their thinking, about their willingness to take in large quantities of information the environment has to offer . . . (*and*) their capacity for quickly changing their point of view.
>
> (Cropley 1972. p. 12)

In recent years, cognitive psychology has merged with certain aspects of evolutionary theory which focuses upon evolution of bigger human brains as the springboard for other creative capacities, and with modern neuroscientific mapping of the brain, into a hybrid perspective. This has fast become the mainstream locus for attempts to understand the creative person, largely as an adjunct of their bigger quest for an understanding of human consciousness, and (in some quarters at least) speculations about the nature of artificial intelligence. So, as we are already beginning to see, the view that creativity is situated within the creative person can take many forms, has many different emphases and stems from many different perspectives.

But the view that creativity happens within the human brain-mind-person is perhaps the common trope which underpins much of this. Most broad accounts of creativity tend to start and end with this rather stereotypical view. We often assume some people, treated as specific and isolated individuals, 'just are' creative. That is, some people are seen as having some kind of innate qualities which give them a *creative personality*, having organized a creative identity for themselves and demarcating themselves from others on this basis. And given this, many accounts of creativity seem satisfied with simply describing these people through interviews and biographies. As we have already begun to say in the previous chapter, for a variety of reasons we tend to reject this person-centric view of creativity. The interviews and biographies of these 'lone genius' creative people tend to indulge in a lot of (self-)selection, and no small amount of (self-)aggrandizement. But whilst we feel this individualized conception is in itself an insufficiently broad view of creativity, it is obviously that the inner psychological dynamics of the human brain-mind-personality have a great bearing upon creativity. Whilst the various ideas emerging from the individualized conception may be wanting in the bigger scheme of things, they are a necessary component of our multi-disciplinary account and form something of a springboard from which to develop our argument overall. Whilst much of this evidence is inevitably quite anecdotal, it is revealing nonetheless. So before we take a critical look at the more rigorous accounts of the creative person flowing from the more current amalgam between cognitive psychological, evolutionary theory and neuroscientific accounts (D'Amasio 2012; Lehrer 2007), let's look at some of the ideas central to the notion that creativity is a personal attitude.

Creativity as a personal attitude

At its most general, it might be that creativity of the individual person comes from a certain personal *attitude* towards life, the world and other people. Many creative biographies and inquiries which bring together interviews with creative people (Gardner 2011; Tusa 2003) do seem to throw up quite common features within a creative life. For instance, in his book *Creating Minds*, Gardner (2011) identifies three key attitudinal features of the creative person. Firstly, creative people seem to commonly display levels of motivation, which entail them spending a longer time thinking about how to do things differently, and the extent to which they have achieved new and better solutions to practical problems. Secondly, Gardner feels that a creative attitude flows from a greater, more sustained determination to focus upon a perceived creative strength or talent, which often becomes a lifelong sense of meaning and purpose. Thirdly for Gardner, this sense of purpose leads to a personal attitude which often exhibits a greater sense of resilience, a willingness to keep working at things which views temporary set-backs as learning experiences rather than insurmountable failures.

In his book *Serious Creativity*, Edward de Bono (1992) identifies several attitudinal features as key sources of creativity. For him, one of the most fundamental of these is *motivation*, which we started to discuss in the previous chapter. For de Bono, the creative person is motivated, for myriad reasons, to spend greater time and energy in the search of something new when everyone else is satisfied with the obvious, or 'orthodox'. Higher than usual levels of motivation lie behind the unsatisfied, unsatisfiable search for creative expression, the restless energy, the endless curiosity or the obsession with finding a solution which many people routinely express as the key driver of their creative spirit.

> Motivation means being willing to spend up to five hours a week trying to find a better way of doing something when other people perhaps only spend five minutes a week. Motivation means looking for alternatives when everyone else is satisfied with the obvious.
> (de Bono 1992. p. 23)

This increased motivation leads to a greater sense of *involvement* in their work. Many forms of human endeavour not usually labelled as creativity entail us becoming involved in what we are doing to achieve an external end. This is what we might call basic goal-oriented behaviour. But the creative person seems to bring, and simultaneously benefit from, a different kind of involvement which is located within the 'creative thing' itself rather than being geared towards an external rewards. Such involvement is expressed as the creative person becoming 'totally immersed', not being able to 'leave it alone', becoming a 'workaholic', having to 'get it finished'. It is what often gives the creative attitude its great energy. As we saw in the previous chapter, this has been called the 'flow' of the creative experience (Csíkszentmihályi 1990), and is part of the 'autotelic' nature of the 'logic' of creativity. This means that the focus is solely *within* the experience of involvement with the creative process itself.

This can mean that the creative attitude has great *resilience*. Creativity doesn't always come when we want it. Sometimes creativity can feel like 'banging our head against a brick wall'. Creativity often goes wrong, but the creative attitude seems to be accompanied by a willingness to accept this and keep going. For example, Marie Curie talks vividly of how she had worked in a miserable old shed, in which she passed the best and happiest years of her life, devoting her entire days to her work. Although a feeling of discouragement sometimes came upon her after an unsuccessful day, this discouragement always led to renewed activity.

And with involvement and resilience comes a greater *experience*. With experience, we know the things that work, we have greater insight into effective working processes, and maybe even what will succeed in the world out there. The creativity of experience is often low-risk creativity which seeks to build upon and to repeat past successes. But nevertheless, it is still often associated with the creativity of great craft. In recent years the *10,000 Hours Rule* (Gladwell 2008) has become well known. Putting the hours into one's craft is often a necessary component because it allows an embodied experience to be forged – thirty hours per week, for forty weeks per year, means that in just over eight years we have a chance of becoming an expert in our craft.

It is this kind of creative experience which often leads to the development of a personal *style*, which can help to consolidate a creative attitude because it provides a firm grounding from which to make choices within one's creativity. Experience and style can enable better *judgement*. Sennett (2008) has argued that the idea of *animal laborens* refers to the basic work we engage in without the need for real involvement, whereas the idea of *Homo faber* refers to our evolved human capacity to combine thought and action within self-directed work. And because we have this capacity there is the need, some would say responsibility, to carefully judge what we do, how, when and why. A creative attitude is in many ways connected to the making of judgements – aesthetic, material, political and ethical – within one's work. The myriad connections between the search for involvement, the experience of experiences, being faced by the need for resilience and judgement seems to somehow be connected to the many reports of creative people developing daily personal *routines and rituals* as an aid to getting in touch with their creative attitude (Curry 2013). But just developing such daily routines and devoting 10,000 hours to one's craft will not in itself guarantee success. Other kinds of experiences are also needed. So whilst a certain attitude which values one's established patterns of creativity is needed, an openness towards new experiences is also a necessary part of a creative attitude. And this brings us away from facets such as involvement, resilience and experience – those which consolidate one's current creative attitude – towards their opposites which signal an attitude of open-ended-ness and exploration. This immediately brings us back to the dialectical idea of creativity introduced in the previous chapter. The elements of the creative attitude which express the establishment of a creative pattern are intertwined with an opposite attitude seeking to go beyond the established, open up new approaches and develop new ways of thinking and doing.

For de Bono (1992) a central feature of a creative attitude is the opposite of experience, namely *innocence*. Innocence is the classic creativity of children. If we do not have the experience to know the usual approach, the usual solution, the usual concepts involved, then we can find fresh approaches. Too much involvement in the way things currently are, too much regular style, risks creative dullness and may serve to restrict the imagination. Because children do not know the orthodox opinion, the common perception, the professional approach, they are more free from any inhibitions in their thinking. So their creativity is often of a different order than the rational, experienced adult. This is why children often have a much more creative attitude. Children know they are children, and so they know that they have a lot to learn. And so, they are often able to see much further than adults. Having a lot to learn given one's self-recognized innocence, and thus being more creative than the more experienced, is but one facet of the contradictory, dialectical nature of creativity.

But the creative innocence often exhibited by children is something we all might experience if we adopt an attitude of *release*. A facet of a creative attitude comes from being released from inhibitions, pressures, fears and conventions. A degree of innocence and release is central to a creative attitude because it helps us to overcome the self-limiting brakes we all too often put upon our creative vision. This can often feel quite counter-intuitive. For instance, we can find value in innocence, and actively initiate a sense of release if we actively embrace our own *ignorance*. A creative attitude often entails actively embracing what we don't know, actively and gleefully exploring the gaps in our knowledge rather than defending the turf of our current experience and expertise. If we appreciate ignorance as a useful signpost directing our attention, then we might better see new learning experiences and so find routes towards new creative destinations. It is likely that most things are relevant in some way. This kind of attitude seems to chime with *divergent thinking* and *ideational fluency* to go beyond the 'normal' logics and rationalities which colour our everyday lives, as discussed in the previous chapter as part of the 'logic' of creativity. For instance, de Bono (1992) has to a large extent made his reputation upon accounts of how this kind of attitude can be developed. He used the term *lateral thinking* to describe a systematic technique to release one's creative thinking from existing strictures. When faced with a problem, we too often mistake the criteria in which the problem is presented to us as the tools we must use to find the solution. Lateral thinking is about finding effective ways to import new ways of thinking from 'outside' of the question, into it. It is *lateral* thinking because it implies *stepping sideways* rather than trying to make progress by going forward along already established tracks. In recent years, the ubiquitous 'thinking outside of the box' has come to mean going for the deliberately wacky and unlikely just for the sake of it. Lateral thinking shows that it is simply about a creative attitude which tries to see the question as it is presented as the 'box', and releasing one's thinking to learn how to bring in new ideas from beyond the terms in which the original question is posed.

Such release mechanisms can help to keep the creativity fresh and alive, because it tends to fuel a more *audacious* attitude, one which is happy to take risks, has the courage to step into the unknown territories, be willing to be mocked, be happy to be an outsider. And this helps us to recognize the importance of *play* for a creative attitude. We have already related creativity to childhood and the benefits of persisting with the childlike. So we have already implied the importance of play for creativity, but as we start to drill down into what are perhaps the more 'public facing' aspects of the creative attitude, we again start to recognize the dialectical interplay of opposites within it. Whilst a playful attitude helps with release and audacity, many creative people also report on a deep sense of *seriousness* within their creativity. In a similar vein, a creative attitude seems to often come with its own degree of *tension and suffering*. Creative people often talk about how they have 'suffered for their art', how it brought many internal tensions and even bordered on madness.

There may be a degree of hyperbole in this, but nevertheless a creative attitude appears to involve strange, contradictory combinations and unclear agendas. Sometimes it is the suffering we experience within our lives that feed back into and stimulate a creative response. Creativity, tension and suffering are often intertwined. It is often a very *disorienting* experience. However, as we saw in the previous chapter, the dialectical interplays within the creative attitude also mean that tension and suffering are often accompanied by a great *happiness*.

But happiness it not a simple thing. Our consumerist society has propagated the idea for many years that happiness comes through getting more of the things we feel we want or need, which is an *acquisition-based happiness*. Such a notion underpins the ubiquitous economistic lexicography such as 'gross domestic product', 'standard of living' and the other facile measurements of happiness. But if we are always asking ourselves whether we are happy or not from this point of view, it is likely we will always be unhappy, because we will always be focused upon what we think is missing. We will become a 'glass half empty' person. An alternative view sees happiness as coming from a sense of involvement and commitment to something bigger than our own life, that is, it can be *value-based happiness*. This form of happiness is intimately linked to the creative attitude in that such creativity is often the vehicle with which the creative person engages with the world in this 'bigger' way. Creativity is connected to value-based happiness in that they are both ways of putting ourselves into things we believe in. But this means that happiness is not a 'state of affairs' which we can 'arrive at' or 'have' (Fromm 1976). If one tries to 'have' happiness, it will disappear. A creative attitude seems to be related to those temporary feeling states which we can sometimes 'be' in. Happiness may not lead to creativity, but creativity through the experiences of tension, struggle and disorientation will probably lead to happiness as we work our way through them. Eleanor Roosevelt is famous for saying that 'happiness is a by-product'. Henri Matisse also said that 'happiness comes from doing a good day's work'. Both are implicitly referring to this notion of value-based happiness as a facet of the creative attitude, in that both see happiness as coming, as a by-product, from doing something to demonstrate ourselves to the world, in the world.

And this is related to the *sense of purpose* which often lies within the creative attitude. Creatively expressing our values to the world and its people is intimately intertwined with finding ourselves in and through this sense of purpose. The philosophy of work often argues that when we are able to express ourselves through a sense of purpose, then such work is at one and the same time more meaningful and more creative. Purpose is usually connected to the attitude of seeking something 'more' or 'better', which is the initial motivation within creativity. But connected to this, many creative biographies report the experience of a *visceral need* to express something in and through their work. And this interpenetration of creative happiness and purpose again takes us back to what Csíkszentmihályi (1990) has called *creative flow*. The happiness–purpose dialectic seems to be expressed within the experiences of having clear creative goals; appreciating a heightened self-awareness from gaining the immediate feedback one gets from one's actions; when distractions, worries about failure and a sense of time seem to disappear. The great sense of happiness and purpose, gained from the dialectical interplays with struggle, tensions and sufferings are sometimes expressed within this sense of creative flow to the extent that there is an experience of the person merging with the creativity itself. This is perhaps the apogee of the creative attitude at its best.

So in terms of locating creativity within the person, these features of the creative attitude perhaps give us somewhere to start. Features such as the ones described above have been expressed, albeit in varying forms, within many creative lives in connection to many different creative disciplines. But given that they are features expressed within the biographies of personal lives, they are inherently anecdotal. In pursuing the nature of the creative person, we can also look at attempts at more rigorous and systematic accounts of the basis of creativity. And in terms of the creative person, evolutionary theory, cognitive psychology and the (recently) connected studies within neuroscience hold some very fruitful lines of inquiry. These three aspects have in recent years become an embryonically consolidated perspective. There are of course other psychological perspectives which lie outside of this, which we can also take into account below, but let's start our discussion of these more rigorous views of the brain, the mind, human cognition and the central facet of self-consciousness as a component of our multidisciplinary account.

Evolution, the brain and the mind

Human creativity is clearly related to the evolution of many capacities to adapt to our environment in the quest for survival which for evolutionary theory and modern neuroscience are connected to the development of the bigger brains of the human species. Neuroscience seeks to describe in detail the specific functions of each region of the brain by 'mapping' its internal neural networks to explain how we process information. It is replete with experiments to show how these myriad neural networks enable creative thoughts to 'bubble up', and more philosophical speculations about how we thus re-process and eventually 'publish' a piece of creative thinking or behaviour (Dennett 1993). Such research dovetails with the older tradition of cognitive research in psychology which emerged from the 'cognitive revolution' stimulated by George Miller and others in the 1950s (Gardner 1985). Cognitive psychology replaced earlier, highly mechanical, behaviourist psychology to focus upon how the human individual actively shaped and determined their responses to the world on the basis of their own perceptions, motivations, expectations, memories and interests. Behaviourist psychology was centred upon the idea that human behaviour is the result of conditioned responses to the external stimuli we get from our experiences of the world. We 'learn' these conditioned ways of responding in various ways, but fundamental behaviourists understood individual actions (creative or otherwise) as simply a novel reaction to certain stimuli, leading to 'unlikely responses'.

Cognitive psychology, on the other hand, took its cue from a critique of this rather mechanical view. Due to the human propensity to actively select and shape their overt behaviour, cognitive psychology argued that processing information coming from the external world is neither a fixed nor objective thing. Rather it is an active process which individuals shape into a personal 'reality' made up from a moving and complex system of interacting parts capable of creating an infinite range of outcomes. And it is this active selection which cognitive psychology places at the heart of creativity. Whilst the 'inner' of individual psychology and the 'outer' of receptions by others combine to make Culture, it is the inner psychological processes flowing from the movability of cognition which is their fundamental wellspring for an account of the creative person. The way the creative person thinks, recognizes, selects, expects, remembers and 'changes their mind' is central to this view. As a result, when considering creativity, cognitive psychologists

> . . . are chiefly concerned with the ways in which people organize information received from the world. The individual is regarded as actively at grips with his/her environment, not merely the passive receptor of whatever it chances to offer him/her. Different people possess differing ways of 'taking hold of' the external world; they receive information in characteristic ways, interpret it idiosyncratically, and store it in terms of all the information processed in the past. Intellectual functioning is thus seen as a highly unified process so that the attempt to break it down into discrete fragments in the way stimulus–response (*behaviourist*) ways is bound to be inadequate. . . . Hence, the cognitive approach to creativity asks about the extent to which highly creative people are prepared to take risks in their thinking, about their willingness to take in large quantities of information the environment has to offer (rather than restrict themselves to a narrow, but safe, segment of it), about their capacity for quickly changing their point of view.
>
> (Cropley 1972. p. 20)

The general contours of this view, and the emphasis upon the selective, dynamic and ever changing nature of such internal mental processes, can be summarized following Smith et al. (1995) within the following range of distinctions:

- **Individual or social** – our mental creative processes can be either purely individual – or they can be the result of interactions with others.
- **Deliberate or non-deliberate** – mental processes can be deliberately chosen by 'paying attention' – or they can be things that happen even though we are not fully aware of them and have not chosen that particular attention.
- **Goal-defined or non-goal-defined** – creativity can come from paying attention to a specific thing, for a specific reason, to achieve a specific goal – or it can flow from being mentally active without any of these specific things, reasons or goals.

- **Subjectively or objectively novel** – creativity can be felt and experienced as 'new', 'necessary' or 'exciting' by the individual carrying out the internal mental processes even though the actual outcome may be none of these things for others. So the creative person can be motivated by subjective experiences. But equally, the creative person might be engaged in internal mental processes that are leading them to something objectively new for the world, even though they may be unaware of this novelty.
- **Continuous or discontinuous** – the inner creative mental processes of the creative person might be something they do all the time – or they might be intermittent and haphazard intervals within their life.

But cognitive psychology's placing of this active thinking person at the centre of their research has meant it has merged with the rapidly developing field of neuroscience, due to the fact that they both share concerns with the way isolated individual subjects actively process information coming from the world. Both disciplines share a concern to generate 'scientific' explanations of these inner mental processes. Cognitive psychology was always very laboratory-based and concerned to use experimental methods to explore cognitive processes. Modern neuroscience has to some extent taken over the mantle of this kind of research, and has tried to explore processes such as human creativity by delving down into the details of neural pathways within the individual human brain. This approach also, sometimes, merges with evolutionary psychology because all three facets of this embryonic tradition of research are very brain-centred, and see the development and functioning of the bigger human brain as the fundamental fact of human creativity. And this is fast becoming an orthodoxy about the creative person.

It also borders upon some very deep debates about the mysteries of human consciousness itself, along with the rather hyped pronouncements which some make about the development of artificial intelligence. Given this, we should say before we go any further that we are not attempting in this chapter to give anything like a full account of this multi-faceted debate. We are not trying to write that kind of book. Rather, we want to dip in and out of these debates to give a flavour of some of the ideas about what the creative person is held to be. We do not apologize for this rather eclectic approach, mostly because we do not really put the idea of the creative person at the centre of our debate. This chapter is to a large extent a staging post for our broader debate which, as already indicated, suggests that creativity is something that is formed from many relationships – with other people, with places, with emerging technical capabilities, with broader contexts – which go far beyond the notion of isolated individual. Research into the creative person can be a starting point for understanding the 'what', and indeed the 'where', of creativity, but it can never be the end point.

This qualification notwithstanding, many have argued that the emerging neuroscientific strand of research is a new and fruitful contribution to understanding creativity:

> . . . we need to introduce a radical, game-changing actor in our narrative: the nervous cell or neuron. . . . Neurons assist the multicellular body proper with the management of life. That is the purpose of neurons and the purpose of the brains they constitute. All the astonishing feats of brains that we so revere, from the marvel of creativity to the noble heights of spirituality, appear to have come by way of that determined dedication to managing life within the bodies they inhabit.
>
> (D'Amasio 2012. p. 32)

Some have suggested that there is a parallel between the mysteries of creativity and the deep intricacies of the brain, which creative people with some aspects of the creative attitude outlined above have always known:

> Neuroscience now knows that Proust was right . . . our senses of smell and taste are uniquely sentimental. This is because smell and taste are the only senses that connect directly to the hippocampus, the centre of the brain's long-term memory. Their mark is indelible. All our other senses (sight, touch and hearing) are first processed by the thalamus, the source of language and the front door to consciousness. As a result, these senses are much less efficient at summoning up the past . . .
>
> (Lehrer 2007. p. 12)

We will leave the hard science of this to others. We would rather note here that the brain is not the mind. When considering creativity, many debates tend to start with some idea of the creative mind, for which the brain is a necessary precondition but not an equivalent thing. As we will discuss in fine detail below, the work of Raymond Tallis (2011) is for us the most insightful of these accounts. The *consciousness mind*, or consciousness, is the label we have chosen to describe the complex series of ever present, ever shifting processes which select, shape, confirm, ignore, remember, forget, re-remember, judge and re-assess what the brain is currently doing. Although the vast majority of this mind-processing is unconscious, it is clear that a lot of creativity happens here, in different ways at different times. But the conscious mind also includes processes whereby the creative person is aware of its own mindful self-awareness. Despite profound differences in perspective amongst the different protagonists in this debate, many arguments in the end agree that some version of self-consciousness is fundamental to creativity.

For instance, in *Consciousness Explained*, Daniel Dennett (1993) argues for the 'multiple drafts' model to understand the interrelationships between the brain and the brain's reflection back on its brain-ness which creates new paths between perception and action. For Dennett, it is central to understanding creativity (and consciousness itself) to see that we do not simply take in signals from the world around us and process them in some kind of brain-centred 'central office', which then produces perceptions in an unilinear and predictable way. Rather, he argues that we produce multiple versions of formed or half-formed perceptions. Some of these perceptions and subsequent (re)actions get discarded, some get 'published' as ideas, feelings, 'findings', etc. Rather than consciousness being analogous to a camera-printer set-up that simply points out to the world and 'prints' what it sees, it is analogous to the various drafts of a book that might get read at different times, edited and re-published. It might be that the ability to see new and interesting connections between things that no one has come up with yet, what we tend to call creativity, is connected to the ability to be much looser about the process of self-editing these various drafts, so that more diverse and unusual versions can get 'published'. A particular version of this central role of self-consciousness might come, literally, from talking to ourselves. In technical language, Dennett refers to this as *vocal autostimulation*. The evolution of language has played a central role in the evolution of self-consciousness because it allows *co-evolution*, the way we evolve our experiences by having experiences of others, just as they have experiences of us. Already we move from the individual person towards relationships as a key factor. Talking to others becomes a way of talking to ourselves, which becomes a route to understanding and developing ourselves. Talking to ourselves and others becomes 'thinking to' ourselves, which becomes 'thinking for' ourselves as we decide upon what is to be 'published' as overt thoughts and actions.

> This private talking-to-oneself behaviour might well not be the best imaginable way of amending the existing functional architecture of one's brain (as it is evolving), but it would be a close-at-hand, readily discovered enhancement, and that could be more than enough. . . . (*and*) Talking aloud is only one possibility. Drawing pictures to yourself is another readily appreciated act of self-manipulation. Suppose one day one of those early hominids idly drew two parallel lines on the floor of his cave, and when he looked at what he had done, these two lines reminded him, visually, of the parallel banks of the river that he would have to cross later in the day, and this reminded him to take along his vine rope, for getting across. Had he not drawn the 'picture', we may suppose, he would have walked to the river and then realized, after quick visual inspection, that he needed his rope, and would have had to walk all the way back. This might be a noticeable saving of time and energy that could fuel a new habit, and refine itself eventually into private diagram drawing 'in one's mind's eye'.
>
> (Dennett 1993. p. 73)

Although they disagree profoundly about many things, as we will see in detail below, the position taken up by Dennett which places a version of self-consciousness at the heart of things is shared by Tallis (2011):

> Humans woke up from being organisms to being something quite different: embodied subjects, self-aware and others-aware in a manner and to a degree not approached by other animals. Out of this, a new kind of realm was gradually formed. This, the human (*creative*) world, is materially rooted in the natural world but is quite different from it. It is populated by individuals who . . . inhabit an acknowledged, shared public sphere, structured and underpinned by an infinity of abstractions, generalizations, customs, practices, norms, laws, institutions, facts, and artefacts unknown to even the most 'social' of animals. It is in this common space that, as selves that actively and knowingly lead lives in conjunction with other selves, our human destinies are played out.
>
> (Tallis 2011. p. 87)

Even the fundamentalists within evolutionary theory seem to accept that sharing, reciprocal relationships between selfish organisms, has something to do with human creativity:

> I think that a new replicator has recently emerged on this very planet. It is still in its infancy, still drifting clumsily about in its primordial soup, but already it is achieving evolutionary change at a rate that leaves the old gene pool far behind.
>
> The new soup is the soup of human culture. . . . Examples of memes are tunes, ideas, catchphrases, clothes fashion, ways of making pots, or of building arches. Just as genes propagate themselves in the gene pool by leaping from body to body via sperms and eggs, so memes propagate themselves in the meme pool by leaping from brain to brain via a process which, in the broad sense can be called imitation.
>
> (Dawkins 1989. p. 61)

So we go from the central idea of the evolution of the bigger brains of humans, through the idea that we use our bigger brains actively to shape and select the way we respond to the world, to the idea that the brain's ability to reflect upon its own brain-ness and generate a self-conscious awareness of its own activities, to become a mind. Despite the theoretical differences and internecine squabbles – between the 'fundamentalists', the 'physicalists', the 'computationalists', the 'pluralists' and the 'humanists' within the still rather confused nexus of evolutionary theory (Penrose 2005), neuroscience and cognitive psychology – the human capacity for active self-awareness or self-consciousness seems to be central to understanding the creative person, to our capacity to think about our thinking, our abilities to re-form and recast our thinking before we embark upon any particular course of action.

Despite the reduction of the human condition to questions of biological evolution in the cause of mere survival which tends to flow from the fundamentalists' view of evolution (which is the main reason we finally disagree with that position), it is clear the human creativity has allowed us to do much more than just survive. Human creativity has enabled us to take advantage of the opportunities presented by our environment to increase our practical well-being. We have thrived to such an extent that we have been able to change the very conditions within which we exist and evolve, not always for the good. Creative self-consciousness has brought a qualitative leap in our collective capacities to go beyond instinctual reactions to do this thinking about the way we think. But self-consciousness on the part of creative people not only means that we are better able to generate and share abstract ideas and plans before we decide upon concrete actions, it also means that we are able to store and maintain shared memories about creativity that can persist beyond the lifespan of any one creative person. Such capacities have given each of us two fundamental creative tools – complex language as a way to express ourselves to others, and Culture as the repository of this shared creativity. So again, we immediately see that, whilst specific 'bits' of creativity are often the product of an individual creative person, this nevertheless involves relationships, and is born of a dialectic between the creative person and everything which is 'not' that person.

The creative loop

The evolution of this creative self-consciousness has enabled what Eric Harth (1995) has called the *creative loop*, which he sees as a multi-faceted and intricately over-lapping series of feedback loops with which the creative person thinks about their creativity as they do it, reflects upon it before, during and afterwards, abstractly plans their plans and assesses their actions. Such creativity is not a one-off act capable of being pinned down to a neurological event in the brain, but is iterative and born out of the on-going inner dialogue the creative person has with themselves, and the dialectic relationship this has with the rest of the world as it takes its original shape, but also emerges (Johnson 2002) out if its own repetitions. The creative loop ensures that the more we learn, remember and pass on, the more creative we get. And the more creative we get, the more we learn, remember and pass on. For Harth, the iterative creative loop enables the creative person to have higher capabilities in propensities such as:

- **Perception** – being able to see things from different angles and appreciate different perspectives simultaneously
- **Imagination** – assessing the potential future prospects of certain courses of action before such actions are carried out
- **Association** – being able to abstractly bring two or more previously unconnected ideas together in thought experiments

- **Projection** – thinking 'into the future' to allow a comparison between various possible courses of action
- **Abstraction** – returning to abstract thought with capacities such as 'theory', to assess the degrees of likely success flowing from different possible concrete actions
- **Planning** – on the basis of combining 'theory' and concrete action, laying out plans which the person and others can refer to for future creativity
- **Collective memory** – developing ways of storing the creativity of each person within shared repositories – Culture in all its manifestations, history, writing, etc.
- **Intentionality** – being able to set out upon creative plans with deliberate and intended plans behind the individual creative acts and projections
- **The design of logical steps** – enabled by having greater clarity about future need, a prolonged sense of creative purpose over time and a focus upon the specific functional outcomes to which our creativity is applied

These propensities allow the creative person to generate greater capacities in the two aspects of human creativity which Harth puts at the centre of things:

- **Imitation** – the ability to see previous combinations of ideas and actions, and thus carry out successful ones again to solve similar problems
- **Invention** – seeing the flaws in imitative creativity to use the above abstract creative capacities so as to develop new responses and arrive at better practical solutions

So for Harth, the creative person is 'defined' by the evolution of these greater capacities in maintaining a mental image of our own being which goes far beyond the instinctual self-preserving behaviour that all animals (us included) exhibit. Harth takes the account of the development from the bigger brain forward towards the self-conscious mind as the wellspring of the creative person.

> The observer of this drama (*of creativity*) played out here is none other than the brain itself, which analyses and re-creates, and then observes its own creations. This self-referent process is the creative loop.
>
> (Harth 1995. p. 45)

Ultimately, the fundamentalist evolutionary account, allied to modern neuroscience, over-emphasizes the biological, and sees the physical functioning of the brain as the locus to explain the creative person. As such, its falls prey to a rather deterministic view of creativity which is unable to adequately explain its unpredictable nature. Human creativity is much more varied and unpredictable than the mechanical picture of brain development and structure allows for. A creative self-consciousness born of greater capacities for self-reflection which increases our abilities to think about how we are thinking before action is fundamental to the *creativity* of the creative person (which is all of us) who has been able to transcend instinctual responses and reflect upon our existence as the basis for devising future actions. Self-reflection and consciousness enable

> . . . a subject who not only sees and hears but perceives what he or she sees and hears, who recalls, projects, associates, imagines, invents, creates. He or she also feels – is happy or sad, hopeful or despairing, elated or depressed, angry or in love. All these

functions, and many more, are subsumed collectively under the heading the mind of man.

They all have in common the fact that nobody has yet succeeded in explaining them as chains of logical steps or mechanistic events.

(Harth 1995. p. 46)

It is instructive, when considering the current predominance of neurological accounts as our current attempt to explain creativity as a chain of logical steps or mechanistic events, to note the common affinities which grow between the defining technologies of an era and the common metaphorical pictures which develop in those times. For instance, previous civilizations which tended to rely upon hydraulic technologies such as the water screw and the steam engine also tended to use hydraulic metaphors to discuss the nature of the human condition. The characters populating Shakespearian dramas were deemed to be influenced by one or more 'temperament' – melancholic, sanguine, phlegmatic, choleric – that formed the 'atmospheric pressure' or 'steam' that coloured their underlying character. We now tend to use electrical technologies and rely heavily upon computers. So we tend to use computer metaphors for understanding the brain as the 'central processing unit' or 'software' that enables human reactions such as creativity. Adopting this historical perspective warns us about the dangers of taking such metaphors too literally. The brain is not a super-computer, it is a brain! Current analyses coming from evolutionary theory and its connections to neuroscience tend to overuse such metaphors. Indeed, there is a 'computationalist' position on this. It thus tends to under-emphasize the role of reflective self-consciousness and feedback within the creative loop within their explanations. The brain-centred nature of neuroscience in particular has an insufficiently holistic view of the creative person precisely because it tends to privilege brain functioning, which to a large extent ignores the larger context of the physical body as a whole, which many people immediately recognize as a key facet of their creativity. This only reproduces the limitations of Cartesian dualism which for many years has been a cultural trope separating mind and body, and privileges the brain. As we will see below, the rest of the body is much more intimately involved in creativity than this brain-centred perspective allows for.

But this point brings us back to the very deep and profound debate about the nature of consciousness – between the evolutionary theory, 'computational' models of conscious and its underlying physicalist perspective on the one hand, and more pluralistic accounts represented by people such as Stephen Jay Gould (2002) and, again, Raymond Tallis (2011) on the other. We will discuss certain aspects of that debate in more detail below, but it is useful to note here that creativity, at least in our opinion, is probably a whole organism experience which cannot be reduced to either the linear picture of evolution nor the neurological structure of the brain alone. If nothing else, the pluralist position reminds us not to privilege any one side of the Cartesian dualism when it comes to accounts of the creative person. The common cultural image of the 'genius' tends to proceed through an account of creativity as flowing purely due to the interior dynamics of 'personality' and the consequent internal flashes of inspiration. But confusingly, physicalist accounts involving rigorously mechanical accounts see experiences as self-deluding over-estimations of what are essential chemical or neurological phenomena. Both views are ultimately unfruitful. Because the cognitive-evolutionary-neuroscientific view operates according to an inherent brain-centred perspective it chronically reduces the rest of the body to a supporting act within the creative person. Other ideas emphasize more a whole-body-centred account.

Evolving to stand upright gave us the *adaptive value* of being able to see further. Hands with *opposable thumbs* allowed full pad-to-pad contact with all the fingers. *Fractionated finger movement* allowed them to all more independently of each other. Increased *nerve receptors* led to greatly increased sensitivity in the finger tips, increasing manual dexterity (try being creative with plasters on all your fingertips). *Proprioception* enabled the body and hand to be aware of each other's relative location and so better relate to the space beyond. For many creative people, the creative capacities of the body, in relation to the brain but not reducible to it, are intuitively known as a key source of their creative skills. The dancer, the carpenter, the musician and the potter all know that the brain alone cannot ever be a sufficient explanation of their creativity. If we are trying to locate creativity within the person, it is rather facile to take the brain in isolation from the *embodied knowledge* which resides throughout the body. Despite the tendency of psychology to over-psychologize matters and approach all human phenomena as purely mental, any sufficiently broad account of the creative person must also take in factors of the physical body. It is clear that the evolution of the body made a new portfolio of concrete actions feasible which enabled the creative loop to expand. The co-evolution of the body and the mind enabled humans to envisage new physical possibilities such that we can act upon our creative thinking, just as we could think about possible actions. The interrelationships between the mind and the body is another facet of the dialectical nature of creativity.

And this means that accounts of creativity which reduce it to brain functioning chronically underplay these sorts of intermediate variables, contextual features and strategic compromises which need to be made. 'Art' and 'science' have for too long been 'two cultures' unable to speak to each other properly on these issues. Pluralist accounts of creativity and its location can and must, obviously, take on board what we know about the nature of the creative person, and evolution is an obvious place to start for any discussion of the human condition. Hence the initial start above. But creativity, and its manifest experience for the creative person, is over-determined. To try to pin it down to any one facet will only lead to a rather reductive account, which the current orthodoxy of evolution, cognitive psychology and neuroscience is fast becoming. So we should take the idea of the evolution of creative self-consciousness as a useful starting point for our account of the creative person, which in itself is only the starting point of a broader, multi-disciplinary account of the location of creativity which takes in relationships, place and other contextual features. This follows directly from the view of Harth, which is why his initial work is so attractive to us.

> What makes the theory of evolution so remarkable is the enormous simplification and unification it imposes on the panorama of life on earth. But a gap remains. We are not just another species. Our ability to reason, our ingenuity, and our linguistic skills place us so far above any competing animal species that many of us feel that something beyond the mechanisms of evolution must have occurred to produce homo sapiens. Or perhaps a unique mutation freed our brains from the constraints of instinct and gave us a (*creative*) mind.
>
> (Harth 1995. p. 61)

This gives rise to the distinctive *creative animation* within human behaviour, characterized by specific *purposes* and *functions* geared towards the transformation of physical matter to meet specific human ends, which the capacities of the creative loop described above allow for. Evolution stemming from adaptation is immanent within life itself, and is something that 'happens to us' by the very fact of being alive. But creativity is stimulated by a broader purposive rationality whereby humans act to transform their immediate environment. However dimly experienced at the time, it is something we *choose* in the broadest sense of the word. Whilst evolutionary change is frozen within our DNA and is always part of the present, creativity comes from purposive acts that differ from this slow trial-and-error mutation of natural selection.

The unilinear picture of evolution is insufficiently pluralist, nor is it open enough to a multi-disciplinary account. This starts to get us into the deeper debate within evolutionary theory, between the 'fundamentalism' represented by Dawkins and the 'pluralism' of people such as Gould. A particularly interesting aspect of the pluralist account of evolution, one which is better able to account for the link between the evolution of creative consciousness and the reported nature of the creative experience, is Gould's idea of *exaptation*. Whilst standard evolutionary change based upon adaptations to the environment are still part of the picture, exaptation allows us to think about how things might also evolve as a result of adaptations which, whilst initially beneficial for one train of development, were creatively 'borrowed' for entirely different uses in response to entirely external factors. Within exaptation, the 'external' meets 'adaptation', and signals at a wholly different kind of evolutionary creation. Maybe the evolution of feathers was originally developed for waterproofing, and was only subsequently 'borrowed' for the evolution of flight. According to this view, adaptations propelling internal evolution become intertwined with an external reason, and thereby make whole new realms of creative (re)action feasible. The whole brain, mind, self-consciousness, creative loop thing is by far the most dramatic example of this throughout human evolution, and is a good way of locating the evolution of the creative person against the often serendipitous, accidental nature of the specific outcomes. What we can do now with our brains-minds is far beyond what we 'needed' for evolutionary survival, and exaptation speaks to the million new creative possibilities which creative self-consciousness affords to give us every day. This picture far exceeds any supposed 'red in tooth and claw' battles between the 'fittest' and the others. Evolution travels in many directions at the same time.

As we will argue in subsequent chapters, it is probably now more accurate to define the human condition as an inherently social condition, which is itself defined by cooperation and collaboration, rather than conflict and competition. Evolutionary perspectives can discuss cooperation and collaborations to some extent, but such discussions still remain within the broader context of competition and the evolutionary advantage to the individual. It seems to us at least that human creativity has gone beyond this, to change the very nature of that (purportedly) competitive context within which the creative person resides.

Some other perspectives on the creative person

If the alliance between cognitive psychology and the sciences of evolution and neuroscience do form something like the current orthodoxy concerning the creative person, there are many other psychological perspectives which can add to our picture.

Freudian psychology is centred upon the unconscious processes that influence our conscious lives. And much of this unconsciousness is formed by our early experiences in childhood, and our memories thereof. So when it comes to the nature of the creative person, Freudian psychology argues that we should take these early experiences into accounts. We should remember the significance of the early 'imaginative activity' which so defines childhood, and the pleasures we got from that imaginative world of play. For Freud himself (1972, 1986), the deep psychological pleasure this brought is something which we are very loathe to give up in adult life, and for some at least, this gives a creative impetus to the rest of their lives. For the Freudian perspective, the creative person is someone who wishes to continue this world of childlike play into adult life more than the norm. Someone who seeks to merge the pleasurable memory of childhood play with the 'seriousness' of adult responsibility, to merge the 'imagined objects and situations' with the 'tangible and visible things of the real world'. For Freud, this merging of childlike pleasures with adult serious-ness, that is, the merging of the world of the imaginative with the 'real', is what gives the creative person their great energy, self-propelling logic and sense of internal tension. To quote Freud at some length:

> The creative writer does the same as the child at play. (S)he creates a world of phantasy which (s)he takes very seriously – that is, which (s)he invests with a large amount of emotion – while separating it sharply from reality. . . . When a child has grown up and ceased to play, and after (s)he has been labouring for decades to envisage the realities of life with proper seriousness, (s)he may one day find him/herself in a mental situation which once more undoes the contrast between play and reality. As an adult (s)he can look back on the intense seriousness with which (s)he once carried in his/her games in childhood; and, by equating his/her ostensibly serious occupation of today with his/her childhood games, (s)he can throw off the heavy burden imposed on him/her by life and win the high yield of pleasure afforded by humour. . . . As people grow up, then, they cease to play and they seem to give up the yield of pleasure which they gained from playing. But whoever understands the human mind knows that hardly anything is harder for a (wo)man than to give up a pleasure which (s)he has once experienced. Actually, we never give up anything; we only exchange one thing for another.
>
> (Freud 1972. p. 72)

In today's psychology, the Freudian perspective may still be the main representative of more philosophical branches of psychology which emanate more from European tradi-tions. Perhaps one of the main characteristics of these (varied) philosophical traditions is the mistrust of the overly 'scientific' approaches which so define the more Anglo-Saxon orthodoxies. Humanist psychology represents a general perspective which, in contrast to the 'analytical spirit' of scientism which approaches the human condition as a series of isolatable propensities, puts the *whole person* back at the heart of things. Perhaps the best known representative of the Humanist tradition of psychology is Carl Rogers (1978, 1980), and he has some very specific things to say about the creative person *per se*. For Rogers, the creative person is something which 'becomes' as a result of the lifetime of experiences which form a particular unique personality. Far from being the result of the development of a big brain understood in isolation from the rest of the body, or the development of certain neural pathways within that brain as a result of certain isolated chemical reactions, or the publication of a particular 'draft' of a particular 'bit' of consciousness, the Humanist perspective sees the creative person as being born of an on-going series of whole-person experiences. Furthermore, the strong link between Humanist psychology and person-centred psychotherapy has meant that the basic human need for self-expression, played out in the context of human relationships, has also figured much more clearly within the Humanist idea of the creative person. For instance:

> Creativity is not, in my judgement, restricted to some particular content. I am assum-ing that there is no fundamental difference in the creative process as it is evidenced in

painting a picture, composing a symphony, devising new instruments of killing, developing a scientific theory, discovering new procedures in human relationships or creating new formings of one's own personality as in psychotherapy. . . . My definition, then, of the creative process is that it is the emergence in action of a novel relational product, growing out of the uniqueness of the individual on the one hand, and the materials, events, people, or circumstances of his/her life on the other.

(Rogers 1978. p. 84)

Further shortcomings of a reductive 'science' of the creative person have been highlighted by more phenomenological perspectives within psychology, which tend to emphasize the ambiguity of perception at the heart of the creativity. Far from being something which can be understood though the analytical spirit of science within evolutionary theory, neuroscience and cognitive psychology, the creative person is seen as someone who responds to a highly over-determined, unknown, visceral and infinitely personal set of ideas, agendas and needs. The creative person is much more ambiguous, and possibly unknowable, than the scientific approach can ever allow for. At the psychological level, the creative person responds to a 'perceptive ambiguity' (Eco 1989), which is the very response which enables them to conceive of ideas and actions which go beyond the conventional. For Eco, it is this ambiguity which 'allow(s) the observer to conceive the world in a fresh dynamic of potentiality before the fixative process of habit and familiarity comes into play' (Eco 1989. p. 39).

Whilst the cognitive view accepts that our perceptions are moveable and changeable, this phenomenological view of creativity takes things further by suggesting that our perceptions of 'reality' are nothing more than passing phenomena with no more claim to reality than any other story. Because everything is much more ambiguous, the prospect of new avenues of thinking for the creative person are opened up, and as is often reported by creative people themselves, the *deliberate choosing* of new ways of seeing becomes much more central to our understanding of the creative person. Those who experiment with drugs to open up the 'doors of perception' and so gain insights into the *how* and *why* of their creativity are implicitly operating from a phenomenological acceptance of an ambiguous reality and the possibility of a creative transcendence of the 'normal'. No scientific analysis needed!

So the phenomenological stance accepts the radically contingent, moveable and less than real nature of the 'reality' of the creative person as its true nature. Far from accepting the neuroscientific mantra that they will soon to be able to measure and predict the neural pathways which lead to the creative person's specific actions, and thus even be able to devise artificial intelligence, the Humanist and Phenomenological perspectives argue that creativity is actually a rather disorienting process given its inherent ambiguities. It cannot be 'coded' because there is no code to reproduce. Creativity is necessarily disorientating and ambiguous.

Creative practitioners have often put this interminable reflecting back upon the disorienting creative process at the centre of their accounts of their creativity. For instance, the idea of *reflective practice* outlined by Gray and Malins (2007) advocates the active embrace of uncertainties about what 'it is', where 'you are' and how it all 'fits together' as a key facet of the truly creative person. A further degree of disorientation created within the audience as a result of the creative work itself is also a progressive part of the interrogation of established views of the world which many art forms refer to.

And this raises another problem within much that comes from the traditional cognitive accounts of the creative person: its tendency to *over-psychologize* the human condition.

That is, its tendency to turn everything into a mental phenomenon which resides within isolated individuals understood as psychological 'units' functioning purely in terms of their own internal dynamic. A moment's thought should suggest to us that creativity only really exists if it has some kind of dialogue with an audience. In what kind of real-world circumstances does any artistic or scientific endeavour really act in isolation from all the relationships which make up life? The controlled laboratory conditions in which cognitive and neuroscientific research proceeds are always, at best, pale approximations of how people think and act. At worse they are held up as sufficiently real conditions, and the mismatch between experimental conditions and the real world is simply passed over.

Some psychological perspectives overcome these inherent epistemological failures by allowing relationships within human groups to come into their thinking. Group psychology, which itself comes from various psychological traditions, sees the individual person, creative or otherwise, as being inherently part of kinship networks with other people, and is fundamentally based upon the idea that such relationships shape and define what the individual thinks and does. Individuals within groups do things which they would not do otherwise, and for a such a social animal as human beings, there can never really be an 'individual' separated out from these relationships and the influences they have over personal behaviour. To try to understand the creative person without taking account of such factors can only ever be an approximation. In the next chapter, we will expand upon how relationships of all kinds tend to shape, and often help produce, creativity in finer detail. For now, let's us simply recognize that relationships between the creative person and the rest of the world are there, and have a profound effect. Recognizing such a basic proposition is the basis for a more *holistic conception* of the creative person, one which is more germane to our overall multi-disciplinary interests. And, as we mentioned above, Tallis (2011) provides in our view one of the best of such accounts.

Intentionality and extensions: a polemic continued

At the centre of Tallis' discussion of the evolutionary-neuroscientific argument is a rejection of the 'stand alone' account of the brain. As we will see in finer detail below, Tallis' more holistic account chimes with a dialectical view of the interrelationship between the brain, the mind, the body and other relationships beyond the individual human entity, which we started to outline in Chapter 1. Creativity, indeed consciousness, is not so much 'inside' the stand alone brain, but in the interactions between brain and world. If we consider sight for a moment, we will immediately see that it is capacity born not of the eyes nor the brain alone, but of the interrelationships between them. Far from being locked inside the dark skull, the brain is connected to the outside world via the eyes and the visual cortex, and the interaction between these parts is what enables light signals to be received by the eyes and made sense of by the brain. The brain alone could not do this. And if we expand this simple piece of thinking out a little, it becomes obvious that is it actually rather puerile to try to understand the brain in isolation from the rest of the body. What the brain does and how it does it cannot really be understood as a separate entity divorced from the body which it does it for and with. And further, the brain cannot really be understood as a separate entity divorced from how that body exists in the real world. All these entities – brain, eyes, light – from the outside world together make sight happen. To focus solely on the brain part of that 'system' will never lead to an understanding of sight.

In pursuing his critique of the 'stand alone brain' perspective, Tallis returns to an older philosophical inquiry into *intentionality*. For him, mental propositions which carry intention, the human activity which surely underpins all creativity, differ from those activities which simply deal with the physical world. Intentionality has the 'property of aboutness' within it. This returns us to some of the points made by Harth (1995) in that intentionality carries with it approximations in the abstract which refer to something outside and beyond themselves. Such intentional approximations stand for *something else* and so form the basis for the personal creative interactions we have with the world. Bertrand Russell (1960) has called this a 'propositional attitude' which can deal with the 'what if' kind of divergent thinking which is exhibited through the many facets of the creative attitude discussed above.

For Tallis, this shows that certain aspects of the creative person exhibit an inverted relationship between the object in the world and their perceptions of it. The orthodox view holds that objects exist, and we then perceive them. But within a creative self-consciousness, we are equally aware that we are dealing with our perceptions just as we generate those perceptions themselves. We do not *just* perceive; we also perceive that we perceive creatively, and imagine all sorts of alternatives upon that basis. Intentionality in its most general sense flows from this capacity. And so perhaps we can say that the abilities of individual people to be creative also flows from this fundamental capacity too. It is self-aware self-reflection which enables us the invert our perceived perceptions back towards the object in the world as we intentionally decide to see it anew, in a fresh light, in a more creative way, as a new possibility. When Dennett (1993) talks of the 'multiple draft' account of human consciousness, he is saying something really quite similar, despite the profound differences that exist between his perspectives and Tallis'. Intentionality, in a dialectical, iterative interplay with self-reflection, is the capacity which allows for the perception, assimilation, mental processing, negotiation of abstract propositions and practical applied thinking, which we call creativity at the level of the individual person. We see things anew, we are aware that we are seeing things anew, we are aware that we can choose the particular way in which we are seeing things anew, and we realize that these new ways of seeing are about something bigger and beyond those thoughts themselves, so that they can be applied to things in the world anew. But also, there is an internal dialectical interaction between these various capacities within self-aware intentionality, which means that the relationships between them 'travel in both ways'. And it is this two-way 'aboutness' of perception and abstraction and back to new perceptions which allows it to be the basis for novel concrete action as it crystallizes into a 'bit' of creativity.

If Dawkins referred to the process of evolutionary change as the 'blind watchmaker', one which creates novelty within the biological world from unforeseen and accidental processes, then Tallis' account refers more to the 'sighted watchmaker' within his account of human creativity. Far from being the culmination of 'blind' evolutionary processes culminating in bigger brains as 'stand alone' entities, his holistic account allows for the fact that we are aware of our awareness, that we can 'see' our creative responses before, during and after we generate them. As the brain becomes the mind, so the mind interacts with the world, and as such it 'sees' itself and the world. And it (re)acts accordingly, again and again during a lifetime of creativity, which can refer back as well as forward. For Tallis, it is this self-consciousness, self-awareness, self-reflection, call it what you will, which defines what it is to be human and why we are radically different from the rest of the animal world. It is this capacity which enables me to write the words I just wrote and to know what they will mean to you. It is this capacity which enables you to read the words I just wrote and appreciate (hopefully – see a small self-reflective joke thrown in too!) what the words mean. We know what we do, and we know that we know it. We see far beyond our brain as something locked inside our skulls just waiting to evolve. We are creative.

We are creative because intentionality enables us to choose between different courses of action before we set out on that course of action. We are creative because we can reflect back upon things before, during and after we think-do-think them. We are creative because we can adapt to new information and insights as we go through this process. We are creative because we can apply these new insights anew to our responses to, and inter-actions with, the outside world beyond the brain. We are creative because we go through these processes again and again at the speed of light. Far from being the passive subjects of a 'blind' process which simply makes our brains bigger, we are creative! To start and end an argument about the creative person with the 'stand alone' big brain thing is analogous to suggest we can 'define' the river Ganges simply by tracing it to its source in a glacier in the Himalayas, and call that 'The Ganges'. This would be to neglect the two river banks which, in concert with the water, create the flow. It would be to ignore the actual flow. It would be to ignore the fact the flow means that it is a 'different' river each moment we look at it. To try to define the Ganges simply as its starting point is to radically misunderstand what it is and how it happens. So it is with the stand alone brain view, which is why a more holistic, dialectical account is vastly more illuminating.

But intentionality itself cannot be the full answer. We need to recognize, again, that for the activities of the creative person to truly come alive, they need to be applied to some-thing in the world. Mental abstractions which simply stay 'in the head' of the creative person and do not find expression would only amount to a rather stultified kind of creat-ivity. In approaching this issue Tallis discusses what he calls *extensions*. These extensions come from our creative ability to develop tools, symbolic representations and relationships which enable our innate creative capacities to grow and find even greater applications in the world. The human capacity (along with some other animals) for developing tools to extend our creative reach and enable new imaginative insights to become feasible is a well-known part of this debate. But the linking of human consciousness and its manifestations in the creative person on the one hand, and the development of symbolic representations within phenomena such as shared language and Culture is less discussed. This is perhaps because there are fewer sufficiently developed conversations between evolutionary biology on the one hand, and social and cultural thinking on the other. Prolonged and ever devel-oping relationships between creative brains-minds have enabled those functioning entities we know as individual people to co-enhance their creativity by the fact of them know-ing each other. Relationships between people for creativity is another kind of extension, because it makes kinds of creativity which individuals could not do alone more feasible. Within this process, Tallis identifies *mimetic skills*, which echo what Harth (1995) discusses as imitation – new forms of creativity born of recognizing the creativity of other around us, and adapting it to new ends. He also identifies *auto-cueing* – born of our abilities to build sustained models of creative planning out of one-off bits of mimetic skills, which we can invoke again and again when the circumstances require. We can 'tell ourselves' what to do, because it is already 'in there'. The actions of the creative person are often born out of the process of internal dialogue whereby our self-reflections are 'stopped, replayed, edited, under conscious control' (Tallis 2011. p. 224).

Clearly all these abilities denote interactions between the creative person and the world of other people. The creative person is inherently a social being, and the 'bits' of creativity they produce are inherently *public* phenomena. As well as his account of perception and the perceived object being a two-way process, so is his account of the creative person and the rest of the human world. It is worth quoting him at length here:

> The development of humans away from the mode of consciousness enjoyed by other primates was not a private, organic event in the intercranial darkness (*of the stand-alone brain inside the skull*): It took place in public, where the visible hand was operating. . . .
>
> Neuromaniacs, obsessed with what lights up in the darkness of the skull, seem unable to appreciate that brains by themselves are pointless . . . brains have a point only if they are attached to organs that deliver behaviour. . . .
>
> After this, it is possible to envisage a dialectic or a ratcheting up between the brain and the hand such that increasing dexterity would drive increasing brain size and shape cerebral organization and the latter would promote increasing dexterity.
>
> (Tallis 2011. p. 226)

The biological reductionism inherent within evolutionary theory and neuroscience, and the over-psychologizing tendencies which reduce the individual to an isolated 'mental unit' inherent within mainstream psychology, both under-emphasize the fact that we are what Tallis calls uniquely *other-consciousness*. In its most general terms, this other-consciousness moves through our developed symbolic extensions such as language and Culture. But it also moves in and through the daily social and cultural conduct of the creative person, in and through the everyday creative interactions the individual person has with others. The mutually effective other-consciousness, which others also have towards us, enables us all to have greater abilities in *meant meaning*, because we can mutually refer to and share each other's meanings and communications. But not only share them, but also know that we share them. We share the shared-ness, which, as we will see in the next chapter, serves to increase its meaning. The creative person does not just put individual 'bits' of creativity into the world, they also put the shared act of being creative into the world of others too. If the creative person is inherently a social being, and their 'bits' of creativity are inherently public, then individual creative people are inherently impacting upon their social and cultural conditions for their creativity, through their creativity, with their creativity. And as such they are changing it. Tallis argues that in this way we develop on the basis of propensities which we explicitly share within a broader network of belief. He uses a metaphorical notion of *pointing* to express this mutually generated context within which the creative person acts, develops and emerges:

> I can see what you can or can't see, I point to it and you see my pointing finger and respond to it, so that we can now have joint visual attention to what was hitherto hidden from, or at least not noticed by, you. The object is thus explicitly located in a public domain that is not mere physical space but of a world had in common . . . through pointing and other pre-visual signs, we have the means by which a human world, distinct from the natural world, is built up, prior to language. It is woven out of a trillion cognitive handshakes.
>
> (Tallis 2011. p. 234)

This idea of a 'trillion cognitive handshakes' which the creative person takes part in is an illuminating image of the dialectical conception of the creative person, because it puts a *relational* notion of creativity at its centre. Because of intentionality and extensions, the evolution of the creative person has involved transcending the constraints of their own individual brain–mind nexus, no longer relying upon their own personality in isolation because we have jointly created out of our co-creativity an 'exographic storage' made from the creativity of myriad others. The many cultural facets of this – its material objects, its endless reproductions, its constant creative conversation and the contours of the daily lives of each and every creative person (which, since we forget, is everyone), as well as institutions such as libraries, museums and galleries too numerous to list. Seen in this light, and through a dialectical lens, it would be a little facile to now try to 'define' what the creative person 'is'. It is everything and it is everywhere. It certainly cannot be restricted to the functioning of the brain–mind nexus as shown up through a picture of some neurons firing inside one individual brain.

Whilst we are not here to claim we have a conclusive theory of human creativity, we are here to offer some ideas about the *where* of creativity, and at this particular juncture some ideas about the extent to which creativity resides within the individual person. Our view is that the creative person is something very different and much more complex than the fiction of the individual operating as a separate 'mental unit' which can be understood by mapping their internal mental or physiological dynamics alone. The creative person is made up from very complex and moving internal dynamics which are as much social, cultural and historical as they are neurological, chemical or electrical. If one stands back from the details, it is actually quite strange that anyone would suggest otherwise! The human brain, the mind, and our capacities for creativity are radically open to the world of experience and does not have anything like a universal, consistent or one-way internal operating logic. The creative person is very much other-conscious, and is shaped by a whole world of dialectical relationships with other people which are in 'perpetual flux and movement' (Tallis 2011). It is a process whereby the creativity of one individual impacts upon the relationships they have with others, just as those others who form those relationships act creativity to shape that very individual. The *creative one* shapes the *creative other*, just as the creative others shape the one. The individual creative person, far from being a stand alone brain or even a mind functioning in isolation, *is* their relationships with others and the world beyond. For that reason the reified things we like to call 'the creative person' in some ways does not exist, at least not in the way it is usually conceived of. The creative person is born of a process of dialectical change, flux and movement. Their personal creativity may be experienced as deeply subjective, emotional, visceral and as something intrinsic to their very being, but it is also born out of relationships with the reality of others, and as such is never fixed. Creativity is intrinsically personal, but at the same time it is inherently relational and contextual. So let's now turn to a consideration of the various aspects of these relationships, a discussion which will shape the contours of this book from now on. Let's turn to the most obvious, ubiquitous, pleasing, annoying, happiness-causing and despair-creating relationships any of us ever have.

That is, the relationships we have with other people.

Chapter 3

Relationships for creativity

> In reality, creativity has always been a highly collaborative, cumulative and social activity in which people with different skills, points of view and insights, share and develop ideas together. At root most creativity is collaborative. It is not usually the product of a flash of insight from a lone individual. The web gives us a new way to organize and expand this collaborative activity . . . (*which*) could make innovation and creativity a mass activity that engages millions of people. . . . Our preoccupation in the century to come will be how to create and sustain a mass innovation economy in which the central issue will be how more people can collaborate more effectively in creating new ideas.
>
> (Leadbeater 2008. p. 37)

Because most of the theories of the creative person discussed in the previous chapter approach creativity as the act(s) of individuals, stemming from their stand alone individual brains, minds, personalities or attitudes, they can never be sufficient explanations. As we stated in passing several times now, it is our firm belief that creativity exist in various contexts, and all individuals live within social, cultural, political or ethical settings. And so this implies the central importance of *relationships* for creativity as much as any other facet of the human existence. The dialectical conception of creativity puts all sorts of relationships, with oneself, with places, with contexts, at its centre. We will return to this idea throughout this book. But for this chapter, let's concentrate upon the social conception of creativity, which puts relationships with other people at its centre. Such relationships take many forms. They can be with others who are:

- very much of the moment – or with those who only now exist as a result of our memories
- physically present – or with others who are physically absent but still very much part of our imagination
- a temporary acquaintance – or with those who are a regular, long-term and established part of our life
- a relatively insignificant part of our life – or with significant others who are of central importance within our lives for all sorts of reasons
- a practical part of our collaborative, co-creative life – or with those who are 'outside' the actual creativity, but who nevertheless impact upon it as audience, customer or client

So relationships for creativity take different forms and have different dynamics. But nevertheless, relationships are always already there. However, for various economic and political reasons, our culture tends to over-emphasize an individualistic view of life and culture, and so underplays the ubiquity of relationships. And this multi-faceted myth purveyed by over-individualism figures larger within discussions of creativity than in most places. So let's spend a little time debunking the myth of individualism so as to put our discussion of creative relationships on a firm footing.

Over-individualism: a polemic continued

When we talk about individualism, we don't mean the rugged 'can do' attitude exemplified by John Muir's frontier spirit, or the ecological self-sufficiency of John Seymour. Nor do we mean the politics of individual identity exemplified by the Feminist and Gay Movements. What we have in mind is the deeper and broader notion of the individual as the repository of all human action which pervades mainstream economics and its cultural corollaries within consumer culture and public political debate. A large part of Western social and cultural thinking has been founded upon this over-individualism, such that it has now become relatively invisible.

In *History of Western Philosophy*, Bertrand Russell (1961) maps out some of the shifting philosophical emphases that have impacted upon political and economic theory since the time of the ancient Greeks. These differing emphases have been played out through various debates between rationality and superstition, and between the various institutions of social authority such as Church, State and markets. But for Russell, one of the major points of this broad history has been the multi-faceted debate between individual freedoms on the one hand and the concern with social cohesion on the other:

> Every community is exposed to two opposite dangers; ossification through too much discipline and reverence for tradition, on the one hand; on the other hand, dissolution . . . through the growth of an individualism and personal independence that makes co-ordination impossible.
>
> (Russell 1961. p. 137)

The Enlightenment was a progressive historical period partly because it challenged overbearing authority, introduced rational argument and eventually brought cultural and political freedoms to peoples' everyday lives (to some extent at least). It led to individualism becoming enshrined within the Western way of thinking, being and living. But this did not happen in a cultural vacuum. In his book *The Philosophy of the Enlightenment*, Lucian Goldmann (1973) has shown how the modern form of individualism emerged as a consequence of a particular cultural-economic context that had been developing since the 13th Century:

> The most important consequence of the development of a market economy is that the individual, who previously constituted a mere partial element within the total social process of production and distribution, now becomes, both in his own consciousness and in that of his fellow men, an independent element, a sort of monad, a point of departure.
>
> (Goldmann 1973. p. 67; my emphasis)

Part of the movement of ideas which characterized the Enlightenment underpinned a progressive expansion of individual freedoms in that it weakened political and religious systems of authority such as the 'divine right of kings' and over-bearing Church dogma.

In doing so it made the prospect of choosing an identity and expressing oneself through one's own actions more of a possibility for more people. This was given great impetus by the growth of the modern market economy. The rising industrial classes could not have it any other way. And this growing sense of individualism has in turn come to affect social and cultural thinking as a whole (another dialectic, between the material organization of society and the ideas which that society creates). Lucian Goldmann again:

> The total social process is seen as resulting mechanically and independently from the individual will, from the actions of countless autonomous individuals on each other and in response to each other, behaving as rationally as possible for the protection of their private interests and basing their actions on their knowledge of the market with no regard for any trans-individual authority or value. It was thus inevitable that the development of a market economy . . . should progressively transform western thought . . . which treats the individual's consciousness as the absolute origin of all knowledge and action. Likewise, the disappearance from human consciousness of all trans-individual authority regulating production and distribution is matched by the fundamental claim of all writers of the Enlightenment that individual reason must be recognised as the supreme arbiter and subjected to no higher authority.
>
> (Goldmann 1973. p. 71)

Many formal and legal proposals flowed from this, which became central to the key social and economic institutions we still have today, which are meant to ensure individual freedoms across the broader context of social, economic and political life. And these institutions continue to market the idea of the individual pursuit of private interest as the best, some would say only, way to create a cohesive society. Perceiving oneself as an individual in these terms continues to be the 'existential furniture' of much of modern culture. Remember what Lucian Goldmann said? 'No regard for any trans-individual authority or value', the abstract notion of individual is still portrayed as the 'absolute origin of all knowledge and action', and individual reason is held to be 'the supreme arbiter'. Over-individualism continues to perpetuate the myth that we are all isolated social, economic and cultural individuals. Today's inheritors of this culture of over-individualism continue to under-value the fundamental significance of the relationships which make up human life – that is, to community and a sense of mutual responsibility to each other which this brings. This is the sub-text which now holds that we are 'customers', 'clients' or 'consumers' rather than citizens.

But the fundamental notion that we are all isolated individuals acting to maximize our own interests never really measured up to the evidence of everyday life, even at the time. For instance, despite his Utilitarianism which has a certain individualism at its heart, Jeremy Bentham also saw *propinquity* – being next to people – as part of his 'felicity calculus'. Even though Utilitarianism put the notion of the greatest happiness for the greatest number at the centre of their politics, it also saw happiness as coming partly from relationships. For more modern sociology, the *propinquity effect* talks of the tendency of people to form associations with others, simply on the basis of an experienced nearness or similarity, as a main factor of everyday life. Simply sharing a location can lead to *residential propinquity*; working in a similar field can lead to *occupational propinquity*; using the same bar after work can lead to *acquaintance propinquity*. Propinquities of these sorts may not lead to deep, meaningful or long-term relationships, but they do often impact upon our (creative) lives. Just 'being around' leads to higher rates of propinquity, which in turn lead to all the experiences which make us what we are. We are shaped, saved, inspired, helped, improved, loved by and protected by our relationships. Our relationships make us, and those with whom we have these relationships are made by us.

As we saw in the last chapter, this culture of over-individualism is as current in the realm of studying creativity as it is anywhere else. But it does not stand up to very much scrutiny here either. To perpetuate the idea that creativity is a solely individual act is a fairly crass denial that creativity can only ever become Culture when there is a relationship between creator and audience. Over-individualism in creativity is to deny the everyday realities of creative people and is what underpins the myth of the isolated creative 'genius'. Thomas Edison had a lot of people working with/for him, and so did Steve Jobs despite all the hype. Despite some rather grand self-mythologizing on the part of such creative people, no one really creates anything in a truly individualized way that is fully divorced from the relationships that made them and led them to where they were when the creativity 'just came'. Creative people not suffering from such individualistic hype not only recognize the centrality of relationships, they actually welcome, indeed celebrate, the fact of co-creativity. The progressive individualism of the Enlightenment was good, but it was not that good. Writing in 1968, at the height of the last cultural-political explosion, and the consequent growth of an alternative, creative way of life, Goldmann wrote of

> . . . a new world vision characterized, despite its retention of the individualistic perspective, by its view of the individual as dominated by dread and the feeling of 'dereliction', especially in his utter powerlessness to understand or master the world around him . . . (*meaning that*) western society is in the process of recovering from the most serious of its inner sicknesses, and is thus taking away (*over-individualism as*) the foundation of ideologies based upon anxiety and despair.
>
> (Goldmann 1973. p. 77)

It has not panned out like that since 1968, because neo-liberalism has re-imposed itself and a culture of over-individualism was re-marketed to us during the 1980s. But the counter-culture never really went away. And within the creative lives of many people today, a rejection of over-individualism is increasingly current. Other social and cultural logics are at work everywhere if one tunes in to seeing them. And many are to be found within artistic circles and scenes – micro-experiments in cultural-economic solidarity being developed by artist-activists in the developing world; creative groups who place alternative social and economic rationalities at the centre of their work; creative work designed to articulate ethical sensibilities which recognize, once and for all, that purposes of mutual care are a greater source of human satisfaction than the individual gain of more and more dumb possessions.

This is a logic of co-creativity which is inherently social, and argues that all individuals can flourish to lead worthwhile and productive lives if they share their capabilities and existential resources. It is sometimes informed by ecological rationalities which reject the social separations at the heart of over-individualism in favour of the more mature view which recognizes that every thing/one is connected to every thing/one else. Various thinkers who represent this kind of view as discussed in this book (Gorz 1983; Illich 1973, 1976; Nussbaum 2011; Roszak 1981; Sen 1999, 2009), even though they might originate from very different perspectives, all recognize the relational nature of life. They all link, in their differing ways, creativity to a sense of *social purpose* which eschews over-individualism. They all tend to agree with the notion that over-individualistic affluence has meant cultural poverty;

an over-stated concern with individual freedom has contributed to cultural fragmentation and disenfranchisement; over-blown individual consumer choice has helped produce cultural banality. And perhaps most importantly for our purposes here, the cultural myths associated with over-individualism continue to give us the image of the lone creative genius, continue to underpin the idea that the individual person is the source of all creativity, and perpetuates the idea that creativity is the preserve of the chosen few individuals who have been touched by the mysterious *deus ex machina* inspiration.

We started to critique this individualistic conception of creativity in the last chapter, and related it to an elitist view. Let's now expand upon that by looking at some of the more thoroughly social ideas of creativity. For all the intertwined social, political and economic reasons touched upon above, let's do away with the woeful cultural heritage of over-individualism and turn to some more likely, more lively, more convivial ways of understanding creativity by looking at the relationships that make it what it is – our greatest source of *shared meaning*, *common joy* and *reciprocal love*.

And let's start this by using a biological metaphor.

A creative ecology

The culture of over-individualism resides within many facets of the social theory – in particular psychology and economics – and holds that we exist in fundamental isolation from each other and pursue our competing interests accordingly. But ecological thinking, dealing with something supposedly even more 'red in tooth and claw', differs, offers an antidote because it rests upon the idea that all species exist in symbiotic relationships with other species, and with their environment. And such ecological thinking is useful for understanding the many ways in which creative people form similarly symbiotic relationships within myriad networks, creative hubs, studio groups and many different kinds of informal creative projects. So much so, that we can perhaps point to the existence of *creative ecologies* of informal networks made up of many temporary but nonetheless very vital creative energies (Shorthose 2004a, 2004b, 2005; Shorthose and Strange 2004). Of course, biological and ecological thinking allows for the existence of competition, but cooperation and collaboration are much more fundamental. The elevation of competition to its current status within thinking about nature is itself the creation of the political over-individualism of people like Herbert Spencer in the late 19th Century. It is not real. Notions of cooperation and collaboration which underpin symbiotic relationships coming from ecological thinking have many illuminating lessons for thinking about creative ecologies. Let's get into some of the details.

The broadest and, perhaps, best known representative of ecological thinking which puts cooperation and collaboration at the centre of things is *Gaia Theory* developed by James Lovelock (1995) and Lynn Margulis (1992). This holds that the earth itself is a living organism, capable of being a self-regulating and self-organizing system of which all living beings, along with the very fabric of the earth, form constituent parts. It is a powerful metaphor with which to start thinking about the centrality of connecting relationships for an understanding creativity. For instance, Margulis' work is concerned to map the micro-interactions that take place within symbiotic relationships as a way to more fully understanding how evolution (itself useful as a broad proxy for human creativity) occurs. The centrality of *symbiosis* within the thinking of Lovelock and Margulis calls our attention towards the study of actual interactions, and suggest that the study of symbiosis within creative networks is a necessary facet of any truly multi-disciplinary approach to creativity. A term first coined by the German botanist Anton de Bary in 1873, 'symbiosis' refers to the fundamental fact of different species living together in and through long-term collaborative relationships. In contrast to the competition-centred view of the world formed by Herbert Spencer's social Darwinism and perpetuated by the evolutionary fundamentalists of the previous chapter, a symbiosis-centred view sees active cooperation and collaboration as the fundamental fact of evolutionary novelty and creativity. It results in what Margulis calls *symbiogenesis*, 'the appearance of new bodies, new organs, new species. In short, I believe that most evolutionary novelty arose, and still arises, directly from symbiosis' (Margulis 1992. p. 43).

Whilst many of the traditional economic and business theories of creativity parallel the social Darwinist emphases upon conflict and competition, a symbiosis-centred conception emphasizes relationships as the true location of creativity. If we compliment the overtly biological lens of Margulis with more social and cultural thinking, we can begin to understand the importance of symbiotic relationships as a crucial factor for the emergence of new creative ideas and possibilities. When Margulis describes the following aspect of symbiosis, she could be describing creative networks themselves:

> At the base of the creativity of all large familiar forms of life, symbiosis generates novelty. It brings together different life-forms, always for a reason. Symbiogenesis (*the way symbiosis leads to birth*) brings together unlike individuals to make large, more complex entities.
>
> (Margulis 1992. p. 12)

However, it is one thing to assert that symbiotic relationships exist, but quite another to map the actual, concrete content and texture of such relationships. In Margulis' terms, symbiotic relationships emerge from the 'community of interactions of once-independent actors', and so the *rules of transmission* need to be uncovered if we are to truly understand the ways in which symbiotic relationships foster creativity. The study of *self-organization* – the way in which systems of mutual interactions are able to form their own emerging context for further self-organization – makes a similar, fundamental point: that uncovering the actual micro-detail of relationships is necessary for a full understanding of such systems. And it is the same with *creative ecologies* – unpacking the nature, texture and tenor of creative interaction is necessary if we are to fully understand what is going on in and through such relationships in terms of how they impact upon and foster creativity. So let's now turn to some of these rules of transmission coming from a biological lens as an extended metaphor for understanding creative ecologies.

For Margulis, symbiotic interactions are self-generating and self-renewing due to their *autocatalytic nature* – *auto* meaning 'self'; *catalyzing* meaning 'stimulating of'. A cyclical series of 'interlocking reactions whose end product is the same as its starting point' means that autocatalytic processes are formed from relationship systems whereby the catalyst for initial action comes from within itself. The initial interaction is in itself also part of the outcome of the system because the detailed collaboration on a particular act of creativity also re-affirms the symbiotic relationship which started the process. Relationships, and the re-affirmation of them, are central to both the nature and the outcome of the processes within creative ecologies. By being autocatalytic – self-starting, such processes are also *autopoietic* – *auto* meaning 'self'; *poiesis* meaning 'the making of' – or self-renewing.

Autocatalytic and autopoietic processes describe how systems of interaction are created by factors which are already within that very system of interaction. For instance, the biological cell is formed through *autopoiesis* – the internal chemical communications between nucleus, mitochondria and everything else inside the cell (which is process) – which can only take place if and when the cell wall (which is structure) is in place. *So structure facilitates internal process.* But the cell wall is itself created by the internal chemical communications. *So process creates structure.* Let's repeat that – *structure allows process*, and simultaneously, *process creates structure.* A dialectical relationship is at the heart of the self-making nature of autopoietic relationships. Now consider how creative networks and the collaborative relationships which animate them are formed. People congregate in certain places to discuss and develop creative ideas and plans (internal process). These places of congregation become recognized as the places to be (structures), so as to benefit from such creative networking. Once the places become so recognized, more people congregate there more often to discuss and develop creative ideas and plans. Creative processes create a 'structure', and this 'structure' allows for more creative processes.

Creative networks, precisely because they are not organized by any Centre, have very little formal structure or membership, have no hierarchy or management, can be understood as *autocatalytic* and *autopoietic* 'structures' with their own particular rules of transmission because they are self-generating, self-renewing and self-organizing. They are sources of great creativity, they can become very robust, reliable and sustained systems of co-creativity, but they are formed out of nothing but informal relationships between people. And if they become vital and energetic, they come to take on a life of their own, a kind of 'identity', as the people who take part in and make them also reflect back upon them and cherish their particular network relationships. That is, creative relationships become more self-reflective, and so more sustained and regularized, and so more self-reflective. The ideas of autocatalytic and autopoietic systems are only metaphors, and there is always a danger of over-applying such metaphors. However, there are more real-world, cultural versions of similar processes of self-organization which help to ground things somewhat. For example, the idea of *mythopoiesis* – *myth* meaning 'collective story-telling'; *poiesis* meaning 'the making of' – is one such notion.

Mythopoiesis describes how collective dialogues (stories, myths, rituals, festivals), which creative relationships often form around, lead to all parties within those relationships becoming mutually self-aware of collectively 'being in the same place' (physically, culturally or emotionally). Such relationships become a sustained two-way dialectical interplay between the myths around which a group coheres, and the process whereby people come together to re-share those very myths. *Stories create groups* and groups create *shared stories*, mostly about their group-ness. Think of how a long-term creative group with a shared history thinks about itself and stays together as a consequence of that shared history. The concept of mythopoiesis brings us a view of creativity

> . . . that is very different from the Greek (*formal logic*) rational and empirical framework which has become the mainstream of western thought. Indeed, the worldview of many indigenous cultures is not based upon linear logic at all. It is first and foremost, mythological. Reality is mythopoiesis – an interesting word, combining the prefix 'myth' and the Greek origin of the word poetry – poiesis – which literally means 'the making'. Mythopoiesis is therefore about the construction of reality from story. . . . People's very sense of who they were, what their human worth was and what values they espoused was transmitted through legendary genealogies, myth, poetry. . . . (*And*

thus, in turn,) (*n*)ormality proceeds from the mythopoietic rather than the other way around. The mythopoietic is more fundamental. I think that this is terribly important: it is why, ultimately, the true bard does not just compose poetry. Rather she or he is gripped by it at the gut level of cultural genesis. Poetics makes the bard.

(McIntosh 2001. p. 49)

What autopoiesis from biology and mythopoiesis from anthropology show is the *emergent* nature of things, that is, how certain processes can lead to shared systems of relationships and rules of transmission which are created simply out of the actions of the various people taking part. There is no external managerial agency nor organizational structure, no unified strategy, no central coordinating mechanism. Systems of relationships of creative networks work because they work, because the people who make them up do their creative work and talk about it with each other. They lead to a shared recognition of being together in the same place (literally or metaphorically). And this often leads to a particular kind of *emergent behaviour*, which is another facet of what we have been calling the rules of transmission within a creative ecology.

To understand this, let's take a short detour and consider a story which Steven Johnson tells in his book *Where Good Ideas Come From* (2010). In April 1838, Charles Darwin found himself on the coral reefs that make up the Keeling Islands in the Indian Ocean. All around him the coral reefs teem with life and diversity. He sees butterfly fish, damselfish, parrotfish, Napoleon fish, angelfish, golden anthias, all feeding on the plankton swimming above the coral itself. Sea urchins and anemones travel the sea bed in search of food this rich environment supplies. Just a few feet away, the dry land of the Keeling Island is almost devoid of life, and Darwin already knows that further out in the middle of the Indian Ocean the inventory of life is similarly sparse. Only at the edges, at the cross-over points, does Darwin see this amazing richness and diversity. This became known as Darwin's Paradox. And it is a useful one for thinking about creative ecologies. As Steven Johnson has put it:

> When we want to answer a question like 'Why has the Web been so innovative?' we naturally invoke thoughts of its creators, and the workspaces, organisations, and information networks they used to build it. But it turns out that we can answer the question more comprehensively if we draw analogies to patterns of innovation we see in eco-systems like Darwin's coral reef. . . . Whether you're looking at the original innovations of carbon-based life, or the explosion of new software tools on the Web, the same shapes keep turning up. When life gets creative, it has a tendency to gravitate towards certain recurring patterns . . .
>
> (Johnson 2010. p. 76)

These 'recurring patterns' are the informal, mutually supporting networks found within ecologies of relationships between different 'species'. The creative ecology is synonymous with such a picture of a natural ecology; both are complex, diverse and rich networks of intimate and moving relationships of mutually beneficial interactions, which lead to multiple sources of creative adaptation and innovation. Analogous to a natural ecology, the creative ecology supports different 'species', and although some relationships within it are *predatory* – in that some feed off others – and some are *competitive* – in that there is direct competition for resources – just as many are *symbiotic* – in that there is a mutually beneficial sharing of resources. And in the bigger scheme of things, the combined effect of all the creative relationships within an ecology is the creation of a more creative environment for everyone. And it is this which leads to the constant adaptation which is often the wellspring of creativity, as each 'species' within the ecology finds their 'fit' with the environment. The importance of such relationships for creativity is highlighted by thinking about Darwin's coral reef as showing how creativity resides within the *spaces between* creative entities, and is animated by the informal patterns of networking given impetus by these mutually interdependent relationships. Human creativity, as opposed to that of butterfly fish and damselfish, often comes from a more self-aware creative coral reef, as creative people consciously work to form and sustain their network environment. So, in returning to the idea of emergent behaviour, we can see it as another facet of the rules of transmission within the creative ecology. In his book *Emergence: The Connected Lives of Brains, Ants, Cities and Software*, Johnson (2002) unpacks the hallmarks of emergent behaviour to describe its recurring inner patterns, and draws our attention to the following key points as a particular attitude germane for creative relationships.

Firstly, Johnson advocates an attitude of *more is different*. The more micro-differences involved within a creative ecology, the livelier they will be. The higher the levels of difference among the creative people who come together, the more everyone can draw upon. Actively seeking to bring more and more creative people together within and though creative dialogue, the more creative everyone is likely to become. This notion can be related to discussions concerning creative *capabilities*. Amartya Sen (1999) and Martha Nussbaum (2011) have highlighted access to key resources as a basis for any creative agency. The more resources for increased capabilities, the more capacity for realistic success each person has, and this reasonable capacity for possible success will form the basis for creative motivation which is required to take things forward to concrete action. So seeking greater difference and diversity, greater reach and depth of relationships, holds great potential for increased creative capabilities in this way. This chimes with points discussed in Chapter 5, concerning the new media landscape. For instance, Clay Shirky (2010) has argued the increased access to new relationships given the Web means that we all now have the potential to draw upon the collaborative ideas of more and more people, and this amounts to an increase in creative resources. We will return to this idea, what Shirky calls *cognitive surplus*, in that chapter.

Secondly, Johnson highlights the efficacy of *encouraging random encounters* within his discussion of emergent behaviour. As we saw with autopoiesis, creative ecologies create, but simultaneously are created by, myriad informal relationships. But they are highly decentralized systems and rely heavily on random interactions. Because these informal ecologies of relationships have no centre or unified co-ordination, the creativity they might foster can be unreliable and haphazard. Without specifically random encounters, practitioners do not stumble over new co-creative solutions, new collaborators and new possibilities so often. Without random encounters they do not get the usefulness from difference. The inner dynamic of creative relationships rests upon the random as much as the planned. Too much planning and focus can 'plan out' innovation and adaptation. Creativity is often located within Centres – public cultural organizations or creative business workplaces. Such formal Centres support creativity in many ways, but they also come with their own fairly closed structures (usually hierarchy), their own agendas (usually managerial) and their own imperatives (usually commercial). And due to all this, they tend to skew the texture and pattern of creative relationships away from the usefulness of the random for new creative thinking. Again, as we will see in Chapter 5, creative relationships are increasingly on the edge rather than within Centres – within peer-to-peer or edge-to-edge relationships – and operate in a way which is analogous to Darwin's coral reef. Organizational structures and managerial agendas dictated by a Centre do not apply. These kinds of creative relationships are much more self-generated and self-determined, and as such they have a very different dynamic. The organizational-managerial view of creative Centres tends to underplay the opportunity costs of too much hierarchy, ego-centric management and over-competitive commercialism for creativity. Centres can be good for creativity, but if the Centre has too much 'status anxiety' the first thing to suffer will be creativity of the working relationships. Emergent behaviour which seeks more random encounters within the network relationships which make up the creative ecology are just as often a source of heightened creativity therein. Encouraging random encounters leads to the creativity of *serendipity* (Johnson 2010) – finding creative solutions by not looking for anything in particular, but rather allowing creative meanderings and other non-specific forms of creative 'travel' to be part of one's everyday life. It also underpins the creativity of *obliquity* (Kay 2011) – the creativity of not approaching things 'head on', but trying different 'angles' out instead. It also offers more real-world potential for finding new 'lateral thinking' possibilities (de Bono 1992) if one gets to speak to and listen to people from disciplines and perspectives beyond one's normal range.

Thirdly, emergent behaviour involves mutually recognizing the *patterns in the signs*. By this, Johnson means standing back from the details and looking for common patterns across the different trajectories of creative work within the creative ecology. Relationships lead to greater creativity when dialogue leads to a mutual recognition that each party has things to offer the other. When it becomes apparent that different parties are (or could be) working on similar issues and so have the potential to become collaborators, even though the overt content of each creative project might at first appear very different, attention to the strange, two-way relationship between problems and solutions is drawn out. We often think of creativity as problem-solving behaviour – we have a problem and we seek a solution in a kind of linear way. But looking for patterns across the signs, and finding mutual understanding through creative dialogue, often shows that just as often there are *solutions looking for problems*. This is something we will look at in more detail in Chapter 7, but it is clear that creative relationships are the only place where the potential joining of problems and solutions in this multi-directional way can happen. Such relationship building can be the key source of the creativity which flows from using certain ideas, tools or techniques designed for one arena, in another arena. It is in the key creative arena where the 'killer app', so beloved by geeks, becomes apparent, and where hacked solutions can be found. Dialogue within relationships is also often the key to *divergent thinking*.

And this is why Johnson, fourthly, puts so much store by *paying attention to your neighbours*. Echoing Bentham's notion of propinquity, the creativity of paying such attention lies in the fact that local information – the ideas within a single creative person's head – can lead to global wisdom if it grows into a more developed joint picture when it is shared, discussed and co-developed within the context of creative relationships. As we will discuss in more detail in the Chapter 5, when we look at the new media landscape through the lens of *swarm logic*, paying attention to the micro-communications coming from your neighbours encourages joint understanding and mutual creative development. And it is these facets of creative relationship building which underpin what Johnson (2010) has called the 'natural history of innovation'. In drawing his history of how world-changing ideas have come to fruition, he highlights various key features which again place relationships squarely within creativity. We will explore these features in full in Chapter 7, when we try the rather hazardous task of saying something about the 'anatomy' of creativity.

As we began to argue in the previous chapter, approaches to understanding and explaining creativity which neglect relationships in favour of the myth of the lone creative person are in danger of seriously underestimating this social context of creativity, and misunderstanding its inner dynamic of transmission. Creativity is never a purely individual act. Myriad relationships form, sustain, re-inform and shape the recurring patterns of the creative ecology. This applies to the relationships between the actual people doing said creativity, but it also increasingly applies to the relationships between creative disciplines. *Convergent relationships* between the different creative disciplines are common now as the tradition boundaries between specific creative disciplines break down. We also see convergence in the changed relationships between the creative producers of culture and their audiences. Traditional hierarchies between producers and consumers are blurring and are being replaced by edge-to-edge and peer-to-peer creative relationships. More on that in Chapter 5. Convergence can also be seen in the changed experience of creative work itself, whereby the traditional distinctions between work time and social time, work space and social space, are disappearing for some. It is clear that these facets of convergence mean that creativity occurs within relationships that are *already cultural*. Rather than cultural meanings coming only from the creative outputs and objects themselves, the relationships within a creative ecology are often already soaked in broader social and cultural meanings and so can almost be the work itself. So there is often a convergent relationship between the processes within a creative ecology and the actual artistic outputs which any one person might create, such that relationships can become the locus of a public cultural articulation. Creativity is almost always born of relationships with things beyond the work itself in some way, whether the individual creator is aware of those relationships or not. And this starts to get us into a more *anthropological conception* of creativity.

An anthropology of creativity

Anthropological research into the formation of human groups and the sustained bonds which are fostered allows us to add something distinctive to this broader social picture of creativity. Anthropology situates creativity against the broad context of how social groups maintain some kind of inner cohesion and speak back to themselves. It views specific 'bits' of creativity – the artefacts, images and texts produced by a particular culture – as signals of internal group processes as much as repositories of something significant in their own aesthetic terms. The material and symbolic culture of any particular group and the outcomes of their creativity within that context is but the expression of deeper ideas and meanings. From this starting point, the anthropological conception of creativity tends to focus upon broad issues of cultural *agency* within a particular setting of relationships which go far beyond the creative acts themselves. So the focus here is upon the 'why' of creativity – its role and function within broad social and economic processes – rather than simply the 'what' of creativity – the concrete material objects which get produced. Due to this, the anthropological conception centres around some key ideas:

- **Intentions** – the expressions between people which speak to shared local traditions and rituals, of which the internal creative motivations of individual artists themselves is but a reflection
- **Causation** – the role creativity plays in creating and sustaining public cultural bonds between those people and the on-going expressions of their shared local traditions and rituals

- **Transformation** – the impact creative acts play in deepening and reinforcing group bonds within the group as they relate to other practical political, economic and technological facets of life
- **Results** – the impact of specific 'bits' of creativity, not so much in terms of the gallery, the cinema, library or shop, but rather in the rituals, ceremonies and other manifestations of creativity as they impact upon social relationships within everyday life

This kind of approach differs from the overly psychological accounts we explored in the previous chapter because it locates creativity very much as a social act with clear sociological functions far beyond the individual. Clearly, relationships between people are the central facet here, but in a way that differs from our account of the creative ecology above. If the creative ecology and explorations into things such as emergent behaviour help us to consider how creativity comes about through relationships *between creative people*, then this more anthropological account locates creativity very much against the broader relationships which creative acts have with the social norms, values, forms of expression and shared meanings of the society within which it resides. This starts to speak of the broad *context* of creativity, something we will explore in detail in Chapter 6. It is worth noting too that this anthropological account also differs from those accounts of creativity which suggest that it is a special activity somehow separate from everyday life. By locating things against the way ordinary people use their creative potential to express common values and shared meanings, reinforce mutually impactful relationships and reaffirm shared rituals, we see a picture of creative relationships which are grounded very much within the regularities of common social and cultural life.

For this view creativity is located within the formation and consolidation of *kinship*. This is partly what gave *Homo sapiens* their evolutionary advantage. Creative works from the earliest times – paintings, ritualized performances, early forms of writing – expressed ideas about shared needs and experiences which helped to foster practical cooperation between people, as well as temper overly aggressive competition. For instance, in his great work *The Golden Bough*, James Frazer (1998) recounts how, whilst expressing ideas of shared kinship, common myth-making and story-telling became what he calls a 'practical magic', that is, a guide to collective conduct between people which embodied ideas about how those people could and should live together in concrete terms.

> Regarded as a system of natural law, that is, as a statement of the rules which determine the sequences of events throughout the world, it (*story-telling*) may be called Theoretical Magic (*myth-making*): Regarded as a set of precepts which human beings observe in order to compass their ends, it may be called Practical Magic (*kinship rules*).
>
> (Frazer 1998. p. 84)

The stories of *Gilgamesh* and *Beowulf* might be our earliest examples, but creativity is still coloured by these kinship meanings today, if we choose to see them in that way. National anthems express kinship values of a certain type, whilst the Glastonbury Festival expresses ideas of kinship differently.

But as we touched upon in Chapter 1, for Dissanayake (1995) such creativity performs a more specific kinship function. By strengthening and sustaining shared beliefs in what is of concrete necessity for effective group cohesion, creativity in all its variations makes what is *necessary* into something *special*. It is this facet of creativity, and its function in 'making special' that which is necessary for group bonds to persist, which gave humans their early evolutionary advantage. The 'software' of human group formation, such as language and

Culture, are emanations of creativity just as much as tool-making and the other 'hardware' facets of human progress ubiquitously lauded when anyone raises the topic of technological progress. The 'making special' function of creativity also helps to socialize new generations into the values of the group in a particularly deep and meaningful way:

> At some point in their evolution, human beings began deliberately to set out to make things special or extra-ordinary, perhaps for the purposes of influencing the outcome of important events that were perceived as uncertain and troubling, requiring action beyond simple flight or fight, approval or avoidance. . . . In ritual ceremonies, then, one can see that making special could acquire even more importance than individual concerns. Because it is used to articulate substantive and vital concerns, it is drawn from, expresses, and engages one's deepest and strongest feelings.
>
> (Dissanayake 1995. p. 33)

Such thinking helps us to locate creativity fully within and against the world of human relationships in a way which adds immeasurably to our understanding of its origins, meanings and function. By situating creativity against this broader context of relationships, an anthropological conception helps us to overcome the problematic over-individualism inherent within psychology-neuroscience on the one hand, and the object-centredness inherent within approaches such as art history on the other.

> The concept of making special . . . casts a new light on the previously troublesome question about the nature, origin, purpose and value of art, and its place in human life. . . . What is relevant is that Homo Aestheticus 'needs' to make special and appreciate special-ness. . . . By using elements that pleased and gratified the human senses – elements that themselves arose in non-aesthetic contexts; bright colors, appealing shapes and sounds; rhythmic movement; aural, gestural, and visual contours with emotional significance – and arranging and patterning these elements in unusual, 'special' ways, early humans assured the willing participation in, and accurate performance of, ceremonies that united them.
>
> (Dissanayake 1995. p. 35)

Marcel Mauss expresses something similar:

> . . . (cultural) exchanges are acts of politeness: banquets, rituals . . . festivals and fairs in which economic transaction is only one element . . . the dances that are carried out in turn, the songs and processions of every kind, the dramatic performances that are given from camp to camp, and by one associate to another; the objects of every sort that are made, used, ornamented, polished, collected, and lovingly passed on, all that is joyfully received and successfully presented . . . is a cause of aesthetic emotion. . . . Thus the clan, the tribe, and peoples have learn how to oppose and to give to one another without sacrificing themselves to one another. This is what tomorrow, in our so-called civilized world, classes and nations and individuals also, must learn.
>
> (Mauss 2002. p. 37)

Collaborative practice

Having looked at the broad contours of various conceptions of creativity which put relationships with other people at the centre of things, let's now consider the question of inner dynamics within such relationships in search of a more detailed picture of how creativity might flow in particular ways, from particular interpersonal processes. Implicit in almost everything we have said in this chapter is the centrality of *collaboration* for creativity. But collaboration can be the result of many different dynamics. Collaboration can come through

- relating to the work of previous generations, or be a deliberately chosen and conscious relationship with someone here and now
- a harmonious working relationship, or the result of critiques and disagreements
- a short-term and spontaneous relationship, or something more long-term and regularized
- a deep friendship, or colder, more professional working relationships
- a deep and shared interest in one sphere of creativity, or due to cross-disciplinary work between people with very different backgrounds

One could probably add more distinctions, but suffice it to say that collaborative creativity can be the result of very different inner dynamics. But nevertheless, some form of collaboration is increasingly key to creativity in our ever more complicated and interconnected world. For instance, from a more business studies approach, Henry Chesborough (2008) highlights the growing need for collaborative creative relationships even in the often macho, overly competitive world of business. He makes a distinction between 'closed' and 'open' approaches to creativity and innovation within corporations.

In a 'closed' approach, management tends to draw tight boundaries around the company to protect confidentiality; assume that all the creative skills needed are already within those tight company boundaries; and focus upon overt competition geared towards getting to market first. In an 'open' approach, management tends to see the interconnections between companies as beneficial for creativity and innovation; recognize that creative skills are often outside of the company and need to be brought in for collaborative co-working; and focus upon such collaborative creativity to ensure getting to market *best* rather than first. This business-oriented view of managing creativity echoes other alternative business models found in the world of the Open Source Movement, peer-to-peer collaborations and myriad other creative micro-experiments which are becoming an increasingly common adjunct to orthodox business plans and models. The entrepreneurial spirit is being complemented by alternative approaches forged by an *alt-trepreneurial spirit* which puts collaborative relationships at their heart (de Guy 2002; Garcia 2007; Perelman 2000). As we will see in more detail in Chapter 5, findings new ways to make collaborative relationships for co-creativity work, whatever their inner dynamic and character, is an increasingly necessary route to creativity itself. Because the collaborative world of peer-to-peer and edge-to-edge creativity, given the Web, are open, self-organized and autopoietic systems, they constantly offer new possibilities for the details of finding particular roots to collaborative working. And we can grasp something of the inner dynamic of these relationships for creativity if we start to see them as resources, that is, as *social capital*.

After first being discussed in the context of education during the 1950s, debates around social capital were given a new life by Putnam (2000) in the 1990s, as he broadened out the scope of the debate to suggest social capital as a useful way to understand the inner dynamic of various social, political and community activities. His central argument is that we can understand access to necessary resources as stemming from, firstly, *finance capital* – the money we can draw upon; secondly, *personal capital* – our knowledge, experience, talent, etc.; and thirdly, *physical capital* – the equipment and other material resources we are able to use.

In addition to these resources, however, Putnam argued that we can also see *relationships* as resources – having a network of contacts; having colleagues or collaborators whose help and advice we can draw upon; knowing people with whom we can trade favours and exchange things within a 'barter economy' – these are all resources just as much as finance, personal knowledge and owning physical equipment. These relationships are what Putnam called *social capital*. Putnam went on to argue that social capital can be in the form of *bonding capital* on the one hand, and *bridging capital* on the other. That is, creative relationships might form on the basis of social capital which grow out of, or grow into, a deep meaning and felt *bonds* between people. Many life-long friendships have grown out of initial creative collaborations. On the other hand, social capital relationships can be born out of simple, perfunctory and temporary relationships which might only persist for as long as the creative 'gig' lasts. Such creative relationships are formed as people are brought together in ways which *bridge* divides in their regular working patterns and everyday lives for a specific 'bit' of creativity, if only temporarily.

But whether in the form of bonding or bridging, social capital is a very different kind of resource which brings its own particular dynamic. Because social capital is relationship-based, it requires that such relationships be kept 'warm' and 'alive'. The other kinds of capital – knowledge, finance or equipment – will 'wait for us' and stay in place until we need to use them. Creative relationships, if they are to be a useful and reliable forms of social capital, need to be maintained – if you don't use them, you lose them as they will simply wither away. This may mean that creative relationships need to be 'invested in' in some way if they are to persist. But despite this particular relationship-based codicil, social capital networks can lead to greater creativity, and creative collaborations can lead to greater social capital.

> To build social capital requires that we transcend our social and political identities to connect with people unlike ourselves. . . . Let us find ways to ensure . . . (*that*) significantly more (*of us*) will participate in cultural activities from group dancing to songstress to community theatre to rap festivals. Let us discover new ways to use the arts as a vehicle for convening diverse groups of fellow citizens.
>
> Art manifestly matters for its own sake, far beyond the favourable effect it can have on rebuilding . . . communities. Aesthetic objectives, not merely social ones, are obviously important. That said, art is especially useful in transcending conventional social barriers. Moreover, social capital is often a valuable by-product of cultural activities whose main purpose is purely artistic.
>
> (Putnam 2000. p. 129)

And this takes us back to the point concerning convergence made above. One of the reasons that social capital awareness has become an increasingly important aspect of creativity is the fact that relationship building is an increasingly necessary dynamic within cross- and/or multi-disciplinary working. As many of the traditional boundaries between creative disciplines, and those between traditional designated 'creative' disciplines and other domains – science, technology, engineering, business, law – converge, finding ways of working with others from other disciplines becomes ever more central to where creativity happens. This convergence is leading to the emergence of new cross-over terrains, and thus many new creative possibilities. But to be able to grasp the nascent possibilities within these new cross-over terrains, a multiplicity of skills in relationship formation and maintenance are now needed on top of the more traditional creative content skills and experience. But not only is convergence putting the need for collaborations with other people *between* disciplines more at the centre of creativity, it is also encouraging more and more people to have interconnecting relationships *within* their own daily creative routines. Many creative people now have a *portfolio career* which entails that they work in different ways, on different facets of their creativity, sometimes for themselves, sometimes for different clients, all within their working week. Many have found a creative identity through relationships forged between the different facets of their portfolio career.

As we will discuss at greater length in Chapter 6, creativity and relationships also rest on the fundamental dynamic of the *dialogue* which takes place between each person involved. For Martin Buber (1992, 2004), any dialogue which flows between two or more people can help to foster mutual understanding, appreciation and fellow feeling. Indeed, for him, such dialogue is synonymous with the creation of a common culture of understanding and tolerance, is one of the main wellsprings of creativity and is the fundamental source of our shared abilities to create inspiration, laughter, tears of joy, the healing of despair, falling in love and the education of our children. A chronically underestimated feature of life, dialogue is perhaps in and of itself the greatest creative medium we have.

But the tenor and grace of dialogue must be consciously attended to. As we will argue further in the polemical section of Chapter 6, not all purportedly creative or cultural places are dialogical, and not all dialogical spaces are creative. Martin Buber's account of dialogical value and its relationship with culture makes some key distinctions. First he identifies *technical dialogue* – purely instrumental discourse aimed at getting information to or from the other person. It has little concern with mutual understanding or appreciation. Secondly, he identifies *monologue* – a discursive position premised upon pre-established notions of hierarchy, whereby discourse between unequal participants masquerades as dialogue. Only after discussing these two interlopers does Buber identify what he calls *genuine dialogue* – discourse guided by sincere intentions to establish on-going, living dialogue between mutually respectful people, with the aim of shared understanding and expanded care as the locus of that relationship. He asserts that genuine dialogue is achieved only if it is an open expression of the possibilities between people who fully appreciate each other. Technical monologue reduces dialogical relationships to the status of 'things' and 'quantities' which only allows for inherently hierarchical relationships. In many different cultural guises today – science, economics and all sorts of technocratic discourses – technical monologues have augmented discourses which seek only to acquire isolated 'bits' of specialist knowledge and have reduced relationships which make up more holistic appreciations of the world to the realm of 'specialised utilization'. Too often, these technical monologues seek to turn the other person into a *means for an end* which is not their own. It is thus inherently alienated and alienating, and redolent of an unethical approach. Within the more 'artistic' discussions of creativity, exemplified by Mr. Tusa, discussed in Chapter 1, this particular kind of technical dialogue proceeds through implicit reference to a pre-established cultural hierarchy between Institutional 'experts' and passive audiences. The other common discursive arena around creativity proceeds in the monologues of the celebrity 'genius' and/or the Marketing Department thereof.

For dialogue to be a more authentic location of creative relationships, it must proceed from something which looks and feels much more like a genuine dialogue for *all* the participants. For Carl Rogers, such dialogue is more genuinely made if it is an expression of *congruence*:

> . . . congruence is a basis for living together in a climate of realness. But in other special situations, caring, or prizing, may turn out to be the most significant element. . . . Caring is an attitude that is known to foster creativity – a nurturing climate in which delicate, tentative new thoughts and productive processes can emerge. Then . . . there are situations in which the empathetic way of being has the highest priority. When the other person is hurting, confused, troubled, anxious, alienated, terrified, or when he or she is doubtful of self-worth, uncertain as to identity – then understanding is called for.
>
> (Rogers 1980. p. 45)

This attitude of genuine dialogue suggests that heightened abilities in simultaneously seeing things from the *inside* – one's own perspective – and the *outside* – the way others see things – are necessary parts of the creative relationship. This requires seeing the subtleties of life and placing a high value upon intuitive understandings. And this means that successful creative relationships can be linked to a heightened *emotional intelligence* flowing from empathy, merged well with a clear-sighted self-understanding.

For Illich (1973) this constitutes *conviviality*, which he understands as 'the autonomous and creative intercourse between persons, and the intercourse of persons with their environment' (p. 11). As such, it helps us re-envisage creative relationships as holding the potential to become 'tools for conviviality', as sites which can help enhance what the aforementioned Sen (1999) and Nussbaum (2011) have called the 'capabilities' necessary for taking creative motivations through to self-determined concrete action. As well as contributing to shared practical wisdom, Illich also refers to conviviality as a value in itself, as a sensibility which embraces an open, mutually caring way of interacting with others. Re-envisaging creative relationships and the dialogue(s) they promise as tools for conviviality helps to recast creativity as a self-organized dialogical community made by mutually respectful partners. Such creative dialogues recast as tools for conviviality encourage people to become active creative producers rather than passive cultural consumers. They help establish places of genuine public dialogue for an authentic authorship of their culture, as replacements for the rather facile notions of the 'ownership' of culture which tend to flow from the Institutional world. Such genuine creative dialogues also help articulate cultural immediacy and appropriateness between cultural professionals and the public to steer emergent co-creative paths working with the vitality of the edge of the creative ecology.

In terms of concrete conversational practices for creative collaboration, Richard Sennett (2013) explores the skills people need to sustain it within everyday life. He bemoans the tendency of our culture to engage in conversations based upon silo-istic thinking and position-taking attitudes. Buber, Rogers, Illich and Sennett all in turn highlight the *de-skilling* of dialogical capabilities as a particular facet of our broader cultural situation, and argue that improved skills for genuine dialogue lie in actively seeking greater attentiveness and responsiveness to the other person. Genuine dialogue as the basis for dynamic creative collaboration cannot flow simply from being in the same space as someone else and taking turns to state already established positions, least of all if one is toting pre-established hierarchies of supposed 'professional expertise' and 'amateurish-ness'. In fact, developing dialogical skills rests upon improving the capacity for creative listening rather than for making declarative statements from an already formed position. Conversational practices conceived by Bakhtin (1981) argue for a sensibility focused upon the dialogue as an *on-going creative process* in its own right, as an *end in itself* rather than merely a means to an end. A more authentic relationship between the listening to, the speaking about, the doing of and the organizing for creativity is at the very heart of any useful creative relationship which embodies and fosters genuine dialogue and collaborative practice.

And this returns us to Buber. One of his main concerns is to reaffirm the inherently *inter-subjective nature of creativity production* as emanating from the intertwining of social, artistic and moral life. Without the shared-ness of the 'inter-subjective situation', it is difficult for creativity to become thoroughly cultural. Creative practitioners can learn much from developing greater self-reflexivity through this *dialogical conception* of creativity, and the dialectical logic of mythopoiesis which it implies. Obviously, this ideal may sometimes happen within certain creative relationships, but a more self-reflexive turn toward genuine dialogue can only improve our understanding of what creativity *is* and *where* it is located. By turning our attention to creative dialogue as a tool for conviviality so as to initiate genuine dialogue as an attitudinal feature for creativity, we might all (self-)consciously work to foster greater creative inter-subjectivity as the fulcrum for cultural growth within our own work and across the broader creative ecology. Genuine dialogue offers the possibility of a strong foundation for an open, collaborative mind-set. In short, it underpins the potential for mutually worthwhile creative relationships.

Whether it is viewed from a sociological or anthropological perspective, whether we refer to dialogue as its cultural epicentre, or use biological metaphors to grasp its collaborative nature, it seems that collaborative practices born of relationships with others are the very essence of creativity. As Keith Sawyer, echoing our critique of the over-individualistic, elitist conception laid out in Chapter 2, puts it:

> We are drawn to the image of the lone genius whose mystical moment of insight changes the world. But the lone genius is a myth; instead, it's group genius that generates breakthrough innovation. When we collaborate, creativity unfolds across people; the sparks fly faster, and the whole is greater than the sum of the parts.
>
> (Sawyer 2007. p. 15)

We will return to Sawyer's ideas in Chapter 7, when we discuss some ideas which we can use to construct a consolidated anatomy of creativity. But before that, as we all know from personal experience, relationships are not always benign. They can also be very frustrating experiences which are shot through with conflict, misunderstandings and other negative consequences. There is a *dark side* to relationships.

The group mind: the pathology of relationships and the damage to creativity

For obvious reasons group psychology places the formation and the inner dynamics of group processes at the centre of things. For this approach, the relationships we have with significant other people and the social rituals, cultural ceremonies and mutual symbols we use to express those relationships are a key facet in understanding the human condition. And although there are different perspectives within group psychology, the central tenet upon which they all agree is the proposition that people do things when they are in groups which they would not do when they are acting as individuals. And this group effect upon individual behaviour often brings negative or counter-productive consequences. But if we want to understand the inner dynamics for creative relationships to any degree of sophistication, understanding groups is necessary, not least because it automatically asks us to consider how two or more people come together to co-shape a situation and deal with each other – another facet of the dialectical conception of creativity we discussed in Chapter 1.

We are all in groups, and we are all in groups all of the time. We are all in different groups at different times. Sometimes we are in a group that we have not chosen, because our membership in them has been *ascribed* to us – our race and gender. Sometimes we are in groups we have consciously *chosen* to be in – our creative profession or network. Sometimes our group membership shifts and changes given changes in our life, some of which we choose and some of which just happen to us – what our age 'means' for us and others. Group-ness has different scales. It can come from, and be about, something quite intimate – our family. Or it can come from, and be about, something more expressive – our creative tribe. Group membership can be something which gives a regularity and shape to our everyday life – our occupation. Or it can be something more fluid – our intermittent friendships. It can be something quite nebulous – our local and regional identity. Or it can be something which we feel we have somehow just 'landed in' – our nationality. Whilst our *ascribed* group-ness is given to us by the perceptions of others, our *chosen* group-ness is actively declared though all sorts of subtle, or not so subtle, signals such as the use of cultural equipment to express our tribal memberships – clothes being the most obvious example. And this chosen expression of group membership is the key route by which we 'present the self' to the world (Goffman 1971), so as to construct and declare our social and cultural identity.

And for all these reasons, group memberships become very powerful influences upon how we think about ourselves, how others think about us, and how we fit into the world or not. Group dynamics are powerful factors for (de)motivating behaviour, for sanctioning or debarring certain ideas and beliefs. Sometimes group memberships enable us, and sometimes they prevent us from being our true self. Groups are often very treasured, emotional places because they give us our sense of place and home, give meaning to our everyday lives, bring feelings of love, friendship and other long-term reliable relationships. We usually feel the need to hold onto our group relationships once we have them. And precisely because they give us so much, they can be very dangerous places full of conflict, tensions and drama. They can easily become like pressure-cookers where 'steam' builds up and often explodes. They can easily lead to all sorts of emotional stuff like guilt, shame and the like. Groups can be the places where irrational behaviour is stimulated and perpetuated, because groups dynamics are very good at creating and maintaining all sorts of illusions and delusions. The inner dynamic of groups has an inherent dark side which can have a negative impact upon creativity. Groups tend to develop a 'group mind', or 'groupthink' (Janis 1982), which is qualitatively different from the aggregate of individual minds which make up said group. This means that the behaviour of the group cannot be understood as simply the outcome of the individual characters involved. The group mind has its own particular, often very peculiar interior dynamic given that *individuals-in-groups* do things, believe things, profess things which they would not as individuals. And again, this can have disastrous effects upon creativity as much as anything else.

Sigmund Freud (1991) has pointed out that the interior dynamic of group relationships is characterized firstly by *mutualism*. This encourages a syndrome whereby 'I will agree with you if you will agree with me'. And this then quickly becomes consolidated by a syndrome whereby 'together we can both/all pretend to be happy/right/safe/moral etc.'. This inner dynamic can then quickly descend into self-granted permission to believe whatever the group feels the need to convince itself of. Individuals-in-groups have real problems disagreeing with each other or seeing beyond their current view of the world. And this can be very bad for clear-sighted and feasible creative ideas.

This is in part fuelled by the tendency towards *suggestibility* which group relationships bring. Groups are much more credulous, easily led or outright dumb than any one individual within them would ever be. Groups tend to sponsor behaviour which more often veers towards a 'herd instinct', and individual behaviour which becomes passive and sheep-like. And this can be very bad for the forward looking and critical thinking which creativity needs.

Thirdly, the group mind often develops a pathological *illusion of invincible power*. Given the interior dynamics of mutualism and suggestibility, groups often tend towards an irrational belief in their own universal correctness. They are very good at perpetuating ideas over time about their own internally self-validating superiority when they look at other groups. And often this comes with ideas about their invulnerability, such that they create and maintain very powerful joint delusions. And this is very bad for reflective practice which sustained creative thinking requires.

Added to this, Freud sees *guilt* as a defining feature of the human condition, by which we learn to repress our personal impulses in favour of more supposedly 'civilized behaviour'. Because groups are the places of so much heightened emotional content, they tend to be places of *heightened guilt*. Inner group processes are able to reinforce their interior delusions by offering or withholding the feelings of membership which we all crave. So they often become microcosms of emotional blackmail.

In his book *The Established and the Outsider*, Norbert Elias (1965) talks at length about how groups, usually through the personas of self-elected leaders, are able to police the behaviour of the individuals within them. The inner dynamics of these group relationships involve pressures designed to produce guilt so as to maintain conformity. Threats to ostracize individuals from the group so as to silence disagreement or dissent are often intertwined with requirements to demonstrate hostility towards other groups and/or individual outsiders, as a way of declaring one's membership of the in-group. This can descend into on-going pressures upon individual members to constantly reaffirm their group solidarity through ever more extreme reactions. The overt behaviour of each individual becomes skewed and shaped by groups in myriad ways. Conformity, threats of internal ostracisms, hostility towards other groups and the need to reaffirm existing identities – none of these behaviour traits can ever be good for the collaborative working and genuine dialogue we have suggested are key to collaborative practice.

Over time, groups also tend to develop a *group mythology* – the ideas and stories about its origins, and the codes of belief which define it. This mythology persists as a kind of meta-story standing above and colouring all the other stories that group members are then able to tell each other. Behaving rationally, maintaining a clear view of the world and acting as a reasonable individual become very difficult if group membership is to be maintained. Again, creativity will inevitably suffer.

R. D. Laing (1997, 1999) has exposed some of the finer details of all this. In particular, once group-ness starts it creates self-perpetuating illusions which become a 'reality' no longer capable of appreciating itself as an illusion. And due to this, individuals come to police themselves before the other processes of group policing get to them. The impact of the group upon individual behaviour becomes that much more profound because the group mind is now *reified* – it has taken on the status of a 'thing' with its own kind of power over the individual, and its influence is ratcheted up another notch. Relationships in groups can culminate in individuals becoming what they are 'supposed to be', and as such they come to 'voluntarily' renounce much of their creative potential. To explore this, Laing (1999) uses the concept of *collusion*. A more refined version of Freud's idea of mutualism, collusion describes the tendency for each group member to act in accordance with what they think the others in the group want from them. This culminates in circular process such that everyone is 'doing it' to everyone else, precisely because everyone is doing it to everyone else, either through overt statements or more subtle, unspoken symbolic expressions.

The inner dynamic of collusion comes from each group member experiencing being under constant inspection, by themselves and each other, such that it becomes a matter of inner psychological comfort for individuals to comply with the assumptions they make about everyone else's assumptions. The circularity of this inherently self-referring, self-validating and therefore internally self-reinforcing system grows over time to become what Laing calls the *group synthesis*. In his book *The Politics of Experience and the Bird of Paradise*, Laing (1967) writes of group synthesis thus:

> I interiorize your and his synthesis; you internalize his and mine; he interiorizes mine and yours. I internalize your internalization of mine and his; you interiorize my interiorization of your and his. Furthermore, he interiorizes my interiorization of his and yours – a logical on-going spiral of reciprocal perspectives to infinity.
>
> (Laing 1967. p. 38)

A further detail in these on-going rounds of group synthesis comes into play when we consider the treatment of individuals who refuse to play the collusion game and so risk the tendency whereby groups *shoot the messenger*. Interior group dynamics are notorious for dealing overly harshly with the person who brings the uncomfortable 'light of day' from outside the group to challenge their self-perpetuating illusions. Instead of risking being 'shot', the individual is compelled to forget the creative 'message', and continue with collusion. As Laing writes in his book *Knots*:

> They are playing a game. They are playing at not playing a game. If I show them I see they are, I shall break the rules and they will punish me. I must play their game, of not seeing I see the game.
>
> (Laing 1997. p. 61)

And again, in *The Politics of Experience*:

> Once people can be induced to experience a situation in a similar way, they can be expected to behave in a similar way. Induced people all to want the same thing, hate the same thing, feel the same threat, then their behaviour is already captive.
>
> (Laing 1967. p. 40)

Once collusion ensures that the group mind becomes self-perpetuating, its becomes preferable to ignore new creative possibilities. In his famous book *Social Theory and Social Structure*, Robert Merton (1952) coined the term *self-fulfilling prophesy*. With this, he identified the process whereby an initially false or unhelpful idea becomes adopted as 'true' simply because it has been expressed. He defines it thus:

> The self-fulfilling prophecy is, in the beginning, a false definition of the situation evoking a new behaviour which makes the original false conception come true. This specious validity of the self-fulfilling prophecy perpetuates a *reign of error*. For the prophet will cite the actual course of events as proof that he was right from the very beginning.
>
> (Merton 1952. p. 110; my emphasis)

We can see the self-fulfilling prophesy at work in the famous *Placebo Effect* – whereby fake drugs are 'believed' to have effects, and so then have that effect; in the slightly less famous *Hawthorne Effect* – where workers being researched changed their behaviour for no reason other than they were being researched; and in the *Observer Effect* – where the behaviour of the atoms being studied by the quantum physicist appear to change simply because they are being studied. It seems that things change simply by being within a process which draws attention to them. The whole 'true' and 'false' thing is a much more slippery slope than we sometimes allow for.

And this troublesome idea can apply just as much to creativity and creative relationships. I know of many examples, and I suspect you do too, of groups of people agreeing to incredibly badly thought-out plans, congratulating themselves of work that was 'good' when it was obvious to the outsiders that it was not. This is almost a defining feature of certain aspects of the art world. Think Nathan Barley. Exploring new directions, being able to reject initial creative ideas when further research has been done, sustaining a critical edge to reflective practice, allowing genuine dialogue as the basis for open collaborative creativity all come under threat from this dark side of the group mind and its particular tendencies towards a reign of error. If individual group members come to hold on too tightly to certain ideas simply because such ideas are bandied around; if individuals behave in certain ways simply because they behave in those ways; if others in the group come to expect such behaviour simply because they expect that behaviour; if group members talk negatively about someone's creative ideas enough times and the person in question ends up displaying that very stultified creativity, then in all these situations collaborative creative practice will suffer. There is a dark side to the mythopoietic processes discussed above.

So although relationships of all kinds, through all sorts of dynamics, for all sorts of reasons, can, as we have explored in this chapter, be good for creativity, they do need to come with a health warning. If we return to the metaphor of the creative ecology, we can recognize that there is great potential for devising and growing mutually beneficial symbiotic relationships to foster greater creativity. But it is also necessary to recognize the existence of 'sharks and snakes' who no one wants to work with. That 'chameleons' and 'talking parrots' also exist which might only be intent on blending into the background noise of the creative relationship and have nothing to add. There is no 'one best way' or any universal answer to these questions; we all need to be our own judge and trust our judgements about the relationships we choose for our creativity. All one can say is that we need to be aware of the pitfalls as well as the benefits of 'getting into bed' with someone to collaborate. Given the point about the dialectical nature of creativity, it is our contention that creative individuals are shaped by their myriad relationships with others. There is no real way out of this, and for the most part it is a mutually beneficial thing. But such relationships can detract from creativity if they are generated, sustained and held onto for the wrong reasons. The inner dynamic of creative relationships is a potentially dangerous thing too if the dark side is left to get out of hand.

So far we have looked at some general points which we feel are useful for situating creativity, explored the nature of the creative person, and now suggested in a rather broad-brush way that relationships persisting between creative individuals are a necessary counterpoint to overly individualistic accounts of where creativity resides. In the rest of this book we continue to broaden things to situate the creative person–relationship dialectic against the backdrop of creative places, the new media landscape and the broader contexts within which creativity takes place. Let's now turn to the first of these broader contextual features, creative places, as the next component of discussing the *where* of creativity.

Chapter 4

Creativity and places

Places matter. . . . They map our lives.
(Solnit 2002. p. 4)

The specific nature of particular places has a large impact on creativity in many different ways. Sometimes places are important for creativity because of their physical beauty, or the way they stimulate memories. Places can represent something we dream of belonging to or escaping from. Sometimes, creative people respond to specific places due to the experiences which others have of them, and what that evokes. Sometimes specific places are important for creativity because they give ready access to other people and creative conversations. Physical places and their concomitant meanings have always been a key factor within creativity. We all exist within places. And so, therefore, does our creativity. There are all sorts of different levels and facets of an affinity between creativity and places, that is, there is a *geographical conception of creativity*.

Creativity is often located within *Centres*. Sometimes such Centres are public cultural organizations, sometimes creative business workplaces. Either way, Centres support creativity in many ways, but they also come with their own structures (usually hierarchy), their own logic (usually managerial) and their own imperatives (often commercial). We often still come up against the myth of the lone 'genius' within a business organization, the perspective that holds up the creativity of people like Thomas Edison, Alan Sugar or Steve Jobs, and tends to ignore everyone else in the Centre. A more organizational view of creativity tends to remember the myriad relationships and processes within the organizational space, as well as relationships with those outside its formal boundaries. It tends to reject the 'lone genius' myth in favour of a more realistic social view. What the organizational-managerial view of creative Centres tends to underplay are the dangers of too much hierarchy, egocentric management and over-competitive commercialism for creativity. Organizational Centres can be good for creativity, but if the Centre has too much 'status anxiety' the first thing to suffer will be creativity.

. . . we observed that ideas come not just from the scientist's bench, but from groups of creative people within the organization, from ideas hunters who uncover ideas inside and outside the organization, from formal relationships with universities and venture capital funds, from efforts to cross-fertilize within an organization across divisional and industry boundaries, and from single creative individuals who may be maintained outside the organization but whose efforts are dedicated to the organizations' needs. A broad spectrum of structural mechanisms exist to ensure a rich discovery competency for the company.

(Chesborough 2008)

But as we will see in the next chapter, *edges* are often now more important within the geography of creativity than Centres. New media have changed the geography of creativity. One facet of this change is the altered relationships between the once all-powerful Centres of creativity such as record labels, TV stations and publishers on the one hand, and those creative spaces/communities previously marginalized by the gate-keeping of that very Centre. Relationships between the Centre and this edge have been changed such that edge-to-edge (e2e), peer-to-peer and Open Source collaborative sensibilities for creativity now by-pass the Centre and often form a much more creative 'non'-place (Augé 2008). The edge has overcome hierarchy, ego-centric management and over-competitive commercialism because it has found an alternative way of doing things. As we will see in more detail in the next chapter, the edge can ignore the Centre and can speak directly to other members of itself.

But within this geography of creativity, it is not just the places *per se*, but the way people navigate across them which also has a big impact on creativity. We have already visited the idea of *propinquity* in the last chapter, and discussed how regular daily contact between people led to a greater sociality, which often forms the basis of the cosmopolitan life of creative relationships and networks found within particular places. For Bentham propinquity could be navigated to through a number of routes. *Familial propinquity* stems from being in the same extended family, which was the major source of social connectedness for thousands of years. But with greater geographical mobility given the advent of a modernized societies, the simple fact of inhabiting the same spaces as others led to greater *residential propinquity* as urban life became the norm for the vast majority. And the process of urbanization was part of the industrialization of society, which also brought greater significance to *occupational propinquity*, as more and more people had daily contact with each other given their similar occupational spaces. More general *acquaintance propinquity*, which comes from things like regularly using the same bar after work and just 'getting to know people', started to occur as the majority had the time and space for such a social and cultural life. To Bentham's ideas we might today add a *lifestyle propinquity*, as regular relationships which stem from having the same cultural habits and tastes as others become far more central to peoples' identity and sense of themselves within a post-industrial society. We might therefore also suggest the idea of *creative propinquity*, being part of the same creative world, the same creative discipline, the same studio group, the same creative ecology, which in general terms is the basis upon which creative network relationships can form and add to the creativity which flows from navigating across the same place.

For Jeremy Bentham, *propinquity* was part of his 'felicity calculus', which sought to measure the pleasure we get from knowing each other. This is how most people now know each other, as a result of inhabiting the same places. And as such, they experience many more things, many more people, which then becomes an experience of a place with its own heightened cultural meanings. For more modern sociology, the *propinquity effect* talks of the tendency people have to form associations with others simply on the basis of an experienced geographical nearness and perceived similarity. These propinquities may not lead to deep, meaningful or long-term relationships. But they often impact upon creativity by leading to acquaintances which foster a broad but shallow kind of networking. The geography of creativity sometimes involves just 'being around' which, by leading to higher rates of propinquity, can lead to the creative relationships and insights which we discussed in the previous chapter.

But at the other end of the spectrum, navigation within the geography of creativity can be much more unknown and haphazard. Creative ideas often arrive when we are not looking for them, through non-deliberate creative wanderings which lead to unexpected avenues for creativity. Steven Johnson (2010) has discussed the importance of *serendipity* within the geography of creativity:

> The English language is blessed with a wonderful word that captures the power of accidental connection: 'serendipity'. First coined in a letter written by the English novelist Horace Walpole in 1754, the word derives from a Persian fairy tale titled 'The Three Princes of Serendip', the protagonists of which were 'always making discoveries, by accident and sagacity, of things they were not in quest of'. The contemporary novelist John Barth describes it in nautical terms, 'You don't reach Serendip by plotting a course for it. You have to set out in good faith for elsewhere and lose your bearings serendipitously'.
>
> (Johnson 2010. p. 49)

And many creative practitioners seem to agree. For example, Henri Matisse talked about how his work always pursued the same destination, even though he used different routes to get there. And this kind of serendipitous creative navigation recalls the importance of informal, open-ended and non-deliberate creative wanderings, which can help in the search for new insights. As we will discuss further in Chapter 7, this recalls Stuart Kauffman's (1996) notion of the *adjacent possible*. If we can see the creative person as analogous to Kauffman's idea of the 'autonomous agent' – the biological organism adapting to the world – and the creative ecology from Chapter 3 as analogous to his idea of the 'biosphere' – the environment within which this happens – then for Kauffman, life is so fertile because autonomous agents respond to the *adjacent possibles* offered by the biosphere. Imagine a palace with an ever expanding number of connected rooms, each with several doors coming off it. Being in the first room gives the possibility of going into several different rooms next. Being in one of these second rooms allows new choices about the third set of adjacent possible rooms. Maybe room 2 was uninteresting, but it was the access route from room 1 to room 3, which contains useful stuff. It also brings access to room 4, and that holds the promise of a choice of room 5. Connecting to possible choices offered by what is adjacent in itself means that further choices opened up. This adjacent possible metaphor suggests that creativity can come from opening unexpected doors so as to travel to other possible adjacent rooms of creativity. And if you see enough adjacent possibles, you have a palace of creativity. This metaphor also allows an overview of the whole palace beyond the particularities of each room, so articulating whole creative journeys of possible 'nexts' – a 'map' of your creativity to allow you to navigate across its terrain.

And again, many creative practitioners seem to agree. For the Buddha, 'There are only two mistakes one can make along the road to truth; not going all the way, and not starting', and for Frank Zappa, 'Without deviation progress is not possible'. So for all these reasons, the geography of creativity and its location within specific places is a key facet of the broad discussion of the *where* of creativity. Creativity always exists within, and responds to its surroundings.

> The right milieu is important in more ways than one. It can affect the product of novelty as well as its acceptance; therefore it is not surprising that creative individuals tend to gravitate towards centres of vital activity, where their work has the chance of succeeding . . .
>
> (Csíkszentmihályi 1996. p. 83)

That is, creativity has some kind of 'fit with its environment'. Often, given the high degree of specificity of the relationship between a particular act of creativity and a particular place, the devil is in the details. But this book is not such a biographical account of specific examples of creativity. Instead, let us stand back from the details and make some broader statements about how creativity is impacted upon by particular kinds of places. And perhaps two of the most important and ubiquitous kinds of place, which have had such a great impact upon creativity, are *the workplace* and *the city*. Let's look at each one in turn.

The workplace

If we go back far enough into history, we would see many places of work as places of great creativity. The artisan developed their craft over many years, had intimate relationships with their tools and skills, had a high degree of control over what they produced and how. But since the industrial revolution and the initiation of the factory system, such places of creative work have become ever rarer. The history of industrialization is also the history of the *de-skilling of work*, reducing it in ever more detail to an experience of mundane, repetitive work which is the experience of work for the great majority today. The sociology of work and organizations, the history of industrial relations, and the finer details of this within Labour Process Theory initiated by the seminal work of Braverman (1974), all tend to suggest that work is now something carried out in places of ever greater managerial control of what is produced and how. This history of the deconstruction of creativity at the heart of this is centred upon *the separation of conception from execution*. Whereas once the crafts-person would have a degree of autonomy over their working processes, this separation is defined by ever increasing control by management to make decisions – conceptions – as well as the fragmentation of work into ever isolated and meaningless tasks given to individual workers – the execution.

The development of managerial techniques was at the very genesis of this separation and the consequent de-skilling of work. The apogee of this was the development by F. W. Taylor in the first few decades of the 20th Century of Scientific Management, a set of managerial principles and techniques which were to become central to the industrial system. The three core principles of Scientific Management were, firstly, to collect all the information about how particular working practices were carried out, which were previously held on the shop floor by the workers themselves; secondly, to centralize all that information in the hands of management, which enabled them to break down complex working practices into separate specific tasks; and then thirdly, to issue specific task instruction to each worker as to what they were to produce and how activities should be carried out. The transformation of creative work into specific isolated tasks was the fulcrum which enabled work to become something stripped of any vestige of control from the person carrying that work out. The crafts-person was reduced to the status of 'hands', almost literally, as the thinking person capable of understanding, planning and carrying out creative work was reduced to the status of the merely a physical body carrying out the allotted task. There can be no clearer example of the reduction of the human being capable of creativity becoming relegated to simply a component of the 'machine system'. The history of the workplace within the industrial system is the direct opposite of any reasonable notion of human creativity.

But this is at the crude end of the industrial organization of work, and for a variety of reasons – general economic conditions, especially during World War II; developments in industrial sociology and psychology; the recognition of organizational culture – the management of the workplace has tried to re-initiate creativity, albeit in rather half-hearted and sometimes disingenuous ways. In the early days of industrial organization, the Human Relations perspective on management grew out of a recognition that trying to encourage a sense of commitment, loyalty and team-ness was good for productivity. In trying to generate a sense of co-operation which was 'spontaneous' on the part of the worker, management went some way to allowing a small degree of discretion to come back into the hands (and minds) of workers (see Roethlisberger and Dickson 2003). Industrial psychology in the 1950s and 1960s took it as part of their mission to understand, and so heighten, a sense of motivation within the workplace. This went another small step along the way towards allowing industrial work to be a source of creative fulfilment for the ordinary worker. These kinds of early development in the organization of the workplace were to some extent progressive, but at best they were very limited and at worst were attempts to purvey a myth that management's and workers' interests could coincide within the industrial system, which many would argue embodied fundamentally incompatible interests.

These developments gave rise to a host of industrial initiatives over the years designed to convey the idea that the industrial workplace could be a place of creativity, as well as benign relations between the worker and their work. 'Industrial Welfare', 'Industrial Betterment', 'Job Enrichment', 'Job Rotation Schemes', even to some extent Post-Fordist management – such initiatives have been given many names over the years. The early history of some of this contributed to the development of Personnel Management as a discrete branch, charged with looking after the welfare of employees. It is instructive that in recent years, given the rise of a neo-liberal political-economic atmosphere and changes in general economic conditions which have seen relatively high unemployment, that the 'caring' attitude implied in the term Personnel Management has given way to the more 'utilitarian' sounding Human Resources epithet. Not a lot of workplace creativity implied there.

At the organizational level, the discovery of organizational culture encouraged the notion that management should seek to actively promote an internal cultural atmosphere commensurate with the joint efforts of management and workers to raise productivity. Whilst there may be some increase in the space for creativity within the workplace here, it is often only for those with higher skill levels or degrees of professional status. The field of 'managing creativity' flows from this, and many people have experienced the workplace as a realm of enhanced 'self-actualization' as a result. But again, the release of creativity within the workplace is still rather limited given this agenda is still about subsuming all activities within pre-established organizational imperatives and hierarchies. The experiences of creativity are rather temporary as the realities of the 'day job' eventually kick in. Again, any reasonable notion of creativity as the human potential for genuine self-directed activities is still a long way away from this rhetoric.

In recent years, the advent of a post-industrial economy, and for many creative people the 'gig economy', whereby the experience of work is of temporary contracts within a self-employed 'portfolio career', are again changing things. The general nature of industrialism and the capitalist relations of production which stand behind that have not really changed. So for the vast majority of people around the world the workplace is still experienced as a place of profound de-skilling and de-creativity. But for many creative practitioners in the developed world, the workplace is now not such an all-consuming, de-skilled and life-damaging arena. This is implied in much of what this book says, either above or in subsequent chapters, but it is instructive that even those concerned with the management of orthodox, formal workplaces have begun to recognize this. The 'open innovation paradigm' (Chesborough 2008) is one particular example of this kind of thinking, trying to more genuinely bring creativity into the formal workplace organization.

Orthodox workplace organizations tend to be large, or at least work towards becoming large, and still tend to operate with clearly defined boundaries between the 'inside' and 'outside'. They still tend to be redolent of quasi-military notions which declare the competition between the 'inside' of the workplace and the 'outside' as the central feature of business, creative or otherwise. But as we have seen, the creative industries often operate in and through informal *networks* which have less rigid boundaries, no hierarchies to speak off and very little in the way of management. Because such creative networks are self-organized, the flow of ideas for innovation tends to occur more organically across the spaces and places that make them up. And this flow of ideas is seen by many as key to the geography of creativity. So the idea of creative collaborations and cooperation with people outside the formal boundaries of the formal workplace is much more important than the universal competition between 'inside' and 'outside'. Because the 'closed innovation' paradigm operates with these spatial assumptions of competition, it tends to set up many barriers, literal and cultural, to creativity spreading and dispersing across the potential landscape of practitioners. Because it assumes that all the creativity needed for the organizational task in hand is already on the 'inside' of the firm, it sets up borders across which the creativity cannot flow. Because it assumes that profiting from creative research and development comes from getting that to market first, such borders become enshrined within Intellectual Property rights, non-disclosure agreements and other passports which creativity must now obtain before it can travel across the potential landscape.

In contrast, the open innovation paradigm sees this closed approach as 'knowledge hoarding', as clinging to an unnecessarily tight and closed geography of creativity. By setting up to many borders between the 'inside' and the 'outside', the closed approach unnecessarily restricts the 'travel' and 'migration' of ideas between different creative minds, and as such leads to missed opportunities for co-creativity which can flow from a more collaborative approach. The closed approach encourages an inward-looking focus which misses the potential in the creativity already 'out there'. As we will discuss at length in the next chapter, the collaborative creative culture of the Web now enables much easier, quicker and more open 'free revealing' of creativity. A continued insistence on a closed geography of creativity often now lead to less creative efficiency and competitiveness, precisely because of its over-insistence on borders, when others are operating in a more open and dynamic way. Highly skilled creative professionals operating with a portfolio career are now much more mobile in navigating across many different creative terrains, and no longer believe in, nor want, a job for life 'inside' the big organization. Such creative practitioners are increasingly willing 'to go it alone' within the new cultural economy by developing their own spin-off companies based upon creativity that could have stayed with the firm if it had been less closed-off. Such creative professionals are often motivated by things that go far beyond simple monetary reward – by the meanings and values inherent within the creative work itself. A more open innovation paradigm lends itself to giving 'breathing space' for the pursuit of these creative motivations within the workplace, and more generally encourages a more creative organizational culture. If the organizational culture parallels the closed-ness of the management processes, then creativity, innovation and the flow of ideas will simple flow out of the workplace as people seek to articulate their creativity elsewhere, rather than flow within and through it.

So, a more open geography of creativity within the workplace needs to be characterized by its own specific assumptions. For example, not all the most creative people work already 'inside' the existing borders of the organization, nor can they be simply recruited, because the creativity of such people is a much more unknown and moveable feast than that. No organization can know what they need to know because, *de facto*, they do not know about that yet. So greater openness which allows creative flow and migration across the borders between the 'inside' and the 'outside' is needed, if only for temporary creative projects. Whilst internal creativity is needed to claim some portion of the potential market value of commercial creativity, co-creativity with external partners can create significant additions to that value, in particular by sign-posting 'killer apps' and already existing solutions looking for problems. The 'inside' of the formal boundaries of the organization need not always be the place of creative origination. Building a better, more open and collaborative geography of creativity which allows better travel across the creative ecology is often better than getting to market first upon stop-start creative business projects. It is often better to get to market *best*, on the basis of more sustained and sustainable creativity. It has taken Big Business and Big Management theories of creativity a long time to recognize this, something that many creative practitioners have known all along, and that the Web is giving greater impetus to – that collaborative, co-creative, cross-boundary, multi-disciplinary ways of working often bring many mutual benefits.

The general conditions of (post)industrialism and the persisting relations of production which define capitalism notwithstanding, such a new geography of creativity within the workplace might indeed bring some profound changes to the experience of work if it allows these collaborative processes to flourish. At the very least, the open innovation paradigm 'blows the gaff' that traditional, macho, quasi-militaristic, overly competitive approaches to the workplace are the only way to organize. Not only does this tend to de-skill and deny creativity, it is becoming increasingly clear that it is not always that good for the creative bottom line either. It may be overly optimistic, but perhaps this emerging approach to workplace organization will lead to a more genuinely creative experience for those working within it, if they are able to pursue creative ideas and projects with the outside world on the basis of mutual exploration and co-creative implementation. New thinking about the workplace such as the open innovation paradigm might be the harbinger of a widespread recombining of conception and execution within work, at least for creative professional work within the developed world. These points are all very broad, and it is doubtless the case that people will experience the workplace in a multitude of different ways. On balance, we can perhaps say that the modern workplace has not been a place of great creativity, and that in the main it has tended to deny creative expression for the vast majority of people. Whilst many people experience work and the workplace as something fulfilling and positive due to the many stranded attempts by industrial management to create such positive experiences, this has had varying degrees of authenticity and success. The workplace is constantly changing, and many new experiments are afoot today which are continuing those changes. For many creative people themselves, it seems that they are increasingly willing to forgo the financial securities which a full-time job brings, in favour of greater creative freedom and meaning which being self-employed brings. Rather than the formal organization, the informal spaces of creative networks are becoming the places where much of the creative economy occurs. Industrial management is increasingly experimenting with new ways to organize the workplace in search of ways to release more creativity, and this is changing the geography of creativity because the relationships between the workplace and the rest of the creative world are being recast, at least in some instances. And of course, as we will see in the next chapter, the Web continues to radically change the way in which creativity occurs, along with the way its outcomes are shared, distributed and disseminated. All these changes are multi-faceted and on-going, so a definitive account of the workplace in relation to the question of creativity is not possible. The devil is in the ever changing details.

So much for the workplace. But another place which has had a long, complex and most profound impact upon creativity is the city. Let's now turn our attention to that place, one of great beauty and danger; a place of great inspiration and despair; the cradle of civilization and a site of great damage to the human spirit; a space of daily human contact and profound loneliness – all features, both positive and negative, which have given great impetus to the creative spirit.

The city

As we have already noted, when Karl Marx referred to urbanization as the 'end of the idiocy of rural life', he was not being unkind to rural people; it was more that he saw cities as allowing people to come together to do politics and culture more effectively. Cosmopolitan urban centres have always been key stimuli for creativity. Florence was the cradle of the Renaissance; Victorian London brought us an explosion of scientific and technological development; Paris between 1905 and 1939 was the place of the key movements within modern art; Los Angeles created 'Hollywood'; Detroit and Manchester gave us Motown and The Smiths respectively.

> As the outer shell of the city grew, so to say, its interior like-wise expanded: Not merely its inner spaces . . . but its inner life. Dreams welled up out of that interior and took form; fantasies turned into drama, and sexual desire flowed into poetry and dance and music. . . . Activities that sprang to life only on festal occasions in ruder communities became part of the daily life of the city. . . . This release of creativity was not . . . one of the original purposes of human settlement . . . but it is through performance of creative acts, in art, in thought, in personal relationships, that the city can be identified as something more than a purely functional organization.
>
> (Mumford 1966. p. 11)

Moreover,

> The city became the home of the pageant, in which all the spectacle and colour of the urban world were on display. On these festival occasions, arches and fountains were

especially built, thereby turning London into a piece of moving scenery. . . . There were platforms and stages upon which tableaux were performed. There was no real distinction between those who participated in, and those who watched, the moving display. . . . It might be in part a definition of Shakespeare's own art. The predilection was for bold colour, and intricate pattern, all designed to elicit wonder and amazement.

(Ackroyd 2001. p. 117)

A complete and exhaustive history of the city is beyond the scope of this one small chapter, and anyway, urbanists have already done that work. Historians like Lewis Mumford, and Peter Hall (1991) have given us great overviews of the history of the city and its origins in technological and socio-cultural processes. Biographers of the city like Ackroyd (2001), along with psycho-geographers such as Ian Sinclair (2002, 2003), have given us various views of the hidden aspects of the city. Many more literary accounts of specific sorts of encounters have shown the city as a 'character' within the narrative. Film-makers and dramatists routinely refer to the city in this way. The city is everywhere.

But when it comes to our more specific question of the geography of creativity, we per-haps need a more focused and sober account. Within his historical geography, Mumford (1966) talks of the 'crystallization of the city'. This implies that the city originated out of things that were happening already, that were 'floating around', in the same way that crystallization occurs from chemicals in a solution. That is, cities and their impact upon creativity did not come about merely as a result of an increase in the pure *size* of things, although that was a factor. Cities and the creativity they tend to foster came about due to *qualitative changes* in social, economic, political and cultural factors as a 'phase transition' from one state to another. The factors that were already within the proto-city led, as a result of their own inner dynamic, to explosions of creativity. There is a dialectic of creativ-ity within this – cities are at one and the same time the drivers and the consequences of these inner geographical dynamics of creativity. For instance, the city and creativity came from, and at the same time stimulated changes in, the *intensity of everyday life* – its speed, its daily regularity of novel creative encounters, the profundity of new meaning, the scope of change to the cultural expressions possible within the everyday. Social, economic, political, cultural and technological life changed in *quality* and intensity, not just due to the *quantity* and size of the changes which created urbanization.

. . . (*the*) new urban mixture (*which*) resulted in an enormous expansion of human capabilities in every direction. The city effected a mobilization of manpower, a com-mand over long distance transportation, an intensification of communication over long distances of space and time, an outburst of invention along with a large scale development of civil engineering and, not least, it promoted a tremendous further rise in agricultural productivity.

(Mumford 1966. p. 4)

For Mumford, these early *structural contours* within the shift from a village-agrarian society towards an urban-industrial-modernized society were intertwined with *cultural changes* to everyday life:

When all this happened, the archaic village culture yielded to urban 'civilization', [*which gave rise to a*] peculiar combination of creativity and control, of expression and repression, of tension and release, whose outward manifestation has been the historic city . . . the city may be described as a structure specially equipped to store and transmit the goods of 'civilization'.

(Mumford 1966. p. 5)

As well as an intensification of the social and economic functions of transportation, communication, technology and engineering, the city immediately became a place of new meanings to life, intertwined with new experiences of other people. This gave rise to a new imaginary landscape for artistic and literary production. It helped to create new places of propinquity such as coffee houses, ale houses and restaurant cultures. A new geography of shared festivity, rituals and ceremonies saw a shift from the Church as the centre of village culture towards the football stadium, the cinema and the studio as the centre of an urban culture. New cultural markets stimulated professional creativity beyond The Court and led to the new cultural drama of 'conspicuous consumption and leisure' (Veblen 1994), as well as consolidating repositories of High Culture such as museums, theatres and galleries. Regularized, professionalized educational institutions such as Universities also located professional creativity within the city. 'The rise of the city, so far from wiping out earlier elements in the culture, actually brought them together and increased their scope and efficacy' (Mumford 1966. p. 6).

But such changes to the location of creativity brought by the city also brought about a corresponding impact upon the *experiences* of life as a creative potential. There were many negative facets to the experiences of the city, such as alienation, anomie and a disenchantment of the world, but urbanization also had many positive effects which relate to the growth of urban creativity. The history of the city saw a growth in a cosmopolitanism born of a growing sense of the individual able to decide upon and (to some extent at least) control their own destiny, which was often given voice through a creative life. This increased emphasis of shaping one's own life and identity often came from new imaginary potentials for self-creation.

Due to the new urban order the city became a symbol of the Modern, set against the rural as a symbol of the 'backward' or 'bucolic'. And as such it called for new creative responses to all aspects of everyday life and culture, as well as opening up myriad space for the burgeoning, professionalized creative trades such as architecture, design in all its facets, literature and film-making. As both a driver and as a consequence of these shifts, the city came to function as a metaphor for an intensified cultural life; to become the geographical 'hardware' of creativity; to symbolize creativity itself. Let's take a short detour to look at this experiential aspect of cities in more detail, before we get to the debate about how it has impacted upon the geography of creativity in more detail.

Creativity, culture and experiences of the city

One way to understand the historical development of this new urban context is to see it as a reflection of a set of over-lapping processes of change, found firstly in the *modernization* of social and cultural institutions; secondly in the initiation of new social and cultural experiences of these changes which we might call *modernity*; and thirdly as the stimulus for a vast range of artistic, literary, architectural and other creative responses to these new experiences which we might call *Modernism*. There is a complex set of dialectical interrelationships within this, between all this as a series of changes to the way society was and is *structured*, the way this shaped how people *experienced* life, themselves and others, and the way creativity was re-shaped to *make sense and comment* on such changes.

The processes of modernization include, in no particular order of importance, secularization, rationalization, bureaucratization, industrialization, professionalization, scientization, democratization, liberalization, centralization, globalization and, increasingly now, digitization. Such processes of modernization changed the basic 'building blocks' around which social and cultural life revolved. Urbanization, giving rise to new patterns of social and cultural life, was and is one of the leading edges of modernization. This has given rise to a whole series of new experiences of modernity within the everyday lives of urban dwellers, which has quickly become the vast majority of the population. This has changed how we experience ourselves as we feel new freedoms about what we can 'be' or 'become' given our identity is now something much more chosen and less ascribed from birth. But this also brings new anxieties about how we fit into the world, new 'existential' problems. It has changed the way we experience each other given that we feel more common, more vital and more meaningful daily interactions with all sorts of new people. But this also brings new experiences of the mass, the crowd, crime and darkness, the Stranger as 'threat'. And the experiences of modernity have changed the way we experience culture in general given new senses of what life is, what the future will be, how life is much more cosmopolitan. But this also changes the normal patterns of everyday life, which have been 'de-traditionalized' such that we experience the world as fragmentation, disorientation, isolation and a loss of community. There are myriad ways in which the negative and positive facets of the new experiences of modernity intertwine and inform each other.

Despite Marx's recognition that urbanization was the end of the 'idiocy of rural life', the Marxist tradition sees the experiences of modernity as linked to largely negative material conditions brought about by industrialization, which culminate in the pervasive experience of *alienation*. This represents a diminution of creativity for the vast majority of the population as they become subject to the machine-like processes of the factory system, and later the broader processes of the commodification of culture, all of which come to stand over people as an alien power. For the Marxist tradition, we become alienated from our innate capacities to 'become more than we are', from the sense of our lives as 'an experiment in freedom'. We also become alienated from our social being, from our innate capacities to make cultural lives through mutually meaningful interactions with others, and as such we become alienated from each other.

For the Frankfurt School theorists – Adorno, Horkheimer, Benjamin and Marcuse – the creativity found within 'the culture industries' was contained in a culture which had become just as industrialized as any other aspect of modern life. For them, the Culture Industries operated according to a Capitalist logic, and as such was characterized by the power of elites operating in the realm of culture and ideas to purvey a 'one-dimensional' logic, with a one-dimensional language and thought, as a facet of a broader Capitalist ideology. As culture became ever commodified, it became an increasingly 'privatized' experience, whereby the collective nature of the public cultural realm was replaced by overly individualized experienced. This tended to replace the self-directed creativity found within previous local cultural traditions with a largely passive 'consumption' of activities designed externally by large cultural institutions and creative businesses. This obviously had a detrimental impact on the experiences of creativity of the vast majority of the population, a situation which is only starting to change in recent years.

For the Weberian perspective, the experiences of the modern city are linked to a broader process of *rationalization*, which itself underpins many of the processes of modernization. Whilst for Weber this had some advantages, there were cultural costs expressed in changed experiences of city life. The leading edge of this for Weber was the initiation of an 'iron cage' of rationalization-bureaucratization, which introduced a particular world-view which was largely inimical to the creative spirit. This new world-view was the cultural underpinning for what Weber called the 'disenchantment of the world', a cultural atmosphere which expunged the more creative, exploratory and spiritual meanings of everyday life and culture. In his book *Modernity and Self-Identity*, Anthony Giddens (1991) takes Weber's arguments forward with his discussion of the 'sequestration of experience'. He uses this concept to compare what would have been in previous times self-directed and relatively autonomous cultural and creative experiences to the current experiences of the city as something now largely directed by professional institutions and 'expert systems'. As these professionalized cultural bureaucracies take over more and more of aspects of public culture, the experience of creativity again suffers, as it becomes a largely passive experience. So there is a common view that the industrial city was not a place of great, free-flowing creativity for the majority. But it did stimulate the few – the writers, artists and film-makers of Modernism – to criticize this new industrial urban experience in myriad ways, which we will come to below.

But there is another general view which sees the experiences of modernity and urbanization as a great, positive step forward for the creative spirit. City life and urban culture brought with it a greater sense of cosmopolitanism, freedom, tolerance of difference, openness. It brought new opportunities for creative expression within everyday cultural life. Urban life and culture are often experienced through a self-conscious sense of being aware of new ideas, more information and different perspectives on the meaning of life. Urban culture is intimately connected to a self-conscious sense of having contact with different people, from different backgrounds on a much more regular basis, as part of one's daily pattern of life. Urbanity brings with it a sense of having more 'sophisticated' cultural experiences given more regular daily contact with more of the cultural stuff of one's society, of 'being more cultured'. It brings with it a self-conscious sense of living a life in and through culture, of making more cultural choices, of having a richer and deeper cultural meanings at the heart of one's everyday life.

Early urbanists recognized cities as the place of a developed cultural life which now included a newspaper culture, regularized scientific and cultural institutions, and established settings for informal political gatherings which gave impetus to the formation of Political Parties. The advent of the coffee house is often identified as the beginning of this new positive experience of city culture, as part of the geography of the 'creative milieu' (Hall 1991) of cities during and after the 17th Century. For example, in his book *The Coffee House: A Cultural History*, Markman Ellis (2004) has a chapter called 'Talking to Strangers', in which he writes,

> Coffee-house conversations, Samuel Pepys had discovered, presented a fascinating panoply of philosophical puzzles. The attraction of the place was never just the coffee, which Pepys did not seem to like much, but rather the potential he found there for social intercourse and companionship with one's fellows – what his age called 'sociality' or 'sodality', the quality of fellowship, brotherhood and company . . . a principle which (*for him*) was the foundation of both the city and the state. In the convivial space of the coffee-house, Pepys found a microcosm of the ideal of sociality . . . a coffee-house only really exists when it is full of people. . . . Through the 1680's the coffee-house remained firmly associated with the production and dissemination of seditious libel (*that is, freedom of speech*) . . . the coffee-houses were deluged by a torrent of newspapers,

periodicals, pamphlets and satires (*and other precursors to what we now know as the mass media*).

(Ellis 2004. p. 104)

Whilst the Georgian coffee house might have been the first of such cosmopolitan, creative city spaces to be so recognized, a similar geography of creativity can be seen in the pub, in the social club (Putnam 2000), in cultural venues offering experiences of all kinds. Which brings us back to the experience of 'making special', and the city as the specific location of that facet of creativity.

As we have already noted, Dissanayake (1995) uses the term 'making special' to talk about how the various cultural rituals, ceremonies and festivals which shape our cultural lives serve to add a greater collective meaning to those particular 'bits' of activity. Although her own research is very much about primitive cultures, making special is a useful concept with which to understand how shared urban experiences bring a greater sense of representing a *collective place* as a 'special' experience of common geography beyond the mundanities of everyday life. The geography of creativity flowing from the development of cities, as people coming together more often within their daily lives, is clearly given added cultural meaning as the new urban cultural rituals bring a making special function. Going to the local festival is not just about the music, seeing your football team play in the FA cup final is not just about the football. The structural facets of the geography of creativity given urbanization, and the social logic of making special, are both aspects of the broader idea that creativity is connected to *doing cultural things together*, in a way that generates a heightened experience of that very togetherness. Obviously making special is not limited to the modern urban setting, but equally obviously the great potential for shared experiences of and through creativity given the aggregation of people within those very settings allows making special to happen more regularly and more powerfully. Again the geography of creativity highlights the social nature of creativity explored in the previous chapter, and suggests that the interaction between the structures of creativity (the place) and the experiences of those inner process (its specialness) is again a dialectical one, driven by a self-organizing and mutually impactful interaction.

The history of the city has always been intertwined with such shared public cultural experiences. From myriad festivals and ceremonies to the cultural specialness generated by sports events, the activities of social clubs and cultural organizations, aspects of everyday vernacular culture, and the greater collectivity enabled by the city have all lent greater making special potential by greater proximities of people. And this, in turn, has helped to stimulate creativity in many forms. Sometimes this has revolved around the cultural specialness of traditional aspects of national cultures, from watching national teams play to celebrations of events of historical significance. But urban making special can also be about more radical challenges to the national traditions, found in the collective cultural actions of many folk traditions and the 'carnivalesque'. This highlights how particular festivals convey the idea of temporarily overturning cultural hierarchies and norms through creative awareness, of 'turning the world upside down for a day'. From music festivals to other collective experiences of the 'impolite', the city enables these outlets for creative making special. Hakim Bey (2003) has discussed the idea of *temporary autonomous zones* in connection to the creation of self-directed public realms of culture away from the normal 'rules' of official institutions.

In both the traditional and radical spheres, the greater proximities of the city enable the more *performative* or *dramaturgical* aspects of creativity to be seen, whereby our cultural lives are coloured by the positive pleasures we get from occupying certain roles. The creativity which lays within the making special offered by the city recalls Goffman's (1971) notion of the 'presentation of the self', and the search for positive self-regard, which can provide a sense of psychological well-being when we receive positive feedback from others. And this, in turn, recalls Veblen's (1994) notion of the public *conspicuousness* of the cultural rituals of consumption and leisure. In short, the city enables a greater sense of 'audience' for these creative expressions of self and cultural identities as something chosen and constantly re-made, as a particular form of creative communication with the collectivity of the city. Creativity almost always needs an audience for it to fully come alive, and the city is the place where that audience resides. In many ways the city has been experienced as a negative. But in just as many ways, it has been experienced as a positive. And in many ways, these negative and positive experiences are intertwined and interconnected in rich and complex ways. We humans seem to have had a bitter sweet relationship with the city since its inception. The city has formed both the stage and the atmosphere, the fertile soil and the annoying distraction, the possibility and the frustration for creativity. It has become the ubiquitous *milieu* at the heart of the geography of creativity.

The creative milieu

If we continue to argue that modernization was carried through by changes to the basic structural 'building blocks' of society, and this gave rise to new experiences which we might call modernity, then the distinct philosophical, artistic, literary, musical and architectural responses to these new experiences can be seen as *Modernism*. It is far beyond the scope of this one small chapter to give a full account of Modernism. It has taken many forms within many different spheres of creativity. As we have already alluded to, some Modernist responses were negative and driven forward by critical responses to modernity. But others have been largely positive and have embraced various articulation of this positivity.

Peter Hall (1991) offers a broad sweep of this history from a perspective which puts creativity at its very centre. Whilst Mumford relates the history of the city largely to technological development, for Hall the essence of the city lay in the increased frequency of people coming together, in much more vivid ways to do new creative things. He argues that throughout history, cities have been centres of creativity due to the way they have developed themselves as *creative milieux* – as geographical aggregations of people and creative activities; systems of symbolic, public cultural meanings; specific places of social and cultural rituals; and propinquities of people – all in constant rounds of mutual development and re-development, affirmation and re-affirmation. This creativity-centred view of the city is, for Hall, best evidenced when we look at specific cities, and what specific things they have done at specific times. That is, Hall's view of the city is very much about how and why specific cities developed their 'golden age'. In particular, he identifies Ancient Athens in the time of Socrates, Plato and Aristotle; Renaissance Florence in the time of Leonardo de Vinci and Michelangelo; Elizabethan London in the time of Bacon and Shakespeare; Succession Vienna in the time of Freud and Klimt; and Fin de Siècle Paris in the time of Art Nouveau, Impressionism, Matisse and Picasso.

> Why should great cities have such golden ages, these belle époques? How do these golden ages come about? Why should the creative flame burn so especially, so uniquely, in cities and not in the countryside? What makes a particular city, at a particular time, suddenly become immensely creative, exceptionally innovative? . . . Why should this

spirit flower for a few years, generally a decade or two at most, and then disappear as suddenly as it came? Why do so few cities have no more than one such golden age? How is it that they fail to recapture the creative spark that once animated them?

(Hall 1991. p. 3)

His answer to these questions firstly suggests that creative individuals come together in cities to earn a livelihood, but they stay to live the 'good life' – a creative life full of purpose. So perhaps a city's golden age is limited to the lifespan of one creative generation. Secondly, Hall argues that as cities create practical problems, so they stimulate creative solutions, which come to symbolize that period in the city's lifespan. Once they are 'solved', other cities take over and have their golden age. Thirdly for Hall, the creativity of a particular city emerges out of the daily 'doing' of life in that place, such that they become self-organizing realms of creativity as each inhabitant responds to their neighbours, a process which has a limited period when they are noticed by the world.

So Hall offers his notion of the creative milieu as a 'tentative verdict' on why certain cities have their golden age. This geography of creativity suggests that certain places in certain points of history bring together creative practitioners of all kinds and enable them to self-organize around certain creative mind-sets, shared cultural concerns, as intensified places for co-creativity. The creativity of such particular places comes from being there, and being there enables the place to generate ever new rounds of creativity. There is a dialectic of the creative person and creative place, such that one leads to the other and vice versa.

For Hall, this idea of the creative milieu is to some extent linked to a Marxist train of thought, because he sees the link between the realm of ideas, culture and creativity on the one hand, and the material conditions of that period in the history, such as the levels of wealth and other practical conditions, on the other. But he also links this to other economic aspects of a geographic lens. Economic facets of this geography highlight how conglomerations of people and processes lead to certain places becoming more affluent, and so more innovative because available investments make more creativity more possible. Silicon Valley is the ubiquitous example used today.

A common misconception sees *size* as a defining feature of the city. But for Hall, the size does not in itself generate the creativity of the city. Many of the cities who have had golden ages are fairly small by today's standards. We would likely experience them as towns if we could go there. Rather, it appears that a certain cultural and economic vitality flowing from enough people coming together to make the creative milieu is more of a precondition for certain cities to become crucibles of creativity. Cities are not just about size, but rather a certain *critical mass of creativity* is the thing.

A second misconception suggests that cities are successful just because they are wealthy. Cities require a surplus (of food, infrastructural development, investment funds) so that the scientist, the artist, the engineer, the researcher, the coordinator is able to concentrate on those things. With no surplus, there can be no creative milieu. But many rich cities have not had a golden age, and many relatively poor cities have. Some degree of wealth within a city seems to be a necessary precondition, but wealth in and of itself does not lead to a creative place of any note. Compare Geneva, immensely wealthy but not known for its creativity, with Lagos, relatively poor but the home of great musical traditions. And also, radically unequal distributions of wealth within cities bring tensions and inner conflicts which eventually seem to destroy the creative milieu. Witness London today. Large amounts of wealth in the hands of few and fewer people, and increasingly subject to creative flight as people seek new opportunities in Berlin, Amsterdam and Copenhagen. As Hall puts it, 'the talent may be more important than the money' (Hall 1991. p. 5).

Over and above these macro-structural facets of the city, Hall identifies four distinct but connected features which are more about the processes of cities, which enable the creative milieu to develop. These points carry strong echoes of points we have made in the previous chapter concerning the social conception of creativity and its location within relationships. But they also prefigure in a broad sense the more detailed points we will make in the next chapter concerning how new ways of working creatively are emerging as a result of the new media landscape. Firstly, Hall identifies how the distribution of *information* as a key facet of the creative milieu of the city. Information becomes centralized by city life. Historically, this has come about as cities became centres of power, fostered by the development of the centres of political administration. This was given added impetus by the increased power of the Church, and then the development of bureaucracies of all kinds. Even more impetus came from the rise of 'expert systems' (Giddens 1991) occupying roles within social institutions, Universities and businesses. This centralization of information has always given the city an immense cultural and economic 'pull', and has always enabled it to be, and be seen as, the Centre in many cultural ways which ran parallel to the centralization of information. Secondly, therefore, cities become analogous with the *knowledge* that such centralized information facilitates. Centralized information is converted into greater knowledge and concentrated into greater creativity and innovation in many fields of human endeavour. For instance, we see this through the work of the early Master Builders responsible for the Cathedral and other great architectural achievements. But it also came through the successes of scientists and those working in others areas of research. But this also grew from the increased cache of the cultural institutions of all kinds. This has enabled the city to become the home of the creative processes of artist studios, publishers, music producers and film companies as much as the artefacts themselves housed in galleries, libraries and museums. And as such this became the stimulant of further rounds of creativity. The city thus came to be seen as, thirdly, the geographical site of *competence*. As institutions and organizations develop new competencies out of their newly centralized information and consolidated knowledge, they become better at their particular form of creativity. And so they gain the 'authority of the urban', meaning that these multi-faceted cultural-economic-geographic processes culminate in the fourth factor, the *reputation of creativity*, which stimulated, and continues to stimulate, ever new rounds of people gathering, information centralization, knowledge consolidation and competence building.

This often means that the golden age of a city's creative milieu is associated with a period of general transition from one 'age' defined by one set of general economic conditions, to a different one. For instance, the cross-over periods from a medieval world-view to a more Renaissance mind-set; from an agrarian mode of production to an industrial mode of production; from monarchic or authoritarian forms of government to more democratic forms. Such periods of general transition are described by Hall thus:

> Because these were all societies in economic transition, they were also societies in the throes of a transformation in social relationships and values, and in views of the world . . . they were all in a state of uneasy and unstable tension between a set of conservative forces and values – aristocratic, hierarchical, religious, conformist – and a set of radical values which were the exact opposite; bourgeois, open, rational and sceptical.
>
> (Hall 1991. p. 285)

For Hall, the vitality of this self-organizing creative milieu helps us to understand how and why cities, as particular kinds of places, are at one and the same time the stimulant and the consequence of creativity. Cities are creative, and creativity is almost always connected, at least in part, to cities. Due to their creative milieu, cities grow their own emergent and self-organizing nexuses of information, knowledge and competence, such that they *become* centres of creativity because they *already are* centres of creativity! Cities become the geographical sites of great creativity because creativity congregates within cities. Creative cities are autopoietic. And especially during times of great economic transition, such as the one we are currently going through – from an industrial to a post-industrial; from an 'old' economy towards a new 'cultural' economy; experiencing new facets of modernization such as globalization and digitization – cities which can embrace these possibilities can also develop new creative milieu.

> The origin of the creative city concept lays in thinking about why some cities seem to have adjusted to, even surfed the wave of, change over the last two (*or now three*) decades. Cities like Barcelona, Sydney, Seattle, Vancouver, Helsinki, Glasgow . . . these and other thriving cities seem to have made economic and social development work for them. Others seem to have been passive victims of change, simply allowing it to happen to them . . .
>
> (Landry 2000. p. 15)

Landry (2000) identifies certain things which the creative milieux of such cities have in common. They have visionary individuals who help to stimulate city-wide ideas, plans and developments. They all seem to have vibrant creative organizations that can support creativity and help to realize it in partnerships with the local population. They have a general political culture with a clear common purpose of embracing creative and innovation industries, which they sponsor as a key part of the future vision for the city. For Landry, such a sense common creative purpose and cultural leadership permeate public, private and voluntary sectors of the creative milieu, which is expressed through imaginative mixtures of public initiatives and private investments, for a similar mixture of commercial reasons and the public good. It is these partnerships, born of imaginative visions keen to express particular values and a sense of civic identity which have enabled some cities to better respond to economic transitions on the basis of their creative potential. For Landry, the modern creative city benefits from cultural policies and planning agendas if they are underpinned by what he calls a 'culturally informed perspective' to make urban planning commensurate with the new opportunities and possibilities, to put creativity at the heart of the city and bridge traditional divisions between particular creative disciplines. They might also help to overcome, or at least weaken, ubiquitous divisions between the public, private and more informal aspects of local, more vernacular aspects of the creative ecology within the overall creative milieu. But Landry's picture of this modern context is sometimes a rather rosy picture. As the polemic at the end of the next chapter will argue, the institutional, the top-down and the policy-led could do much more to stimulate the creative milieu of their locale if they were to embrace a more open dialogue with the informal and vernacular. As Holden (2006) has argued, the debate the 'cultural system' of civic policy-makers and cultural professionals have is too often only a *conversation with itself*, and as such is a rather 'closed conversation'. But more on that below.

Landry argues that the geography of creativity within these successful cities also exhibits some common inner dynamics which have underpinned their successes. Such cities see creativity as a *resource*, and have sought to pro-actively shape a response to the transitions towards the post-industrial or cultural economy. They have been able to forge a new civic future to replace previous city identities based upon some form of industrial heritage. They have, or are doing this, by supporting creativity in the form of business, or simply in terms of 'developing talent'. Often the local university has been at the centre of such support, and again the creativity of the city is fuelled by itself in self-organizing ways. People are creative and stay in the city to do their creativity, because others are there too, doing the same.

Often the creative milieu has been able to develop a 'unique niche' by generating a particular cultural reputation or city identity by coming to be seen as a 'centre of something special'. There are echoes of Dissanayake's (1995) more anthropological notion of 'making special' as a location of creativity here. This sometimes enables the creative city in question to become a 'destination', again drawing in other creative practitioners and cultural visitors. This is another facet of the dialectics of creativity which informs most of this book: the existence of the creative city encourages more creativity within it, due to the internal dynamics and flux of that city.

Some cities seem able to retain, release and utilize the talents and skills of their creative people. Whilst some cities seem content to ignore this, the creative cities seem to be good at bringing into a collective vision, often through effective networking, the talents of all their citizens. For Landry, this is sometimes down to good leaders with smart, culturally sophisticated policies, able to simultaneously 'let go of the reins' whilst opening up city-wide dialogues. Often this entails referring to their already existing local traditions, and valuing what they are already good at. This can take the form of re-vitalizing their distinctive local traditions, festivals, public rituals to enable the city 'tell its stories back to itself', and so strengthen its own sense of itself. Such cities seem to benefit from the kind of mythopoietic growth we have already touched upon, whereby people are brought together to share common stories in ways which encourage a shared sense of a common city culture, which in turn encourages the re-telling of those common collective stories. The ideas of mythopoiesis and autopoiesis help to explain how (a) the 'structures' – the city itself as a shared location, and the shared stories it tells – enable people to creatively come together to re-energize (b) their cultural 'processes' – their collective meanings and capacities for creative relationship building. And just as they do this, the 'processes' allow the 'structures' to become more shared, more recognized and more collective. A vibrant creative milieu enables greater, more meaningful coming together, and the very meaningful-ness of the coming together helps the city to be more creatively aware of itself. A enables B, and at the same time B strengthens A!

And when this works well, born of an authentic cross-city culture shared in vital and dynamics ways, the city is able to take its creativity more seriously. Whilst many cities and their 'management' give lip service to 'culture as development', many approach it in an over-mechanical way and adopt a top-down view of 'Culture' as a proxy for economic development. Cities which can develop their creativity through more self-organized means, allowing for all their voices to be heard, are better able to articulate a more genuine creative milieu as the locus of its future and the felt experiences of its creative population. Successful creative cities seem to be those which recognize and articulate what is already there within its creative milieu.

And this adds exponentially to the quality of urban life and experience within those places, making retention of talented people and the attraction of further creativity much more likely. As well as the creativity itself, creative cities benefit by being places of cosmopolitan experiences, leanings, social cohesion, diversity, integration and tolerance. All the positive experiences of cities which people have valued for at least two thousand years. A creative city tends to be a happy city, and an authentic creative milieu is both the cause and consequence of that. Yet again, we see that creative cities are creative places because they are creative! They are self-organizing and emerge organically from the dialectical interplays between the myriad internal processes which make them up.

But as we have started to intimate, the role of the Official, the Institutional and the Organized is often over-emphasized. If we are to draw an adequate picture of the location of creativity, it is necessary to recognize that culture and creativity is *always already everywhere*. When approaching the geography of creativity, we might go back to first cultural principles and suggest that when one puts more than two people who speak the same language into a room, we already have culture! But this of course depends upon which definition of culture we are working with. The 'artistic' definition of Culture tends to come with a capital C, and denotes that Culture is the name we give to the agreed highlights of artistic, musical, literary or philosophical production which we experience in the gallery, concert hall, library, museum or lecture theatre. But culture and creativity are fundamental facets of everyday life for all of us, and make us what we are (or are not). This is to work with another definition of culture, which sees it, and creativity, as a much more ubiquitous facet of *everyday life*. So when we think about *the* location of creativity in the city, we would do well to remember that it is not only found in the programmes of the shiny Official Cultural Centres. It is also located within the informal creative ecologies and relationships which, as we have already noted, make up the informal creative ecologies and networks of any vibrant city. It is just as much in *the hidden city* and in the works of those operating on the edge.

We have already made a distinction between different elements of the overall cultural economy of a city, between the public sector – the agencies and institutions which use public money and expertise to support culture and creativity; the private sector – the commercial businesses operating within the cultural economy; and what Landry calls the 'voluntary sector' – the diverse landscape of community groups, charitable organizations and temporary projects which work in and across the cultural sector for many different reasons. Landry makes the point that the truly creative city does not come about via the activities of one sector of these sectors alone. For him, the successful creative cities are able to make partnerships between these different facets for mutually beneficial growth in the creativity of a city. This in itself begins to show a greater awareness of the multiple links and potential working relationships between 'Centres' – either literal geographical city centres, or professional organizational Centres – and the edges of the city – the outlying districts of the city, or the more temporary and informal activities not associated with professional organizations.

> A creative milieu is a place – either a cluster of buildings, a part of a city, a city as a whole or a region – that contains the necessary preconditions in terms of 'hard' and 'soft' infra-structure to generate a flow of ideas and inventions. Such a milieu is a physical setting where a critical mass of entrepreneurs, intellectuals, social activists, artists, administrators, power brokers or students can operate in an open-minded,

cosmopolitan context where face to face interaction creates new ideas, artefacts, products, services and institutions and as a consequence contributes to economic success.

(Landry 2000. p. 133)

By 'hard' infrastructure, Landry is referring to the buildings, facilities, venues, meeting places, hubs which support the creativity of any particular city, as well as the broader services infrastructure such as transport, health services and general amenities which allow the city to function on a daily basis. By 'soft' infrastructure, Landry is referring to systems of 'associative relationships' which make up networks (face-to-face or digital) which enable the citizens of any particular city to connect, generate ideas, 'do' the culture of the city and generate creative 'flows'. Landry is starting to recognize its more informal aspects:

> These networks may include social ones such as clubs, regular meetings in bars or informal associations; common interest networks such as business clubs or marketing consortia; or public-private partnerships involving (*say*) financial support structures and devices whereby public and private resources and ideas can be creatively brought together and their creativity harnessed.

> (Landry 2000. p. 133)

However, Landry and others do often underestimate the vitality and importance of the hidden, the informal and the edge in their geography of creativity. There is a tendency to misunderstand key differences in the way the informal creativity of the city is motivated, shaped and differs from its overtly institutional and professionalized facets. A key aspect of this difference lies in the way in which the creativity of the informal tends to be more autotelic. That is, its creative acts tend to be motivated more by intrinsic reasons that are *already within* the creativity itself. The organizational world of creativity, heartfelt and meaningful though it may be to the professionals involved, remains a set of institutional arrangements driven forward by money, contracts, professional divisions of labour and extrinsic rewards (commercial or public value). The world of Official City Creativity would not happen unless it was the 'day job' of many people. By comparison, the informal creativity at the edge is born of varying motivations, and moves through very different, more informal working relationships. It tends to be created by a different constituency within the city, often the recently arrived, the outsiders, those not high up within the Official Cultural hierarchy of the city, those without any formal organizational positions. The informal creativity of the city edges is often keen to articulate a very different image and meaning of the city, of *their city* and what it means to them. And because of all these specific factors, the creativity of the informal edge often comes from much more underground and hidden places.

The hidden city: a polemic continued

> I could tell you how many steps make up the streets rising like stairways, and the degree of the arcades' curves, and what kind of zinc scales cover the roofs; but I already know this would be the same as telling you nothing. The city does not consist of this, but of relationships between the measurement of its spaces and events of its past: the height of a lamppost and the distance from the ground of a usurper's swaying feet: the line strung from the lamppost to the railings opposite and the festoons that decorate the course of the queen's nuptial procession; the height of that railing and the leap of the adulterer who climbed over it at dawn . . .

> (Calvino 2002. p. 44)

Because cities have grown up in organic, piecemeal and haphazard ways, due to the activities of many different groups of people over many years, they have many layers of creativity with varying degrees of visibility. And so, recognizing the more hidden aspects of this adds depth to our geography creativity. The hidden, left over, half-forgotten bits of the city's place, its lives, its collective memory are always in tension with the current, the Official and the Institutional. There is another aspect of the dialectic of creativity here, the hidden and the forgotten understood as the *now absent*, which forms the context for the obvious and remembered as the *currently present*. And this interplay between the absent and the present is the conceptual tool with which we can understand the tensions between the forgotten and the lauded; the underground and the 'polite'. Highlighting the absent as partly what frames the present within the city draws our attention to the cultural processes which shaped what is to be (de)valued, (dis)respected, (dis)enfranchised, (de)selected, (un)authorized and (un)recognized. And much of the creativity of the hidden city flows from particular contestations within such factors, an interplay which, in the end, gives us the distinction between the *Officialized* and the *otherized*. But it is these otherized bits of creativity, those which are initially deemed to be 'beyond', which give particular creative cities their character, flavour, texture, meaning and cultural 'imaginary'. It is the particular forms of contestation which drive those particular creative articulations. So it is necessary for any thorough geography of creativity in the city that we appreciate these more hidden aspects, and appreciate the forgotten, overlooked and outside. The creativity of the city can lie in many places beyond the Official. As Kevin Lynch (1960) once wrote:

> Looking at cities can give a special pleasure, however commonplace the sight may be . . . a thing perceived only in the course of long time spans. . . . At every instance, there is more than the eye can see, more than the ear can hear, a setting or a view waiting to be explored. . . . Nothing is experienced by itself, but always in relation to its surroundings, the sequences of events leading up to it, the memory of our past experiences. . . . Every citizen has had long association with some part of his/her city, and his/her image is soaked in memory and meaning. . . . Whilst (*this image*) may be stable in general outlines for some time, it is ever changing in details. . . . There is no final result, only a continuous succession of phases.
>
> (Lynch 1960. p. 51)

Any picture of the creative city worth its salt needs this memory of the past, that which is soaked in multiple and contested meaning, those continuous successions of phases. Understanding the city for a geography of creativity thus suggests the need for a *deeper sense of legibility* to our reading of it. This almost automatically calls for a *broader sense of recognition* to overturn the overly hierarchical notion of authorized creativity in the city, as the city. This calls for a *greater sense of memory and (re)discovery* within any assessment of creativity within any particular city. A new image of the creative city which takes account of the hidden thus seeks a *self-aware re-orientation* which enables ever-new contests between traditional accounts of the city creativity and new ones to be a part our geography. And this raises questions about *visibility* and *imagine-ability*, questions about what is to be deemed see-able, and therefore readable and writeable within the city.

Such questions have been central to the actual creativity of the hidden city for many years, perhaps ever since cities were the preserve of the artist and the activist. They have always called upon active creativity to turn its gaze back onto the city as a contested terrain, rather than a benign place before the serious work of creative output takes place. The city is a place of creativity partly because it itself has so often been the subject of those considerations, those critiques, those moments of resistance.

And recently arrived, the outsider and the outcast often have the best perspective. Their hidden creativity from the edge is often given its impetus when they seek to articulate their particular cultural *politics of place*. It is often a creative response to place, seeking what Lynch calls the *apparency of place* — creativity which seeks 'a more vividly comprehensible appearance' of the city born of ever new articulations of what is there, what used to be there, what might be there, what could have been there and what ought to be there. In search of this apparency, artists, writers, film-makers, philosophers and psycho-geographers have for many years been drawing our attention to accounts of the *forgotten city* just as much as the *obvious city*; to the *vernacular city* just as much as the *Official city*; to the *informal city* just as much as the *Institutional city*; the *temporary city* just as much as the *confirmed city*. To make these points is only really to work with a reasonably developed conception of culture. The 'artistic' definition of culture which refers to the literary, musical, cinematic highlights of a particular society and period in history is all very well, but clearly it is in and of itself insufficient. More normative accounts of culture which focus upon the norms and values of a particular society or period of history have much to add. But we can only really do full justice to the normative if we allow for sub-cultural discussions, which give an airing to the myriad norms and values of specific groups within any broader 'host culture'. If we accept that city culture is as much the expression of these norms and values within the everyday lives of real people in ways which make sense to them, then revealing these hidden, forgotten, vernacular, informal and temporary aspects of creativity in the city becomes an obvious necessity.

The 'devil' of revealing the hidden of any particular city and its creativity lies in the detail of 'thick descriptions' which come from ethnographic or anthropological research. But the general proposition for a geography of creativity which takes account of the hidden city expressed here suggests the need for a depth dimension to take into account the uncertified, the non-specialist, the 'amateur', the unheard, the misunderstood, the discredited, the impolite and the transgressive outcomes of the creativity of the city in all its richness and vibrancy.

Perhaps the psycho-geographic tradition is one of the most developed perspectives when it comes to attempts to capture these facets of the city. Its use of relatively aimless, haphazard wandering through the city has become its way of uncovering its lost layers of history and meaning. This offers the possibility of an approach to reading the city and its creativity which allows the city to 'speak for itself' concerning its 'edges', and to speak about theses 'edges' as locations of micro-cultures and their arcane creativities. Psycho-geography reminds us to cherish the crummy and the shabby of city creativity. It is in and of itself a creative response to the creative city, one which is able to grasp the city's own feelings, its temperaments, its competing 'logics', its sense of itself through an approach which is more literary and poetic than economic and sociological.

> Walking is the best way to explore and exploit the city; the changes, shifts, breaks in the cloud helmet, movements of light on water. Drifting purposefully is the recommended mode, tramping asphalted earth in alert reverie, allowing the friction of an underlying pattern to reveal itself. To the no bull-shit materialism this sounds suspiciously like fin de siècle decadence, a poetics of entropy – but the born-again flaneur is

a stubborn creature, less interested in texture and fabric eavesdropping on philosophical conversation pieces, than in noticing everything. Alignments of telephone kiosks, maps made from moss on the slopes of Victorian sepulchres, collections of prostitutes' cards, torn and defaced promotional bills for cancelled events at York Hall, visits to the homes of dead writers, bronze casts of war memorials, plaster dogs, beer mats, concentrations of used condoms, the crystalline patterns of glass shards surrounding an imploded BMW quarter-light window, meditations on the relationship between the brain damage suffered by the super-middleweight boxer Gerald McCellan . . . and the simultaneous collapse of Barings, bankers to the Queen.

(Sinclair 2003. p. 68)

This hints at an approach to the geography of creativity which notices everything; which notices the everyday as well as Official; which drifts through the different creative realms and tribes. But it does so with a 'purpose' and 'alertness' to recover the left-overs to penetrate the impenetrable and find meaning within that which has been designated as unworthy of our attention and so 'meaningless'. It proposes an approach to the geography of creativity which seeks to touch base with the ephemeral and temporary, to revalue manifestations of the 'non-cultural' as something readable, understandable and the product of deep human creativity. It is an approach to the creativity of the city which denies the universality of the 'systems logic' which guides the cultural policy-maker and planner, and the concomitant elitism of such top-down views of creativity in favour of celebrating the everyday nature of the creativity of real people within a place, about a place, about *their place*.

There are a thousand more things we could say about the interconnection between creativity and place, about how particular creative people have responded in their own particular ways to a specific place. But we do not intend this book to be that kind of book. Our main concern in this chapter has been to draw some broad contours of how places and creativity intersect, as part of a broader theme of trying to locate creativity. But of course, the geography of creativity is no longer restricted to physical spaces and places. In many respects, the Web has lifted creativity out of specific places, such that it now as often as not resides in 'non-places' (Augé 2008). New media tools which allow creative production, new forms of communication, new ways to distribute and disseminate creative works out to the world, what we might for brevity's sake call the *new media landscape*, is now an equally important location of creativity. And the new media landscape is developing its own particular ways of working, its own inner dynamics which in themselves seem to be changing the way many do their creativity, forge their creative relationships and express their shared concerns. So let's now turn to the new media landscape as another important facet of our tour across the different locations of creativity.

Chapter 5

The new media landscape

When we think of where creativity resides, and when we think of developing a broad multi-disciplinary account of this, and when we think of going beyond the orthodoxy of the individualistic conception, we now have to think about the impact of the Web. Over the past twenty years the Web has changed a lot of things, perhaps not so much or so fundamentally as the early hype told us, but still a lot has changed. Any broad account of the location of creativity has to take it into account. This is but one current phase in the much longer relationship between creativity and technology. But it is a particular one, with particular characteristics which have a bearing upon the *what, how* and *where* of creativity. New creative processes, ways of forging creative working relationships and ways of getting work out there are clearly developing in lots of different ways. This is because new media and the Web have forged new practices of creative origination, but over and above that, new processes of production, dissemination and consumption. It has led to new spaces for creative relationship building leading to new forms of co-creativity. This new media landscape brings shifts in business-oriented creativity for a mass market towards the customization and personalization of cultural production and consumption, which represent new forms of interaction between producers and consumers.

However, we should be careful of the hype within all this. In his book *Uncanny Networks*, Lovnik (2004) argues that despite the new possibilities offered by the Web, genuine cross-disciplinary creativity has not really happened. He argues that new media have so far only really been used as specific tools within discrete arenas of creativity. He notes that within assumptions about new media there has been little reflection or actual practical take up of the potential of the Web for genuine collaborative, cross-disciplinary creativity. Maybe that is still to come, but this is not the ringing endorsement of the new media landscape as a great stimulus for collaborative creativity. There are, however, as we will see below, many other voices who take a different view, that the Web in general and the new media landscape in particular has fast become a space of new creativity, new sensibilities and motivations which drive that work, and new forms of cultural dissemination and distribution. We ourselves tend towards that view, not least because we have ourselves used them whilst publishing books previously to this one. As we will see, the edge, the DiY, the self-organized, is now much more able to get on with things without the permission of the traditional Centres.

A second key point for us within this chapter is the concern to move our debate away from considering the new media landscape as just a list of discrete new creative tools, software packages and the like. We want look at the issues concerning how the new media landscape might impact upon the nature and character of creativity and its inner practices in a more general sense, so that it can be part of the broader debate of situating creativity. But we are still a little worried about the over-hyping thing. In contrast to Lovnik, Lunenfeld (2000) argues that narratives about the new media landscape often start with 'perverse' and overly hyped accounts of 'digital culture'. These accounts tend to bring highly disparate arguments into rather dubious over-arching theories in which *everything* can be included. And so they sometimes end up not saying *anything*. Instead, Lunenfeld offers what he calls 'screen grabs' – accounts which offer snap-shots of particular activities occurring at particular 'moments'. Lunenfeld sees this 'screen grab' approach as being useful for discussions of the new media landscape because it can offer a 'compromise' view between the idea of the new media landscape as a never-ending list of creative 'tools' on the one hand, and the over-blown theorizing on the other. For Lunenfeld, this is better able to embrace the 'ambivalence' between the too-specific on the one hand, and the too-theoretical on the other. He sees this ambivalence as lying within a 'dialectic' between the theoretical and the practical.

Whilst we have referred to the dialectic of creativity throughout this book so far as a useful way to establish where various aspects of creativity lie, we do not use the notion of dialectics in exactly the same way as Lunenfeld. He uses the idea of dialectics in a more Socratic way, simply to establish an argumentative position. Notwithstanding this, his dialectical starting point does call our attention to the need to position the creativity of the new media landscape as a novel interplay between the specifics of new 'tools', and the broader contexts of social, economic and cultural implications. In our view, the 'screen grab' approach can't really do that because it is still too focused upon the particular. In our view the novel forms of creativity flowing from the new media landscape lie between the 'diverse' (Benkler 2006) interpenetrating opposites of creative motivation on the one hand, and the explosion of new practical opportunities offered by new media on the other. A dialectical interplay of (new or existing) motivations lead to the grasping of new opportunities made feasible by the new technology on the one hand, whilst at the same time these new technical opportunities stimulate new motivations on the other. This is where creative movement, change and flux come from. New opportunities for creative production, dissemination and distribution clearly set up all sorts of new interplays within the inner movement, flux and 'logic' of creativity itself. New directions become possible, new expressions become feasible, new ways of making creative work public in global ways which were simply not possible before come within reach. The interrelationships between the *what* of creativity, the *how* and *why*, and the *with whom* are all given new impetus by the new media landscape. These new dialectical interplays between inner motivation on the one hand, and concrete, practical, technical capacities on the other, mean that motivation and agency are brought into new and more fertile interrelationships. This particular point again echoes broader points already made through references to the capability theory developed by Sen (1999) and Nussbaum (2011) – creative *opportunities* sit in a dialectical relationship with creative *motivations*. New opportunities can release motivations, just as new motivations can focus and help to realize opportunities. And this leads to new creative movements. It is this key point, as an aspect of our broader dialectical idea of creativity, which informs the rest of this chapter.

But there is another facet to this. The anthropological conception first raised in Chapter 3 suggests that creative relationships also bring, and are re-affirmed by, the 'making special' function of creativity. New meanings, new senses of trust, conviviality and dialogue can flow from this, such that the development of shared meanings becomes the important locus of the thing. We think something similar can sometimes be seen at work within the new media landscape. As we will see below, some theorists are identifying not just new ways of developing concrete collaborative practice, but also a whole new sense of shared cultural meanings. Perhaps this is becoming a new subjectivity which sits in dialectical relationship with the new objective possibilities which new media make available? Let's get into some of the details.

The new media landscape and the creative commons

As we have already noted, creativity is often located within *Centres*. Sometimes such Centres are public cultural organizations, sometimes creative business workplaces. Either way, Centres support creativity in many ways, but they also come with fairly tight hierarchical structures, managerially oriented ways of working and a set of imperatives decided upon somewhere else, external to the actual doing of the daily work. The populist, or journalistic, view sees the Thomas Edisons and Steve Jobses of this world as the leaders who 'do' all the creativity, and everyone else in the Centre is made relatively invisible. The view of creativity and innovation coming from business studies or organizational theory tends to be better at remembering the myriad relationships and processes within the organizational space, as well as relationships with those outside its formal boundaries. It tends to reject the 'lone genius' myth in favour of a more realistic holistic view of the organizational culture which sets the tone for these interrelationships. However, what the organizational view of creativity-within-Centres tends to underplay are the dangers of too much organizational hierarchy, too much ego-centric management style and too much competitive commercialism. The business studies approach to 'managing creativity' tends to see the creativity bit as easily taken for granted, and so focuses upon the management bit of bringing it into line with the pre-established imperatives of the organization. Centres can be good for creativity, but this is not always the case. Organizational cultures are fragile, and require sensitivity which management all too often get wrong. Often because they don't understand the true nature of creativity and its genesis within informal relationships and collaborations. As we saw in Chapter 2, the edge of informal, emergent, self-organized creative networks are sometimes much more creative places than Centres which usually come with tight structures, heavy managerial agendas, too much ego and too many barriers to open discussion.

But such Centres are increasingly being by-passed. The landscape of opportunities being opened up by new media in particular, and new ways of connecting via the Web in general, have changed the concentration on Centres of creativity, as well as creativity in Centres, in many profound ways. It is not news, but the once all powerful Institutional Centres of creativity such as record labels, TV stations and publishers are becoming relatively less powerful, and the informal creative spaces and communities on the edge, previously marginalized by Central gate-keeping, are becoming much more vibrant places of creativity. Relationships between the Centre and this edge have been changing such that edge-to-edge (e2e), peer-to-peer and Open Source collaborative sensibilities for creativity can now circumvent Centres. The creative edge has overcome the over-bearing hierarchy, ego-centric management and over-competitive commercialism because it has found alternative ways of doing it yourself (DiY) and doing it all together (DIAT). The edge can now ignore the Centre to a large extent, and speak directly to other members of itself.

If we want to locate creativity, we should recognize that it has been at the edge, between creative peers, for quite a while now.

> Because of e2e, innovators know that they need not get the permission of anyone – neither AT&T nor the Internet itself – before they build a new application for the Internet. If an innovator has what he or she believes is a great idea for an application, he or she can build it without authorization from the network itself and with the assurance that the network can't discriminate against it.
>
> (Lessig 2002. p. 43)

> The web gives us a new way to organize and expand this collaborative activity . . . (*which*) could make innovation and creativity a mass activity that engages millions of people. . . . Our preoccupation in the century to come will be how to create and sustain a mass innovation economy in which the central issue will be how more people can collaborate more effectively in creating new ideas.
>
> (Leadbeater 2008. p. 87)

The creativity within and across these new spaces between peers is now often more fertile because it has created and distributed a *surplus* of creative ideas and thinking which we can all now draw upon and share. This is leading to 'collaborative spirals' of creativity according to Clay Shirky (2010).

One of the first points which Shirky makes concerns the nature of *aggregated creativity* – the processes of creativity which flows from, and into, those spaces which are comprised of the input of multiple creative people in concert with each other, either specifically and deliberately, or in anonymous and temporary relationships. He makes the point that people increasingly co-use their creativity for an aggregation which signals a shift away from purely individual creativity and towards a more collective endeavour, which echoes the broader social conception of creativity we have already considered. But it also echoes many other even broader social theories from a wide range of discrete areas of research. In particular, the philosophy of work and the centrality of free time as an existential resource which can be used for collective social activities, as a demonstration of self-determined action beyond the purely privatized realm, which is discussed most effectively by Andre Gorz (1982). But Shirky's particular example also echoes the aforementioned ideas of Illich (1973, 1981) concerning how certain configurations of technology can become 'tools for conviviality', as well as the ideas of Mauss (2002) and Hyde (2006) concerning the 'gift economy'. All this is summed up by Shirky when he writes, 'the use of social technology is much less determined by the tool itself; when we use a network, the most important asset we get access to is one another' (Shirky 2010. p. 14). This 'access to one another' gives credence to the social conception of creativity given that it situates aggregated creativity as something we co-create and share, something we offer to others and simultaneously draw upon. For Shirky, a key location of creativity is people's common desire to make the world a better place, and they will help others in these endeavours if they are invited to do so. By forging these spaces of co-creative space in the new media landscape, increasingly by using relatively common technologies, people help each other overcome creative problems which were previously insurmountable barriers. This is, for Shirky, the most important lesson of the cognitive surplus facilitated by the new media landscape – how one person's problem can be shared and quickly lead to co-developed solutions which then become common solutions to which everyone has access. This is a particular case in point of the more general point about creativity as relationships explored in Chapter 3. But in this particular nexus, the social nature of creativity moves with a changed cadence and location. Whereas old media encouraged passive consumption of the creativity of others, the new media landscape now provides myriad opportunities for active co-creative production with others throughout the world. This starts to re-situate creativity back within a broad public cultural location which persisted before over-individualization and its 'enclosure' driven by privatization and commodification. As Shirky puts it, 'The simple act of creating something with others in mind and then sharing it with them represents . . . an echo of that older model of culture, now in technological raiment' (Shirky 2010. p. 19). Whereas media during the 20th Century were predominantly a culture of the single event experience to be consumed, the new media landscape represents a new culture of aggregated creativity between many producers as an on-going dynamic relationship redolent of myriad opportunities for self-determination and self-expression. The context of new media allows co-creators to travel through many iterations together, rather than simply speaking from the edge to the Centre. Because it allows the edge to speak to others on the edge without any permission from the Centre, it allows active co-creation to also by-pass the social and economic logic of commodification which had previously controlled the heights of mainstream cultural production and dissemination.

A critical take on this sees the relations of creative production as being transformed away from what Karl Marx has called 'money relations', into something new and more inherently social, a *creative commons* not subject to enclosure. And as more and more creative producers take up the opportunities presented by this renewed commons, they become more self-aware of it and add a new round of vitality to it. There is a dialectical interplay here between the new technological capacities presented by this on the one hand, and newly developed social relations which are forging a new culture of common creative life on the other. There is often a 'new sensibility' (Marcuse 1969) at work here with which, as we will speculate in more detail below, the edge is pre-figuring broad social, cultural and attitudinal changes. In more critical parlance, the cognitive surplus has become a commonly owned and accessed resource. Ideas and information are no longer owned and controlled by a small elite, or perhaps in this context a professional creative class, in ways analogous to the way the economic surplus of industrial society was, and still is. The new media landscape of the creative commons means that creative resources are no longer 'owned' by anyone in any meaningful sense, but are accessed by the self-organizing community which creates those very resources themselves. As such, the surplus is inherently, already and always, *distributed across* the creative commons. And this hints at a radical transformation of 'surplus value' into something no longer owned as 'creative capital', but something which can be an addition to a more radically democratized realm of creativity. Although not in any kind of complete way, the creative commons is a new location of creativity, because it is at one and the same time a new 'structure' for creative production and the expression of different values which promote new ways of interacting. As well as a new 'structure' of co-creativity, it is also a new place of creative relationship building and a broad cultural expression of the human pleasures of adding to the collective supply of creativity.

And this new media landscape impacts upon the inner dynamics of the creative process itself. Aggregated creativity and the creative commons makes the two-way combinations of problems and solutions much more likely by enabling existing 'solutions' to find their 'problems'; it enables the creativity of divergent thinking through the aforementioned processes of obliquity (Kay 2011) and serendipity (Johnson 2010) to become more feasible. Cognitive surplus and aggregated creativity enables greater 'right to roam' across creative commons which have been de-enclosed. As we will see in detail throughout Chapter 7, changes brought about by the new media landscape signal new routes from creative origination to practical application along paths freed of gatekeepers and 'toll booths', to create open fields of possibilities with many ways to cross. These newly realized, newly realizable opportunities amount to Sen's (1999) vision of new relationships between motivations to act and the capabilities to carry these motivations through to something concrete. This allows the intrinsic motivations within any particular creative person or project to be expressed in a way which can more feasibly lead to an extrinsic articulation. Creativity thus has a much better chance to become an autonomous expression of something beyond the logic of the market. Shirky echoes Csíkszentmihályi's (1996) broader, more contextual analysis of the creative process and 'flow' when he writes of how intrinsically motivated creativity is made more viable by new media, and so leads to increased motivation:

> Taking on a job that is too large and complex can be demoralizing, but taking on a job that is so simple that it represents few challenges can be dull and demoralizing. The feeling of competence is often best engaged by working right at the edge of one's abilities. . . . This feedback loop (*dialectic*) of personal and social motivation applies to most users of cognitive surplus.
>
> (Shirky 2010. p. 79)

The creative commons goes to the very heart of where creativity is to be found because, over and above broader questions about its social and cultural location, it represents new ways of balancing motivations, skills and competences, new interrelationships between creative origination and overall creative development. The new possibilities of aggregated creativity offer new interrelationships between the 'desire for autonomy and competence' *within* one's creativity, and the 'desire for membership and sharing' *from* one's creativity. Aggregated creativity adds to the general picture of a non-individualized account, and hints at a whole new vision of what creativity *is*, *is for* and *who* it is for.

Aggregated creativity also adds a further aspect to the dialectic of creativity in that it highlights how new interrelationships between what is *expressible* and what is *viable* lead to a newly *amplified* creativity, born of new mixtures between technical capacities, newly expressible motivations, new forms of collaborative practices and a newly democratized public creative realm. This amplification is the result of new dialectical interplays, resulting from new fertile mixtures between interpenetrating factors. This dialectic of creativity is summed up by Shirky when he writes:

> The real change (*for our understanding of the location of creativity*) comes from our awareness that this (*cognitive*) surplus creates unprecedented opportunities, or rather that it creates an unprecedented opportunity for us to create those opportunities for each other. . . . All this is already happening. It's novel and surprising, but basic change is complete. What has not yet happened, what is in fact still an open question, is what benefit will eventually emerge from our ability to treat the world's cognitive surplus as a shared and cumulative resource . . . (*creativity is now located within a*) positive normative and ethical valence towards the process.
>
> (Shirky 2010. p. 184)

Given all this, and as we will argue in more detail below in concert with Benkler (2006), this new location of creativity represents the possibility of a whole new *political economy of creativity*. But these are all very big, broad points, and there is still the need to avoid the aforementioned hype! These things are very easy to say, but is there any real evidence within actual, concrete creative practice that such changes are coming about? Let's now turn to more detailed discussions concerning the inner dynamics of the creative commons to test some of these assertions about a new site, texture or cadence of creativity within the new media landscape.

Free revealing: the inner dynamics of the creative commons

In contrast to the ecological metaphors we explored in Chapter 3, Zohar and Marshall, in their book *The Quantum Society* (1994), attempt to identify a new cultural paradigm by using quantum physics as their guiding metaphor:

> We can think of society as a milling crowd, millions of individuals each going his or her own way and managing somehow, to co-ordinate sometimes. This is the Western way.
>
> We can think of society as a disciplined army, each member a soldier marching in tight, well-ordered step. Individual differences as suppressed for the sake of the uniform performance. This is now a discredited collectivist way.
>
> Or, we can think of society as a free-form dance company, each member a soloist in his or her own right but moving creatively in harmony with the others . . .
>
> (Zohar and Marshall 1994. p. 8)

Zohar and Marshall identify 'mechanistic' thinking which fosters 'an unbridgeable gap between human beings and the physical world' such that human creativity tends to be reduced to an increasingly small part of orthodox social and economic organization which tends to move through an over-emphasis upon technocratic orientations. For them, this over-emphasis upon fixed roles and bureaucratic organizational remits operates according to a logic of isolated, separated and interchangeable parts which negate the aggregated notions of creativity we have been discussing. The modern 'cult of the expert', the increasingly prevalent detachment of the everyday lives of creative people from the isolated bits of information or experience, tends to split apart the potential within the creative commons, and favour the reproduction of sterile Centres of creativity.

In contrast to this mechanistic thinking, Zohar and Marshall focus upon the contours of a *holistic sensibility*, characterized by 'new pattern of social and political relationships', and a 'new emphasis on unity and integration' (Zohar and Marshall 1994. p. 6). This holism emphasizes creative interdependence and the mutually interpenetrative links between people which go beyond the individual–collective dichotomies within accounts of creativity which we have been tussling with.

> We need to evolve a new alternative, a third way that mediates between the self-centredness and fragmentation of extreme individualism and the imposed communality of extreme collectivism.
>
> (Zohar and Marshall 1994. p. 8)

Their quantum metaphor provides something of a base from which to explore in finer detail the inner dynamics of the new media landscape and the creative commons offered by people such as von Hippel (2006). His discussion of how the new media landscape 'democratizes' creativity is perhaps the most developed accounts of these inner dynamics.

> The on-going shift of innovation to users (*as distinct from innovators who are geared to supplying only for external market demand*) has some very attractive qualities. It is becoming progressively easier for many users to get precisely what they want by designing it for themselves. . . . Open, distributed innovation is 'attacking' a major structure of the social division of labour (*between creative producers and consumers/audiences*).
>
> (von Hippel 2006. p. 27)

In contrast to some of the more pessimistic views of the new media landscape, notably Lessig (2004) who sees an increasingly prevalent closing of the creative commons given the corporate use of copyright law, von Hippel's discussion of the creative potential of new media emphasizes the increasingly open access it offers for creativity to be 'distributed' within and across new digital communities. The democratization of creative processes, linked as it is to new concrete technical capacities and distributive network facilities, enables greater facility for creative motivation to be taken through into concrete co-action. Echoing Shirky, he sees this is residing in the fact of more possibilities for co-creativity between more and more connected people. It also moves through the possibilities for easier and more far reaching public dissemination, such that communities of users and their audiences start to form self-organizing creative networks.

For von Hippel, the key point of the new media landscape as a location of creativity lies in the inner dynamic by which virtuous circles of co-creative relationships become *creative spirals*, as each round of development simultaneously solves collective problems and stimulates new phases of joint creative agenda setting.

> Products, services, and processes developed by users become valuable to society if they are somehow diffused to others that can also benefit from them (*who in turn offer their own new products, service and processes for others*).
>
> (von Hippel 2006. p. 77)

As such, *many-to-many* creativity, as well as *many-for-many* creativity, develops its own 'multiplier effect'. Creative possibilities are passed on to new potential users and inherently set the scene for further rounds of co-creativity. This many-to-many creativity quickly becomes a public creativity as once private aspects become *freely revealed*. Within von Hippel's account, this free revealing is a new key location of creativity – between myriad people connected via the Web, which simultaneously generates and is generated by a new ethic of aggregated creativity. It provides a view of creativity which echoes the 'making special' function (Dissanayake 1995) we touched upon in Chapter 3, by giving the creative commons a new daily texture and continuous sense of common meaning. This is the ethic of free revealing, whereby people pass on their creativity to the many, and receive it back from the many. Over recent years this has become a ubiquitous part of the location of creativity as its ethics, routines and etiquettes have become ever more normalized and reliable as part of the inner workings of the creative commons. It is a new emergent, self-organizing location of creativity which goes far beyond orthodox accounts.

And von Hippel drills down into the details of this in various ways. The dynamic nature of peer-to-peer creative production is a particular narrative within studies of the new media landscape. The Open Source movement, although not directly equivalent to the peer-to-peer discussions, nevertheless has a similar logic to the creative commons at its heart. We can overdo the differences between these areas of debate. The edge-to-edge nature of public disseminations within the new media landscape are again of a slightly different emphasis, but still revolve around the common nature of creative processes and outcomes. As we have seen, similar processes have been identified by those of a more mainstream business studies orientation within the Open Innovation Paradigm. But differences of emphasis notwithstanding, these openly collective sites of creativity all have free revealing at their heart in some way or other. Whatever their origins, ethics or culture, 'free revealing is often the best practical option available to user innovators' (von Hippel 2006. p. 80).

These accounts of creativity recognize that creativity which is co-produced and publicly disseminated is a non-zero-sum game. That is, freely revealing one's creativity to allow others to use it does not then mean that we ourselves can no longer use it. Quite the reverse: the more it is revealed the *more it is available* to everyone, then *the more of it* there is to be so available, then the more there is for each person, because free revealing encourages others to freely reveal too. Unnecessary caution and over-protection of one's creativity becomes coterminous with closing down one's access to the bigger world of the creative commons, and one's 'right to roam' across such 'common land'. The sensibility of free revealing is something like affirming one's group membership in the greatest tribe of all, the rest of humanity at its best. Denying the creativity inherent in the very act of free revealing itself is analogous to denying the benefits one might gain from the creative multipliers on offer. Non-disclosure agreements and the like become the opposite of creativity and the collaborative spirit upon which it all too often rests. They may be good for business in very limited circumstances, but as von Hippel himself points out, it is rare that the freely revealed 'bit' of creativity will be unfairly 'passed off' by someone else anyway. Collaborators are more keen on co-developing the general ideas, principles and general innovations then stealing particular 'bits'.

The fact that many highly successful creative innovators not only have gone on to reveal their creative ideas, but have taken an active role in pre-publicizing their free availability, is testament to the benefits they have seen in doing so. There are concrete incentives in actively telling the world what you are making freely available. For von Hippel, these concrete incentives include:

- the potential for developing a better version of the creative project in question after it has been co-developed with/by others
- being able to contribute to a public-ethical space through one's creativity, stemming from a genuine belief in free revealing as a broad public good
- being able to put one's self and one's creativity at the heart of a creative community, so as to benefit from and contribute to a 'collective action model' of creativity, and so help to generate a sustained future based upon further spirals of creative work to come

Such benefits and the subsequent rounds of co-creativity depend upon a mutually shared sense of a regularized community of creativity which is able to self-organize across time, albeit in highly informal, network-based ways. Echoing the more general points made in Chapter 3, communities of long-standing relationships are again seen as a key facet of creativity. Again we see that the locus of creativity lies in the development of personal relationships of co-creativity, flows of information and knowledge within and across these relationships. It also increases general and particular levels of competence based therein. The free revealing inner dynamic of the new media landscape discussed by von Hippel echoes the 'creative milieu' outlined by Hall (1991) in the last chapter, the 'natural history of innovation' outlined by Johnson (2010) which we have touched on in several places, and the internal dynamics of *swarm intelligence* outlined by biologists such as Miller (2010) which we will explore shortly.

There is an interplay between the *specific* creative communications of free revealers and more *general* creative revelations, which helps to shape a public realm. This is perhaps the broadest dialectic at work here, the creative interplay between personal information and public co-creativity. These characteristics give the creative commons its inherent characteristics, born of a process whereby

> . . . improving tools for communication are making it easier for user innovators to gain access to the rich libraries of modifiable innovations and innovation components that have been placed in the public realm. . . .
>
> Today . . . user firms and increasingly even individual hobbyists have access to sophisticated design tools for fields ranging from software to electronics to musical composition . . . with relatively little training and practice, they enable users to design new products and services – and music and art – at a satisfyingly sophisticated level. Then, if what has been created is an information product, such as software of music, the design is the actual product-software you can use or music you can play. . . .
>
> Democratization of the opportunity to create is important beyond giving more users the ability to make exactly right products for themselves . . . the joy and the learning associated with creativity and membership in creative communities are also important, and these experiences too are made more widely available as innovation is democratized.
>
> (von Hippel 2006. p. 123)

The characteristics of this location of creativity bring us back to the notion of a creative ecology – an environment of mutually supportive interactions between different creative 'species' as a defining metaphor. The more that people freely reveal, the more information and knowledge flow there is, and the more user innovators have access to. The more cognitive surplus people have access to, the greater the incentive to become part of such a creative community and freely reveal. The creative commons seems to emerge from an inner self-organizing dynamic very similar to the autopoietic structures and mythopoietic cultural processes discussed in Chapter 3. And given all of this, we can perhaps say that free revealing is a way in which the different creative 'species' are actually creating a richer, more fertile, more self-sustaining and reliable environment for the creative ecology to inhabit and thrive within. Such free revealers find a good 'fit' with their environment by creating one anew for themselves! Similar to the human species as a whole, we do not now merely survive by adapting to the environment, but also thrive by changing that environment. The new media landscape, at least in part, is just such a new environment self-organized by its inhabitants.

And a way of getting a broad picture handle of this, still using ecological thinking, in a way which does not collapse into a 'particularism' of focusing the micro-details of new platforms, software packages or particular projects, is to consider swarm intelligence.

Swarm intelligence: back to the creative ecology

First, a short detour. There is an enormous and still growing body of work that discusses the ecological movement. Some facets of this are obviously well known, whilst some are less so. The current scientific focus upon global warming, the manifest political negotiations around policy and the cultural exhortations to live more sustainably are at the more well-known end of things.

But the ecological movement in its current form also includes much deeper and more long-term philosophical concerns, which raise fundamental and very useful questions for other aspects of contemporary social, economic and cultural life. One element of this, useful for our current discussion, are the lessons provided by the idea of holism, which we have already touched upon. Similar to Zohar and Marshall, Spowers (2003), in his book *Rising Tides*, contrasts the 'mechanical world-view' with what he call the 'new world-view' characteristic of the holistic thinking of the ecological movement. For Spowers, the new ecological world-view has grown out of a rejection of industrial-economic concerns to gain mastery over nature. Historically this has been driven by a series of interlocking agendas that reduces nature to a resource to be controlled and exploited, propagated by industrialization, the scientific interrogation of nature, the commercial market exploitation of natural resources and the managerial reduction of nature (and by extension humanity) to controllable variables. But these historical manifestations have been accompanied by cultural facets which are connected to our current notions of creativity as an individual pursuit, and as something *exotelic* – what creativity can do in terms of aims outside of itself – rather than *autotelic* – what creativity is about according to its own inner meanings. At the broad cultural level, this atomistic thinking, in contrast to holism, has given us:

- **Positivism** – the reduction of the natural world to a series of isolated variables to be studied in isolation from the natural context which connected them, and ultimately gave them their meaning. This also involved a 'scientific arrogance' that to this day insists that science is the only way to have knowledge and that positivism is ultimately the only way of doing 'science'.
- **Rationalization** – the reduction of knowing and thinking to the confines of what is pre-established as the reasonable and rational. This culminated in the insistence upon 'rational' Institutions (bureaucracy, management and policy-makers) as the final arbiters of purportedly rational decision-making, social co-ordination, authority and legitimacy.
- **Individualism** – the growth of an underlying cultural of individualism as the locus for free-will, the articulation of economic and cultural behaviour and arbiter of social and economic progress.
- **Technologization** – the growth in our reliance upon technology accompanied by a fetishization of technology and a techno-fix obsession, which involves an unwillingness to accept that, sometimes at least, technology ceases to be part of the solution and becomes part of the problem.

At the heart of many of these facets of the mechanical world-view is a cultural alienation, due to its atomism. An approach to the world which insists upon breaking it apart to analyse its 'bits' in isolation from each other. For such atomistic thinking, the very idea of locating something such as creativity within a broader sweep of interrelationships with things which appear 'beyond itself' is simply a non-starter. Hence the approaches which focus solely upon the isolated individual brain, mind and separate psychological 'unit'. But the new ecological world-view asks us to embrace a less atomized, less dualistic and ultimately less fragmented idea of the world, and of how we as collective beings fit together with each other and nature. Hence the dialectical, multi-disciplinary approach which informs this book. As Spowers puts it, 'ecology teaches us to recognise the complex inter-relation of countless systems' (Spowers 2003. p. 57).

So the new ecological world-view seeks an understanding which is balanced between the individual and the environment, which overcomes atomism in favour of a more holis-tic account, and recognizes the intimate interconnections between us all and between us and our environment. It seeks a better harmony by rejecting the privileging of the individual and recognizing the true nature of the dialectical interrelationships which give things their meaning and movement. And our discussion of creativity should be no different.

We now return to the details of the new media landscape, the specific inner dynamics of this as a new form of co-creativity and the more general proposition of the creative ecology. We can find a case in point of holistic thinking if we consider the idea of *swarm intelligence* as a way of summing up how this location of creativity is played out. The idea of swarm intelligence rests upon understanding the interconnections within a system of creativity rather than approaching things as isolated units of creative action, and it thus gives us a deeper understanding of aggregated creativity and free revealing.

For instance, Peter Miller's (2010) account of the inner dynamics of swarm intelli-gence found in many different eco-systems highlights the nature of collective decision-making. The key facet for this ecological view of aggregated creativity, one which chimes with the broader social conception, lies in the fundamental recognition that the ability for creative decision-making within a swarm does not lie with any one individual biological entity. Rather it emerges from the sum of many individual actors responding to each other. Swarms are formed when groups of individual animals coalesce to create and sustain a self-organized super-entity far beyond each individual itself. According to this ecological view, such self-organized groups can innovate far faster, operate with greater agility and respond to changes in their environment in far more sensitive ways. This is because their creativity is born of myriad micro-messages within the swarm which can be mutually heard and acted upon, rather than from one 'order' or 'decision' from 'above'.

This is premised upon a degree of openness and porosity with the group, and of the group to its environment, such that distinctions between the 'inside' of the swarm and the 'outside' become relatively unnecessary. The edges of the swarm are difficult to distinguish from the Centre. Miller could be describing the new media landscape and the creative commons, when he writes the following about the nature of swarm intelligence:

> Nobody's in charge. Nobody's telling anybody else what to do. Instead, individuals in such groups interact with one another in countless ways until a pattern emerges – a (*dialectical*) tipping point of motion and meaning. . . . No ant ever understood the (*final*) purpose of its own labour, why it needs to complete the job, how it fits in. . . . Ants aren't smart . . . ant colonies are smart.
>
> (Miller 2010. p. 6)

For this ecological view, swarm intelligence stems from three key factors, which again very much echo the way the new media landscape of the creative commons works:

- an absence of central control of the group given this decentralization of command
- the distribution of decision-making throughout the group
- a multiplicity of actions and interactions within the group until a collective choice has been arrived at

As Miller puts it,

> Taken together, these mechanisms explain how the members of a group, without being told to, can transform simple rules of thumb into meaningful collective behaviour.
>
> (Miller 2010. p. 11)

Through these relatively simple 'rules', it appears that swarm intelligence regularly occurs when sufficiently large numbers of individuals, all having mutual effects upon each other, operating within something they understand as a collective 'system', simultaneously come to feel a kind of 'responsibility' to, and received creative guidance from, that system.

This dialectic of responsibility to and guidance from a self-organized system leads to the *amplification* of certain behaviours geared towards a joint creative solution. The internal dynamics of swarm intelligence shows that each individual amplifies the behaviour of its immediate neighbour, such that collective behaviour ripples through the system as a whole. Early successes in the search for a creative solution to a specific problem are built upon as the proposed solution is tested, and if it is amplified again, ripples even more thoroughly within the system. Amplification leads to further amplification, such that it becomes another form of aggregated behaviour.

Swarm intelligence is another exemplar of a radically non-individualistic location of creativity, one which places it very much within relationships between individuals. Instead of being 'straightforward and linear', this view sees creativity as decentralized and distributed, emerging from *sustained and mutually impactful internal reciprocations*. This view locates creativity within a system of thinking-acting-rethinking-reacting, where trial and error feedback loops generated by internal micro-messages are acted upon and tested. Inside this swarm intelligence, learned adaptations flowing within horizontal relationships lead to collaborative decision-making. No one is in charge, everyone is active, and everyone is acting upon everyone else. Creativity is but an aggregation of this. If human beings are to learn to more fully adopt such a swarm intelligence, then we should seek a diversity of knowledge, encourage friendly competition to forge collaborations and develop better ways to hear each other. No one mind can be as creative as this potential swarm intelligence.

This is a very strong echo of the aggregated creativity of free revealing and cognitive surplus offered above by von Hippel and Shirky, respectively. As Miller implies, *diversity trumps ability*. The creativity of finding novel combinations of older ideas is vastly increased by swarm intelligence. This is especially the case if *confirmation bias* – holding onto existing ideas simply because they are our current ideas – is avoided and new information is responded to openly and genuinely. It is especially the case if the swarm intelligence is applied to testing each idea as it comes in and responses are also kept genuine. Especially if there is a *singularity of purpose*, however temporary, within the swarm mind which pays sufficient attention to the interests of the whole. With these factors in place, real world ecologies – ants, bees, shoals of fish and birds of many kinds – have been shown to benefit the wisdom of the crowd. Creative thinking can cascade through the swarm.

If this ideal form of swarm intelligence occurs, it can lead to what ecologists refer to as *stigmergy*, a term first coined by Pierre-Paul Grasse during his study of termites. Stigmergy refers to the process whereby each individual within the swarm is stimulated to act by the actions of their immediate neighbour, and vice versa, on the basis of what they have both achieved together. This notion speaks to the creativity of reciprocal actions stimulating further reciprocations, leading to sustained *indirect collaboration*. In this case the 'structure' of reciprocal relationships becomes the guide to further individual action within the context of reciprocation. This is another echo here of the 'logic' of creativity, concerning emergent behaviour and autopoietic systems. Swarm intelligence in the natural world and aggregated creativity within the edge to edge of the new media landscape are but two observable manifestations of self-organizing systems which have a dialectical logic at their heart, and as such offer a much more revealing picture of where creativity is located.

In addition to the ecology of ants and fish, the analysis of swarm logic has shown the role of *adaptive mimicking* within flocks of birds. Again, the role of myriad internal micro-messages between individuals within the system is key to this. It is by paying great attention to the activities of one's immediate neighbour that each individual can pick up messages about what the whole flock is doing. This aspect of swarm intelligence again confirms the emergent nature of this form of decision-making, as internal systems of communication *within* lead to coordinated creative actions *throughout* the system. Individuals within such systems of swarm intelligence copy the actions of others, just as those others also copy the actions of other others. This gives us a picture of creativity flowing from direct interactions with relatively few others within the system, but which can still stimulate bigger changes throughout that system, because adaptive mimicking leads directly to a *collective vigilance*, whereby all members of the flock benefit from the vigilance of just the few. This again shows the great benefits of collective action and collaboration. The benefits of collective vigilance can accrue from collaborative creativity which spots new opportunities as well as threats.

But can we really apply this ecological thinking to the real world of human creativity? There are dangers in taking metaphors too literally and over-applying them. I think we can find strong parallels between what the biologists studying swarm intelligence say about such a 'logic' and other areas of study within the human, cultural world.

For instance, there are some strong similarities between the way swarm intelligence offers a creative place in which individual animals can multiply their collective creative effectiveness and the work of Sen (1999), which we have touched upon several times already. In his discussion of *substantive freedoms*, Sen argues that real freedom involves processes which allow people to articulate and express their needs, wants and decisions through their own self-directed concrete action. Without a degree of this capability, without a degree of capacity to act, freedom becomes merely an abstract notion. And central to this capacity to act is the question of the *opportunity* which people have to achieve a *degree of success* through such substantive action. Without freedom of process, opportunities cannot be taken up, but without opportunities no amount of formal freedom will lead to a capacity for success within action. And central to all this is the question of *available resources*. This is how Sen defines the idea of substantive freedom, which is central to his *capabilities conception* of creativity. The 'process aspect' and the 'opportunity aspect' of substantive freedom need to form something of a whole if personal motivations, inspirations, values, purposes and all the other drivers of creativity are to come to full fruition.

This capabilities conception is useful for our current discussion concerning the location of a particular kind of creativity within the new media landscape and the creative commons. We can see this new media landscape as an example of increased capability, as a key intermediate resource which allows greater substantive freedom. The new practical, technical and social opportunities released by the new media landscape can be seen as resources because they open up all sorts of opportunities for greater creativity, more regular self-directed creativity, with more people, in a way which makes all sorts of new prospects viable and feasible. The new media landscape increases substantive freedoms to act creatively because it is now a new 'principal determinant of individual initiative and social effectiveness. Greater freedom enhances the ability of people to help themselves and also to influence the world' (Sen 1999. p. 18). Through the lens of the capabilities conception we can see the new media landscape as what Nussbaum calls 'a set of (usually interrelated) opportunities to choose and to act' (2011. p. 20). And given this, the new media landscape is an exemplar of what Illich (1973) has already called 'tools for conviviality'.

This increase in substantive freedom to choose and to act on the basis of the greater opportunity and capability which new media provide can be about individual agency. But clearly it is just as much about the realization of greater opportunity and capability enabled by new combinations of people. The new media landscape can be seen as enhancing *internal capabilities*, but it is just as much about increasing *combined capabilities* as the location of creativity. The capabilities conception of creativity along with the considerations of the inner dynamics of free revealing and aggregated creativity and the ecological metaphor of swarm intelligence start to suggest a *new political economy of creativity* if decentralized, self-organized and emergent processes made feasible by the new media landscape become new opportunities and make new collective resources accessible; if internal and combined capabilities of people and groups are enhanced; and if substantive freedoms are increased to allow myriad creative motivations to be taken through to concrete action. The arguments made by Sen and Nussbaum represents a particular contribution to the political economy of human development writ large, but Yochai Benkler (2006) represents a much more detailed account of how the new media landscape represents the possibility of a new political economy of creativity. So let's turn to his work to look at some of that detail.

A new political economy of creativity

Starting from a point concerning the political economy of information, knowledge and culture as features which are central to human freedom and human development, Benkler (2006) argues that changes in political and economic relationships that brought about new media technologies are bringing about a fundamental shift in the *information environment* which underpins the *organization of creativity*.

He makes a key distinction between what he calls the *industrial information economy*, characterized by the proprietary ownership and control of information used in the services of profit maximization on the one hand, and a *new information environment* on the other. This has strong parallels with the more specific points about free revealing and aggregated creativity made by von Hippel. But Benkler's new information environment can also be seen as key to changes within the organization of creativity brought about, and simultaneously driven forward by changes to, the *relations of creativity*, due to a dialectical interplay between the following facets which have developed over the past twenty years or so:

- the specific technologies of creativity
- the forms of economic exchange which underpin those relationships of co-creativity
- the ways in which creativity is produced, distributed, received and consumed
- the social experiences and meanings associated with these new creative-economic relationships
- the emergence of non-proprietary forms of cultural exchange

In detail, Benkler argues that this new information environment becomes a new organization of creativity, one which is increasingly geared towards non-proprietary forms of creativity and exchange, because it holds the potential for:

- more active creativity in one's life to replace the rather passive experiences of Art and Culture which many currently experience within commodified culture
- an expression of human capacities as an expression of substantive freedom, self-expression and purpose
- a more open and self-determined cultural realm which enables more critical and self-reflective voices
- a series of creative forms which by-pass the Official Centres of Culture, and the 'experts' and 'leaders' who occupy them
- avenues towards a democratization of the organization of creativity

According to Benkler,

> New patterns of production – non-market and radically decentralized – will emerge . . . specifically, new and important cooperative and coordinated action carried out through radically distributed, non-market mechanisms that do not depend on proprietary strategies – plays a much greater role than it did, or could have done, in the industrial information economy.
>
> (Benkler 2006. p. 3)

These general political and economic changes signal the specifics of edge-to-edge creative production, peer-to-peer creative distribution, driven by swarm intelligence, as a shift from the old industrial information economy towards more sustained collaborative relations of creativity. Creativity is now much more thoroughly located at the edge and less and less restricted to Centres, whether that is physical, spatial Centres or metaphorical economic or Institutional Centres. Creativity is less fixed to physical space of any kind – creative hubs, offices, studios, etc., cities or indeed countries. Because creativity is increasingly located in Augé's (2008) non-places, this leads to the 'removal of physical constraints', which has three key profound implications for Benkler.

Firstly, the non-proprietary nature of this new organization of creativity will continue to undermine the commodification of creativity characteristic of the industrial information economy, and continue a relative return of creativity to the realm of human freedom and autonomous self-expression. Over roughly the same time that the new media landscape of the Web has been developing, the old industrial economy of 'heavy' industry has been increasingly replaced by a post-industrial economy. This has seen the 'weightless', the 'cultural' and the 'experiential' outputs of the creative industries come to the fore. For Benkler, the next round in this broad political economic shift will be the replacement of the proprietary nature of creative output with non-proprietary forms of creative exchange.

So secondly, this new political economic context will create, and simultaneously be created by, myriad non-market creative motivations, by what he calls 'diversely motivated user-innovators'. Taken together, contextual and motivational facets of creativity will increasingly lead to non-market forms of aggregated creativity. It will mean that that the open and the edge-based will become the normal location of creativity. As it becomes more common, it will become more feasible. And as it becomes more feasible, it will become more common – a dialectic of motivation and opportunity. And such a dialectic suggests the possibility that it will become

> . . . available to anyone connected to the network, from anywhere, (*which dialectically will lead to*) . . . the emergence of coordinated effects, where the aggregated effects of individual action, even when it is not self- consciously cooperative, produces the coordinated effects of a new and rich information environment.
>
> (Benkler 2006. p. 5)

Individual creativity will continue to contribute to aggregated creativity to facilitate the new information environment, and in turn this will encourage individual creativity in and through aggregated efforts. Creativity will increasingly be located within this dialectic of individual motivation and a newly formed context of aggregation facilitated by the new media landscape.

With this kind of thinking at its centre, Benkler represents a view which goes beyond the idea of the new media landscape as merely a litany of new software programmes and the social media facets of new media. He represents the view that the new media landscape should be seen as a location for new forms of creativity and creative exchange in its own right, changing as it does the very culture by which information, knowledge and culture is accessed, distributed and used within the creative act. And the endless motivations for creativity will mean that these ever-new opportunities will be grasped for ever-new creative purposes as expressions of greater autonomy and self-determination.

> Human beings are, have always been, diversely motivated beings. . . . We act instrumentally, but also non-instrumentally. We act for material gain, but also for psychological well-being and gratification, and for social connectedness. There is nothing new or earth-shattering about this, except perhaps to some economists. . . . The result is that a good deal more that human beings value can now be done by individuals, who interact with each other socially, as human beings and as social beings, rather than as market actors through the price system.
>
> (Benkler 2006. p. 6)

It is clear that much of this has already happened, but that much of it is yet to come. Time will tell concerning the extent to which it will grow to become a fully developed alternative economic culture which truly transcends commodified and proprietary contexts for creativity. The democratizing possibilities within the new media landscape may well be 'contained' by the corporate system (Marcuse 1964). That has happened before. But the scale, scope and inherently decentralized nature of new media and the Web will make such containment difficult for the corporate world. The 'tools for conviviality' are already in place and are far beyond the control of any Centre. And if free revealing for aggregated creativity represents a 'new sensibility' (Marcuse 1969), then the combination of new tools and this new sensibility perhaps represents a *new mode of creative production* which is already upon us, if only in embryonic form. If diversely motivated creative people are able to grasp new possible interrelationships between these new practical opportunities and new non-proprietary motivations, then perhaps this starts to speak of new *relations of creative production*. Perhaps the broad dialectic between new modes and relationships of creativity articulates possibilities of heightened social being which transcend our current instrumental economic culture, and we can start to envisage the creativity of the new media landscape as a contribution to the renewal of an ethical cultural and economic context. The 'devil' will be in the historical details, as this emergent process plays itself out in and through the real creative actions of real creative people and groups. What is clear, however, is the degree to which the processes and 'structures' of creativity have already changed as a result of the new media landscape, as well as the degree to which such changes will continue to recast the nature of creativity further into the future.

Putting questions of big political economy from Marxist or otherwise perspectives to one side for the time being, what is also clear is the way in which the new media landscape stimulates fundamental changes to the location of creativity.

> The result is a flourishing non-market sector of information, knowledge and cultural production, based in the network environment, and applied to anything that the many individuals connected to it can imagine. Its outputs, in turn, are not treated as exclusive property. They are instead subject to an increasingly robust ethic of open sharing, open for all others to build on, extend, and make their own.
>
> (Benkler 2006. p. 7)

If the dialectic of opportunity and motivation enables greater space for what Benkler calls 'enhanced autonomy', it will improve the capabilities for creative people to do things 'for and by themselves'. But at the same time it will become a site of creativity defined by 'loose communities' which are freer from hierarchy, 'which operate outside of the market sphere' (Benkler 2006. p. 121). This might in the future become a location of creativity which is more public, more accessible, more transparent, more malleable to the needs of more people. It might become a stimulus for greater democratic engagement such that it becomes something like a 'new folk culture', a non-zero-sum game for co-creativity from which everyone can potentially benefit. As such it might become a new *public realm of creativity*. A new creative commons which promises greater 'right to roam', which resists the digital 'enclosures' of the increased copyrighting of culture (Lessig 2004), and returns us to the fundamental *social and ethical value of creativity*. The growth of a creative commons might turn out to be the most profound liberation of human creativity in both spirit and in concrete terms. This is what Benkler means by a new 'commons-based peer production' as the ethic which increasingly shapes the location of creativity.

But there will be a lot of cultural politics to get through before this happens.

The outcast and the outsiders: a polemic continued

In *Ecology as Politics*, Gorz wrote,

> What is essential is not to define a new coherent political scheme, but to suggest a new imaginative attitude . . . to change the logic of our development.
>
> (Gorz 1983. p. 62)

And in *One Dimensional Man*, Herbert Marcuse wrote of

> . . . two contradictory hypotheses; (1) that advanced industrial society is capable of containing qualitative change for the foreseeable future; (2) that forces and tendencies exist which may break this containment and explode the society.
>
> (Marcuse 1964. p. xv)

Marcuse went on to articulate the potential for a 'Great Refusal', by which he meant a broad cultural resistance to an ever encroaching ideological control which moved through social and cultural means, rather than overt political messages. And within this he high-lighted the role of

> . . . the outcasts and outsiders . . . (*whose*) opposition hits the system from without and is therefore not deflected by the system, it is an elementary force which violates the rules of the game and, in doing so, reveals that the game is a rigged game.
>
> (Marcuse 1964. p. 121)

Having spent enough time over the past twenty years or so working and researching within various arenas which we might call cultural governance – within the cross-over terrain between public cultural agencies populated by cultural policy wonks on the one hand, and cultural organizations populated by cultural professionals with a mixed cultural economy agenda on the other – I think I can make the following point. The general cultural governance arena tends to be happy with, clear about and largely receptive to the creative businesses, because they are the particular face to creativity which fits with the key criteria and priorities of cultural governance writ large. They firstly fit with the economic impact agendas of local or regional economic growth, job creation and business development. Creative businesses also tend to come across as the easily identifiable, measurable, sustained and professionalized aspects of creativity within a particular area. For this reason, they tend to be the kind of creative people which the world of cultural governance gravitates towards when it is seeking to work with partner organizations and businesses to develop cultural strategies and the like.

But these established, official creative businesses are but a small part of the creative ecology which persists in many places. The independent, more DiY aspects of the creative ecology tend to be seen as more problematic by the world of cultural governance, despite protestation to the contrary when these issues get aired. The world of cultural governance tends to find the more 'impolite' edge of the creative ecology less easy to identify in the first place, less easy to work with because they are seen, often wrongly, as being less professional and sustained. Their contribution to the local creative economy is often less easily measured, and so they are often simply invisible to the cultural economists. This is often because their ways of working are informal, or what the cultural economists would call 'fragmented' – they do not have a central trade association of professional bodies which is easily contacted as a spokesperson for the industry. The work of the DiY, of the independent, of the edge is often of an overtly non-commercial type; it is sometimes in direct challenge to the commercial, Capitalist world. And so, despite the great creativity of the independent edge, despite their great contribution to the cultural and creativity of their places, they are too often too readily designated by the official world, usually implicitly, as the outsiders and the outcasts. We will argue strongly in the next chapter that this represents a big missed opportunity for cultural policy-makers and other professionals, and for cities as a whole. Better, more genuine dialogue between the edges of the creative ecology and the Centres of cultural planning, cultural delivery of all kinds and for the civic development agendas more generally could be beneficial for all concerned. Often the neglect of the outsiders and outcast is not even a matter of actual policy, but a consequence of unspoken elitist assumptions, a failure of research to find out who the people at the edge are and what they are doing, or simply something flowing from the personal prejudices of the people on the ground. During many years of practical, hands-on working with the independent creative edge, I have seen how this works, and how damaging it can be to the creative ecology.

And now we see that a whole world of creativity has opened up across the new commons, which has many new informal ways of working together based upon free revealing, encapsulating aggregated creativity. The outsiders and the outcast are inventing new, regularized ways of working with each other which by-pass the official Centres, they are using tools which are not restricted to any one physical space or place. They are operating according to a different creative logic, if the idea of swarm intelligence is anything like a reasonable metaphorical insight of the creative commons. The edge, the supposed outsiders, the putative cultural outcasts are where the creative energies reside more and more.

If the official world of cultural governance persists with the pre-established demarcation between their 'inside', and the informal world of 'outside' creativity, if they persist with their overly economistic focus upon creative business and fail to engage with 'the street' in any meaningful, sustained or supportive way, then their approach will always culminate in a one-dimensional approach which at least is far less rich and diverse of creativity than it could be. At worst, it will damage the thing it is claiming to support, and culminate in 'containing qualitative change' to our collective creativity and culture. The aggregated creativity of the creative commons represents a new way of working, perhaps a new value system which motivates that creativity. It is simply not sufficient for the official world of cultural governance to see this new world of aggregated creativity as simply people who 'use the Internet' for their work, as an integral part of their 'business plan'. But of course they do! We all do! No, it is also now necessary that the official world of cultural governance genuinely starts to see the edges of the creative commons – the culturally disenfranchised, the impolite, the hidden and underground facets of the creative city in all its depth and richness – as an equally creative contribution to the overall creative ecology that is just as worthy of credibility, recognition, hearing and support, in whatever shape that might be.

The current creative business foci, agendas, and rhetoric stand as models for the reductive collapsing together of creativity, business, industry and a consumerist 'lifestyle'. As we will argue at more length in the next chapter, this reductive stance and its consequences are precisely what Marcuse means by the containment of qualitative change in particular, and by one-dimensional thinking and language in general. Despite the myriad activities of creative businesses which profess to offer greater choices within the market, their wider consequences tend towards offering us a culture which we do not author for ourselves. In the rhetorical universe of many over the past twenty years, the way the creative industries have been conceived of and spoken about is but a recent version of a longer history of new cultural values and creative productions being assimilated 'back into' the mainstream economy and so commodified as a *passively consumed* series of events, as something extrinsic to one's own life and capacity for creative expression.

But as the quotation from *One Dimensional Man* above argues, it can be instructive to recognize two contradictory trends within contemporary culture. One tends towards the greater consolidation of capitalism as it limits creativity to the pre-determined nexus of market mechanisms, the priorities of public cultural organizations, and the 'cultural experts' and 'leaders' which populated what John Holden (2006) has called the 'cultural system'. The other is exemplified by the new sensibilities of free revealing, aggregated creativity born of a deep and broad sense of co-creativity and swarm intelligence. As well as a different creative 'logic' and different processes of production, distribution and dissemination, there are also different values at work here. The outsiders and the outcasts may at one time have been just that, and felt that as their position. But this is no longer the case. For the outsiders and the outcasts of the creative commons today, it is the Centres that are largely irrelevant, easily ignored as of no importance to what they do and how. It is for the Centres of cultural governance – national, regional or local – to up their game and come to a new settlement with this edge of outsiders and outcast if they are to do well at their job. As Marcuse wrote, 'Solidarity and community do not mean the absorption of the individual. They rather originate in autonomous, individual decisions, they freely invite associated individuals' (Marcuse 1969. p. 39).

The mutuality, solidarity and de-institutionalized forms of cultural exchange exemplified by the creative commons have been forging myriad DiY cultural public spheres over recent years which echo this sense of being freely invited into a sense of association quite precisely. As such, as we have seen, they hint at a new political economy of creativity. The forging of such new relationships between politics, culture and technology is by no means a new phenomenon – indeed, it has a long history. The development of the creative commons given the new media landscape is but another manifestation of this history. But it appears to be one with its own particular expression potential of *expanded creative autonomy*. The rise of aggregated creativity, both in process and through its easily distributed outcomes, makes many, many things possible, indeed easy, which were previously held onto very tightly by the Centres. Whether in terms of (self-)expressions of new ideas, or resistances to old forms of control, the outsiders and outcasts of the last twenty years have now become their own self-organized and emergent centres of creativity, and as such they represent a very vital sphere of creativity, culture and politics, which increasingly informs people's everyday lives and the choices. The creativity of the outsiders and the outcasts may or may not culminate in actual artistic or overtly political outcomes, but it is moving in and through seemingly mundane processes by which people live their lives through mutual trust, collaboration, aggregation and respect. And this in itself represents, at one and the same time, both the vehicle of change and the ultimate destination. In developing the tools of aggregated creativity, the creative commons of the outsiders and outcasts confirm not only an 'ownership' of their own creative capabilities, but also the 'authorship' of their own culture as *actively produced* rather than as passively consumed. Rather than being an aspect of a wider consumerist society, they are signalling the continued possibility that creativity, along with the culture(s) it leads to, is still a viscerally felt and intrinsic aspect of life. As such, it is a vital, energetic and successful version of Marcuse's 'Great Refusal'.

But of course, this small polemic notwithstanding, there are many other facets to this debate. There are contextual features far broader than the development of the new media landscape to consider. The polemic we have just presented is but one way of seeing the myriad interactions between the broad context within which creativity resides on the one hand, and the nature, texture and cadence of creativity on the other. So let's now turn to a more detailed consideration of how and why these broad contextual features impact upon creativity itself, and have a bearing upon its location.

Chapter 6

The broad contexts of creativity

. . . creativity results from the interaction of a system comprised of three elements: a culture that contains symbolic rules, a person who brings novelty into the symbolic domain, and a field of experts who recognize and validate the innovation. . . . (*Therefore*), creativity does not happen inside people's heads, but in the interaction between a person's thoughts and a socio-cultural context. It is a systemic rather than an individual phenomenon.

(Csíkszentmihályi 1996. p. 11)

The location of creativity within relationships, places and the new media landscape reveals the specific ways in which creativity goes far beyond the orthodoxy of the brain or mind as the locus of the creative person. But beyond these specific locations there are much broader contextual features which we need to take into account for a fully developed discussion of the *where* of creativity. It is located within, or at least against, the backdrop of broader historical, economic and political contexts, which are themselves shaped by broad institutional and cultural systems. These systems are born of the many established creative paradigms which shape both its production and the way specific 'bits' of creativity are received (or not), and fields of 'expert opinion' which authorize and validate what 'counts' as creativity. These contextual features have varying degrees of breadth: some revolve around the particular cultural systems as they impact upon creativity within specific arenas of work, whilst others are rather more general and relate to how society-wide institutions such as the market and public investments stimulate and/or constrain concrete creative practice.

These general points underpin what has been called the *systems perspective on creativity*, developed by Howard Gardner, Mihaly Csíkszentmihályi and others. Its fundamental point is to argue that, far from being the outcome of individual creative talent, creativity must be located within these broad contextual systems if it is to be properly understood. For this systems perspective, creativity in all its manifestations emerges from multiple inter-actions between three different spheres or levels of activity. The creative person actively developing new ideas, outcomes or innovations within their chosen creative discipline must interact with the *cultural domain* (what Kuhn (1970) more famously has called the paradigm), because this goes a long way to defining the urgent questions, theories, fashions, models and prescriptions of that very discipline. And this interaction between person and domain sits in an interrelationship with *the social field*, which is a system of institutions and gatekeepers who have the cultural and economic power to select, promote, publish and exhibit certain 'bits' of creative work, and to *de facto* ignore others. The social field is the 'expert system' which, for good or ill, ultimately passes judgement on the relative merits of particular 'bits' of creativity given their institutional positions as commissioning editors, judges of competitions, critics, curators, buyers, etc. And then of course, in the world of commerce, the ultimate 'field expert' is the consumer.

The systems perspective takes a rather neutral and benign view of this social field, but one might readily see some problems with this 'expert system', given their power, biases and that fact that they are not always that 'expert'. Ever wondered why it seems so easy for the sons and daughters of celebrities to get their work reviewed, get the part, get the investment or the contract? It is highly likely that the 'expert system' is far less meritocratic, far more nepotistic, and generally far less informed as to the full panoply of creativity out there than the systems perspective suggests. But nevertheless, it is a fact of creative life. Many creative practitioners have recognized the important impact of the domain–field context upon their creative work, in both the arts and the sciences:

> Close historical investigation of a given speciality at a given time discloses a set of recurrent and quasi-standard illustrations of various theories in their conceptual, observational and instrumental applications. These are the community's paradigm, revealed in its textbooks, lectures and laboratory exercises. By studying them and by practising with them, the members of the corresponding community learn their trade . . . discover what isolatable elements, explicit or implicit, the members of that community may have abstracted from their global paradigm and deployed as rules in their research. Anyone who has attempted to describe or analyse the evolution of a particular scientific tradition will necessarily have sought accepted principles and rules of this sort.
>
> (Kuhn 1970. p. 25)

Others, however, have seriously questioned its impact:

> History generally, and the history of revolutions in particular, is always richer in content, more varied, more many-sided, more lively and subtle than even the best historian and the best methodologist can imagine. History is full of accidents and conjectures and curious juxtapositions of events, and it demonstrates to us the complexity of human change and (*its*) unpredictable character. . . . Are we really to believe that the naïve and single-minded rules which methodologists take as their guide are capable of accounting for such a maze of interactions?
>
> (Feyerabend 1993. p. 24)

So, to develop our multi-disciplinary view of creativity, the systems perspective is a necessary addition, given that it is probably the most developed account of how contextual features such as the domain and the field impact upon creativity itself. The systems perspective is one of the most sophisticated contextual views because it takes account of the ways in which of each of the three facets – person, domain and field – exert a mutual impact upon each other as they interact. The great creative person will affect and change the domain and field, just as the field and domain influence their work; developments in the domain will be picked up or rejected by the field and thus may impact upon subsequent generations of creative people; the power of the field 'experts' will skew what fads and fashions the creative person, and the communities thereof, congregate around. So there is a mutually impactful three-way interaction across the various facets of the system. So this contextual picture is itself another example of a dialectical view of creativity, whereby opposites are always and already influencing, possibly defining, each other. We have situated creativity against such a dialectical conception throughout our argument, and we will return to a more fully developed notion of dialectics in the next chapter.

Both Gardner and Csíkszentmihályi explicitly refer to a dialectical notion of creativity at the level of contextual influences. More of that below. But let's first consider the broad contours and fine details of the systems perspective on creativity more thoroughly.

The creative domain

Csíkszentmihályi (1996) and Gardner (2011) argue that the only satisfactory answer to the question of the origins, nature and location of creativity comes from the observations of how individual actions are impacted upon by the external settings within which they are conceived and disseminated. Discrete individual creative acts cannot and do not exist in isolation from the world which receives them, makes sense of them and selects them (or not). For them, the creative domain is made of, and at the same time perpetuates, a set of 'symbolic rules and procedures' which form the basis of what the creative person is initiated into as they learn the contours of their specific discipline. This symbolic system shapes, steers, validates and authorizes the disciplinary tradition, its high points, its current debates and issues, the terms of success for any practitioner at that point in the history of their discipline. These domain 'rules' are in turn situated within, and simultaneously inform the host culture as a whole, and the interactions between the specific domain and culture writ large is in itself another aspect of the interactions within the system as a whole. For the systems perspective, the domain impacts upon individual creativity in that it defines what is to 'count' as current knowledge, current fashion, current 'cutting edge' research, viable innovation and necessary technological applications. It forms the contextual atmosphere of shared assumptions, working models, received histories and revered texts (in all their written, visual and other material manifestations) of a particular discipline. The education which each individual goes through to become an initiate into their chosen creative discipline is in effect the socialization of each person into these symbolic rules and procedures. And any creative individual may respond to the domain in many different ways. They may choose to work squarely within the verities of the domain as it is currently defined. Or they may choose to work on the 'margins' of it, looking to push things forward by criticizing it, and so re-developing its symbolic certainties. Or they may choose to reject particular received symbolic rules and procedures as the locus of their creative work. But in each of these directions, the creative act is still in some way a reaction – positive acceptance, guarded and critical reaction, or outright rejection – of their domain-specific starting point.

As we saw in Chapter 1, Policastro and Gardner (1999) have provided a 'robust generalization' of creative people, a kind of typology of these different reactions to the domain. Each 'type' of creative person has a different trajectory. Whilst this is only an ideal type demarcation, and the real world of creativity will likely be much more nuanced, a consideration of these types show that different responses to the domain are nevertheless reactions to it in some way or other. Their 'robust generalization' of types of creative people includes:

- **The master** – the person who works fully within the domain, accepts its shared assumptions and works to become a master exponent of it – in the arts, Billie Holliday or Helen Mirren; in the sciences, Richard Dawkins or Bill Gates.
- **The maker** – the person who works on the margins of the domain to challenge some of its basic assumptions or styles so as to change the domain from within, and perhaps create a new version of the domain. This change can be evolutionary or, more rarely, lead to a genuine revolution within the domain – in the arts, Marcel Duchamp or Vivienne Westwood; in the sciences, Charles Darwin or Albert Einstein.

- **The introspector** – the person devoted to exploring their own interior meanings and motivations, but who still has a relationship to the domain, in that their published work is received and eventually accepted as part of the canon. The person then becomes one of the established domain representatives – in the arts, Virginia Woolf or Franz Kafka; in the sciences, Isaac Newton or Paul Dirac.
- **The influencer** – the person seeking to derive broader ideas, arguments and plans designed to change the world around them by working within the domain so as to change it – in the arts, Pablo Picasso or Angela Davis; in the sciences, Alfred Nobel or Tim Berners-Lee.

When discussing the creative person, Csíkszentmihályi makes a distinction between *autotelic* and *exotelic creative personalities*. As we have already seen, the autotelic person is someone motivated to pursue their creativity as an end it itself, as a self-defining objective. On the other hand, the exotelic person is more motivated by the external rewards that can come from their creativity. It is the creative domain, and in turn the field of 'expert opinion' which to a large extent determines the distribution of these external rewards of recognition and authority, and so the exotelic creative person is often motivated to accept and work thoroughly within the domain in search of this. The currently ubiquitous creative business entrepreneur seeking their creative success within the world of business and supplying to the market is perhaps the most obvious example of someone working solely within the domain for exotelic reward. It is this world of business economics and the impact of the market which in more general terms forms the strongest domain–field nexus for many creative people. Indeed, it can become such a strong and ubiquitous domain–field nexus that some mistake it for an inevitable 'reality' beyond which nothing else makes much sense as a creative trajectory. Within a capitalist economy and culture, the market is always already everywhere. But obviously, many other 'types' of creative people are motivated by things other than commercial business success, which brings us back to the whole question of the motivations lying behind creativity as part of its 'logic'.

Csíkszentmihályi's (1997) own research into creative motivations and the extent to which they experience *flow* in their creativity does indeed show that many creative people, perhaps the majority, are autotelic. As he puts it:

> The autotelic person needs few material possessions and little entertainment, comfort, power or fame because so much of what he or she does is already rewarding. Because such persons experience flow in work, in family life, when interacting with people, when eating, and even when alone with nothing to do, they are less dependent on the external rewards that keep others motivated to go on with a life composed of dull and meaningless routine. They are more autonomous and independent, because they cannot be as easily manipulated with threats of rewards from the outside. At the same time, they are more involved with everything around them because they are fully immersed in the current of life.
>
> (Csíkszentmihályi 1997. p. 36)

In this case, their relationship to the domain, and beyond that to the field, is less direct, but nevertheless even the autotelic creative person is likely to be affected by the underlying domain-centric assumptions of their particular creative discipline. But our own research into creative motivations has shown that the autotelic response to one's own creativity is by no means universal. Creative entrepreneurs within an increasingly significant new cultural economy are more and more turning to more exotelic approaches as new, viable business opportunities on the basis of one's personal creativity open up. So the domain will be a necessary and important contextual feature as they base their creative plans upon supplying to external market demand for external rewards. But it is also clear that many creative people are navigating new settlements between their own autotelic interests and the exotelic demands required for worldly business success. Such *creative alt-trepreneurs* – entrepreneurs with an alternative value system – are increasingly resolving the tensions between their own internal creative desires and the external contextual demands. Many of these 'types' of creative practitioners are to be found navigating new mixtures of the autotelic and the exotelic within the new media landscape which we discussed in the previous chapter.

The cultural field

> The second component of creativity is the field, which includes all the individuals who act as gatekeepers to the domain. It is their job to decide whether a new idea or product should be included in the domain . . . creativity occurs when a person, using the symbols of a given domain such as music, engineering, business, or mathematics, has a new idea or sees a new pattern, and when this novelty is selected by the appropriate field for inclusion into the relevant domain.
>
> (Csíkszentmihályi 1996. p. 68)

For the systems perspective, this field of 'expert opinion' can come in many different forms. It is made up all those people who have accrued some kind of cultural authority to make selections, pronouncements and choices about what is designated as creativity worthy of public attention. It is the system made up of the 'cultural expert', the 'cultural leader', the 'taste maker', the critic, the curator, the buyer, the reviewer, the investor, the publisher, the commissioning editor. It is the system whereby some people are authorized, usually due to their occupation of some kind of institutional position, to make public judgements about the work of others. As such, they have a very powerful contextual effect upon what 'counts' as creativity, what is invested in, what is discussed, what receives public dissemination.

They can be very powerful allies for creative people, and to a large extent determine who is to achieve that particular kind of 'success'. But at the same time, they can be a very powerful hindrance to anyone wishing to pursue a creative career which hinges upon public display and acclaim. It is probably true to say that the field ignores more people than it takes notice of, and that for public creative success the need to get noticed by them often outweighs the quality of the creativity itself. Because the field experts have the power to select, circulate, authorize, validate, promote, sponsor, review, popularize, exhibit, publish and bring to market, recognizing the need to speak to them and get them to listen is a key component of creativity for many today. And this system is inherently self-selecting, and so deeply undemocratic, non-meritocratic, shot through with cronyism and unfair.

For the systems perspective, the working definition of the creative person is someone who has had a significant impact upon the domain, but it is in large part the field of 'expert' opinion that decides if and how this domain impact has come about.

> Creativity is an act, idea, or product that changes an existing domain, or that transforms an existing domain into a new one. . . . It is important to remember, however, that a domain cannot be changed without the explicit or implicit consent of the field responsible for it.
>
> (Csíkszentmihályi 1996. p. 69)

But this is a very limited and reduced notion of creativity, one which takes us back to the elitist conceptions of Mr. Tusa (2003) which we were so critical of in Chapter 1. The field of 'expert' opinion comprises the 'ground troops', the 'office staff', the 'management committee' of the new cultural economy. And as such, they have a particular type of power to determine the context of creativity. For Lukes (2005) power comes in different guises. Sometimes power is distributed in a *unitary* way, in that some people have all the power, all of the time. But at other times power is more *situational*, in that some people have specific types of power at specific times, in specific situations. And the field is made up of certain people who have situational power for very particular reasons. And it is not always on the basis of their actual 'expertise', so much as their institutional position that they can accrue this power. Are we really to believe that these self-selected 'experts' really have the refined taste and insights to be able to make such universal pronouncements upon something so rich, diverse, complex and ever changing as creativity and culture? The field 'experts' can simply be ignorant of the many, many things beyond their own world-view. And to make such pronouncements on the basis of ignorance quickly descends into arrogance at times, situated within a highly self-referential way of seeing the cultural world which brooks no challenge from outside of that self-validating position. Dubious tastes, elitist conceptions, often highly nepotistic ways of working, and sometimes just plain wrong views often masquerade as 'expertise'. We have touched upon the dark side of groupthink (Janis 1982) in Chapter 3, and one suspects that many elements of the field of 'expert' opinion suffer from this. The fact that J.K. Rowling's *Harry Potter* manuscript was rejected by so many publishers before it finally got 'taken up' is evidence of this.

But their power to shape and determine the context of creativity does not really come from their personal qualities and refined taste, so much as their institutional location. And it is this which gives them their particular type of situational power. Going back to Lukes (2005), he identifies the 'one-dimensional' facet of power, defined as a situation whereby person A has the ability to make person B do something they would not otherwise do. This is the most basic and obvious form of power. The field 'experts', however, tend to have what Lukes calls the 'two-dimensional' facet of power, defined by a type of power which enables person A to make person B do something they would not otherwise do, whilst simultaneously using their power to ensure person B of the legitimacy of that power relationship. So the two-dimensional facet of power comes with its own internally self-validating form of *legitimation*. In this sense, it is a type of power that is pre-cloaked in a sense of *authority*. And it is this air of authority which is key to understanding the way that the field of 'expert' opinion wields its power over the context of creativity. Such authority can be accrued by various means. *Charismatic authority* flows from the legitimacy a person gains due to their own personal qualities – their previous creative track record, their standing within a particular community, their status among 'believers', their ubiquity within popular cultural channels, their personal charm – think Simon Cowell or Stephen Fry. Their opinions, tastes, levels of intelligence, knowledge of the creative field may or may not be any greater than other people's, but their authority is gained from elsewhere. *Traditional authority* flows from the legitimacy a person gains due to some kind of traditional narrative, myth or cultural orthodoxy – think The Queen or the average Oxbridge Don. Again their 'expert' opinion on a new piece of creativity may be no more credible than anyone else's. Indeed, they may be so out of touch with the provenance, meaning and significance it has for others that their 'expert' opinion is simply discountable. But they get their legitimacy, and hence their field authority, from the fact that they have always had it, due to the very fact that they are who they are and have been ascribed as such by some tradition or other.

Finally, we have purportedly 'rational' *bureaucratic authority*, which flows from the fact that certain people have a formal position within the hierarchy of an institution, which invests in them the power to make decisions, choices and judgements. Their legitimacy comes from their institutional position, and thus enshrines that form of authority – think of the commissioning editor of a publishing house or a TV company, or the fashion buyer for a high street corporate brand. They are often people who have a particularly pre-set world-view with a rather limited set of tastes and opinions. But their legitimacy, and hence their field authority, comes from the fact that they have 'The Job' to make such choices and so decide to 'take up' certain things which fit their own agenda. And so they have the power to ignore other things. This form of legitimacy and authority is the most common form in today's new cultural economy given that it is to a large extent ordered by large institutions who shape and select what is to 'count' as creative. They have the largest say in what is to be popular culture and the degree to which each individual creative idea is to receive public dissemination.

We may think that the form of cultural authority enjoyed by the field is a deeply unsatis-factory state of affairs, and indeed it is. With something so subjective as the way we receive and appreciate creativity, you might think that accruing the cultural authority to define another person's career due to something as mechanical as an institutional position is highly questionable, and you would be right. But nonetheless, this is a very significant part of the context within which creativity exists. As we saw in Chapter 5, one of the most significant aspects of the new media landscape and the new public distribution system it and the Web offers is the redistribution of power it brings to circumvent this rather ossified system of field 'expert' opinion. It is a major criticism of the systems perspective as a whole that they take a far too neutral and benign view of the creative field and its activities. The peer-to-peer and edge-to-edge locations of creativity are challenging and undermining its power and authority in many, many ways on a daily basis. But it is easy to forget that it is still very early days for the Web, and the power of the creative field over the contexts within which creativity must work is still in place for large swathes of culture. The creative field must still be dealt with in some way, which means that 'getting your work out there' still requires negotiation, discipline, resilience, testing, patience and clarity – many of the aspects of the creative attitude we touched on in Chapter 2. This is the case for various reasons, but not least of these is the fact that the main way in which many creative people experience the domain and field context of creativity is in the form of this thing we call *the Economy*.

The economy

It might be thought that the point which suggests that the economy is a key feature of the context of creativity is a rather banal point, and indeed it is. The economy is the context of pretty much everything. We hope we can save ourselves from such banalities by delving into the details of this, because the nature of the economic context which pertains most directly to creativity has particular features beyond the broader economic compulsions of earning a living and paying the rent. There are more specific things going on here given the nature of the 'new cultural economy', or the 'weightless economy', which have par-ticular impacts upon how the creative entrepreneur situates their work (de Guy 2002; Flew 2005; Hartley 2005; Holden 2006; Shorthose 2004b, 2011).

Over the past thirty years or so the creative industries have become recognized as a discrete industrial sector, as an increasingly important contributor to most developed economies, as a key employer and a major factor in economic development. But there was a time before this when people still dismissed the *economic conception of creativity*. The rise of the creative industries emerged from the recognition of a growing post-industrialism during the 1980s, as many developed Western economies restructured their industrial bases away from heavy industry and towards the service economy. As traditional manufacturing sectors moved to the developing economies of Brazil, Russia, India and China, their contribution to the economies of the developed world started to reduce somewhat. This meant a shift towards a 'weightless' economy, as the economic significance of stuff which was weightless – services, ideas, images, meanings and fantasies – began to outweigh stuff which was 'heavy' – cars, ships, tables and shoes. And the creative industries were a key part of this contextual shift from heavy towards weightless. All industrial sectors produce either *objects* – for example, a car – or *services* – for example, the legal services of a lawyer – as the basis of their business plan and the thing which they supply to the market. But the creative industries were one of the leading edges of the contextual shift towards the weightless economy because they also supplied very specific things. Although the creative industries supply objects – for example, a piece of fashion – and services – for example, the role of the graphic designer – they also provide *meanings* – for example, what an advert tells you about what the object 'means', or why the celebrity endorsement is important for you. They also provide *experiences* – for example, what the visit to a cultural venue adds to your quality of life, or how the creative city now 'feels'. These meanings and experiences are key to shifts in context location of creativity, and have brought very profound changes to the way in which creativity is forged if it is to successfully relate to its contexts. For creativity to thrive as an industrial sector such as design, not only must the design function, but it must also convey the 'right meanings' and 'feel good'. But these economic-cultural shifts are but the latest turn in even broader contextual shifts in the very *structures* of the economy, which have continually impacted upon the way work, life and culture writ large is now *experienced* (another dialectic).

Economists make a distinction between *extensive* and *intensive* economic growth. Extensive economic growth comes about when more and more land, raw materials, resources, people or machinery are brought into the economy. Growth comes about because there is just *more economy out there*. This is what happened during the industrial revolution, first in Europe and then around the world from around 1700 onwards. It is what has been happening in India and China over the past thirty years. But that stuff is largely over now in the West, despite what professional politicians and their associated economic technocrats would have you believe.

Intensive economic growth comes about when the same amount of resources is used, but used in smarter ways. Growth comes about because the economy is *made more productive by innovations*. That is the fundamental contextual imperative now for advanced Western economies, and is a fundamental reason why we have witnessed the increased economic importance of creativity. This is why the 'cultural' or 'weightless' bit of the economy is also forging a 'new' economy. The business of creativity; the technologies involved in its production and dissemination; the systems of supply and distribution; the ways in which people consume creative outputs and what this means to them; how creativity within entrepreneurship must therefore understand itself; relationships to competitors and collaborators; what this means for public culture – all these factors have changed radically in recent years. And they continue to change. We explored one broad aspect of this in Chapter 5 as it pertains to the new technologies of the new media landscape. But there are broader and deeper contextual shifts at work as we move from an 'old' to a 'new' economy. Building on ideas developed by Coyle and Quah (2005), we can perhaps summarized these shifts as follows in Table 6.1.

And these contextual shifts have big implications for creativity, especially those creative acts geared towards commercial agendas and supplying to the market. It is less and less possible to rely upon anything stable in terms of organizing for business, producing and supplying to markets, relating to customers and creating for broad public cultural experiences. Everything in the 'new economy' column is about change, adaptation, innovation, learning new skills and collaboration, rather than the standard assumptions about traditional entrepreneurial attitudes and business planning. The nature of 'employment' for most creative people is now routinely unstable and based upon short-term contracts, projects and gigs. But it is perhaps the changing nature of the market which presents the most fundamental contextual shift for creativity, as it changes from one defined by mass consumption, through to customized consumption, and then, in the near future, towards personalized consumption.

To grasp this, let's step back and take a historical detour. The first industrial revolution was brought about by, and at the same time created, all sorts of technological changes which culminated in a business model based upon mass production. This only really made

Table 6.1 From the old to the new economy

	Old economy	New economy
Nature of markets	Stable	Dynamic
Scope of competition	Regional and national	Global
Organizational structure	Hierarchical and bureaucratic	Network-based
Sources of value	Raw materials and physical capital	Creative skills in innovation
Organization of production	Mass production	Flexible production
Key drivers of growth	Investments in fixed capital and labour	Investment in innovation and intellectual capital
Key technological change	Mechanization	Digitization
Source of competitive advantage	'Economies of scale' given large scale of output and lower unit costs	'Economies of speed' given innovation and flexibility of output and better market position
Importance of constant R&D	Low	High
Relationships to other firms	Competitive	Collaborative
Skills	Highly job specific	Highly transferable
Education	One-off training for specific job	Constant life-long learning and 'up-skilling'
Nature of employment	Highly stable	Highly unstable within the 'gig' economy
Nature of market	Highly stable based upon mass consumption	Rapidly changing customization and personalization of consumption

economic sense if it was accompanied by mass consumption. Precisely because Henry Ford's way of making cars was based upon making lots of lots of them all the same, he was able to sell them relatively cheaply. But this meant that everyone bought the same thing. As he famously quipped, 'You can have a Model T Ford in any colour you want, so long as it is black'. And this mass production–mass consumption nexus of producing in large numbers and selling the same product to large numbers of people has been with us ever since. The advertising arm of this industrial model would have us believe that you are buying expressions of your own 'individuality' and 'difference' every time you buy a T-shirt from Primark or a car from Toyota. But step back and ask yourself what kind of individuality you are getting from consuming mass produced products. Is your T-shirt really that different from the next one? Is your Toyota really that different from the Nissan next door? Probably not. So they are myths to overcome before we can really get to the point about the coming world of customized and personalized consumption.

As with the broad historical link between economic development and technological development, so with the digital revolution. It has similarly been brought about by, and at the same time created, all sorts of technological applications which are fundamentally changing within the market context. Precisely because Nike now has the technological capabilities for you to design your own training shoes, within certain prescribed limits of choice, they can sell one-off customized versions of the basic product at viable prices. This new, digitally based production–customized consumption nexus means that not only can you have Nike shoes in many more colours than Ford's black, you are also invited to 'design your own' shoes.

The next round of this shift in the market context for creativity, which we are on the cusp of, will be based upon the shift from customization towards personalization. If customization is about designing your own products within certain prescribed limits, then the new personalized production–consumption nexus will be the expansion of a creative business model based on 3D printing technology, such that the prescribed limits of choice which characterize customized consumption will wither away and be replaced by a fully personalized consumption. Very soon you will be able to design and print your own shoes with little or no need for the pre-established settings of Nike's Web interface, or anyone else's.

But this is one picture of how the market context for creativity is going to change. A broad historical lens offers a degree of corrective to the hype which often comes with this view. If we set the shift from mass, through customized, towards personalized production–consumption into this broader context, we can start to suggest some more considered ideas about what it might mean for the context of creativity itself (see Table 6.2).

If we unpack some of the details of Table 6.2, it draws our attention to the following key points. Firstly, the 'production technology' column charts the historical shifts from small-scale production space towards the more large-scale factories of mass production, but then sees a return to the relatively small-scale production units. The creative industries have tended to be at the forefront of this shift in scale, such that now many creative people work in 'small- and medium-sized enterprises' (SMEs) of twenty people or less, who often work on franchised projects and gigs for the bigger organizations. Many creatives work in micro-businesses of five people or less, and either supply to bigger organizations or directly to the market. This return to small-scale places of industrial creativity is underpinned by the aforementioned contextual shifts towards a new economy, and the ever-present need for innovation, flexibility and speed of reaction to changed contextual situations – technological,

Table 6.2 The changing nature of industrial production and consumption

Production system	Production technology	Industrial relations	Business supply chain	Nature of consumption	Broader culture
1700 to 1750 **The early 'putting out' system**	Largely cottage-based	Relatively free from managerial control	Irregular production and supply	Highly localized	Local and regional
1750 to 1830 **Batch or 'table' production**	Small workshops	Early forms of industrial relations	Developing market systems	Early consumer culture	Embryonic mass culture
1830 to 1980 **Mass production**	The factory system and 'heavy industry'	Fully developed industrial relations	Fully developed supply chains	Mass consumerism	Fully developed mass culture
1980 to present **Customized production**	Post-industrialism and the 'weightless economy'	SME engaged in constant networking	Smart-targeted production and supply	Niche consumerism and customized consumption	Multiple and layered cultural identities
Present to future **Personalized production**	A return of small-scale batch and very high levels of innovation	P-to-P, e2e, and Open Source creative relations	Personalized production and supply	Emerging personalization of consumer markets	New media and 'many-to-many' cultural transmission

economic and cultural. But the subtext of the 'production technology' shift is within the new kinds of competitive advantages which 'economies of speed' – being quick to innovate, adapt and be flexible, and being small and having an inherently creative mind-set – now offer. Situating creativity within the market context requires that we recognize these very broad historical-economic shifts as much as the mezzo level facets of the creative domains and fields offered by the systems perspective. Creativity is now squarely within the economy in its broadest sense, as much as within the personal motivations of individual creative people and their dealings with those domains and fields.

The 'industrial relations' column of Table 6.2 charts the shift from a context defined by 'managers' seeking ever greater control over what 'workers' do, how they do it, when, where and for how long during the day – that is, *industrial discipline* – towards a context defined by ever greater collaboration between the different parties involved – a paradigm of *cooperation*. The *open innovation paradigm* we have mentioned above is but one of the current public articulations of this. As we have seen, this points to a new organization of 'industrial relations' precisely because it facilitates greater collaboration and cooperation. But beyond these tweaks to still fairly traditional business models, the edge-to-edge, peer-to-peer and Open Source relationships for creativity, which we explored in Chapter 5, add to our picture and suggest a much more radical and far reaching shift within the 'industrial relations' which now define the context of creativity.

Taken together, the 'business supply chain' and 'nature of consumption' columns of Table 6.2 chart the more specific shifts in the way market creativity is consumed. It charts shifts towards personalized consumption, and the corresponding shift in the market conditions of creativity discussed above. But just as this specific shift in market context needs to be understood against the broader story of shifts in 'production technology' and 'industrial relations', it also needs to be located within the 'broader culture' implications set out in the final column of Table 6.2. This shows the broad shift in the *cultural context* of creativity, over and above its technological and economic facets. New forms of customized and personalized consumption continue to impact in all sorts of unforeseen ways upon the *generation and transmission* of culture as a whole. And this is opening up all sorts of new relationships between individual creative acts and ways of 'getting it out there'. It is leading to a convergence between the previously separated cultural 'producer' and the cultural 'consumer'. The traditional cultural organizations and Centres, what the systems perspective has called the field, now no longer have so much power to select, shape and deny the creative person and limit the reach of their voice. DiY cultural transmissions of all kinds – self-publishing, self-broadcasting, many-to-many ways of distributing culture and myriad other creative experiments 'on the edge' – are replacing the power of the 'Centre' in all sorts of ways. A new cultural context, which is creating, and at the same time being created by, new forms of cultural transmissions is opening up a context for active public creativity which is going far beyond the traditional, largely passive forms of 'channel' oriented Culture.

Once, the vast majority lived in and through fairly stable and long-lasting cultural traditions. However, we are living through the early years of a *cultural diffusion* away from the context of Official Institutions of Culture, with their 'expert' opinion and gate-keeper capacity, towards a cultural context whereby people engage in their own creative experiments, disseminations, systems of distribution, crowd-sourced funding and investment arrangements and assessments of cultural value. The interrelationships between the creative person and/or group, the domain and the field is changing to form a new, freer and more dynamic cultural context for creativity. And all of this has profound implications for creativity, for what gets produced, how and why, by whom, for whom, and how/when it gets distributed and seen.

The public sector

Whilst it is necessary to recognize shifts in the market context of creativity, it is also necessary to recognize that this context, along with the domain–field nexus, is a *mixed economy*. As well as a market, the broad context of creativity is also shaped by the very important, very significant and very powerful influences of public sector agencies of many kinds. The particular role of the public sector within cultural provision is deemed necessary, by everyone except 'market fundamentalists', because reliance upon markets alone for the social and cultural outcomes will result in 'market failure'.

To understand market failure, think about what would happen if we all had to pay for our own street lighting. We would each put a street light outside our own house and pay for the running of said street light. But we would not want others to get the benefit from the street light we were paying for. So we would only switch on our street light when we were benefiting directly from it, which would be the few minutes per day when going out or coming home. So the streets would be full of lights, but they would each be switched off for the vast majority of the time. The potential for lit streets would be there, but there would be almost complete darkness after the sun had gone down. There would be massive individual investments made in street lighting, but darkness would prevail. This is but a thought experiment, but it points out why public investment for a provision which benefits society as a whole is sometimes superior to reliance on the market, and why, despite the current neo-liberal hegemony, the market can and does fail. This is especially the case within certain sectors of society, and the investment in culture and creativity is one such sector. So the context of creativity includes aspects which are heavily affected by the role of public sector institutions which invest public money in cultural and creativity. This is vital because reliance on markets alone would mean that only creative output which promised the biggest sales would get produced, and this would lead to an under-provision, both in terms of the *quantity* of non-market viable creativity, and also in terms of *quality*, as the lowest common denominator of taste would prevail. Reliance on markets alone would mean that the creative outputs which could attract most advertising revenue or private business sponsorship would be produced, which would lead to a chronic under-representation of other cultural voices and a lack of diversity. Anything challenging, provocative or critical would not get made.

This means that the logic, priorities and processes of the various public sector agencies are a key facet of the context within which creativity takes place. The public sector presents particular opportunities for creativity, because public sector agencies often become customers, clients, investors and sponsors in lots of different ways for different reasons. Public sector institutions often invest in particular creative practices by giving grants and funding; they seek to develop infrastructure for local creativity by building buildings and other facilities for production and dissemination of all kinds; they often help with such dissemination by marketing particular places, sponsoring events and festivals; they are often the customers of creative practices given that they have procurement money to buy creative products and services in the same way as the commercial sector.

But the public sector also forms part of the context of creativity in that they have a broader public cultural role. At the local level, they have a civic role which involves using culture and creativity for neighbourhood regeneration, helping to develop 'creative cities', encouraging inward investment and tourism, and sometimes seeking to develop the branding of their city as part of local economic development. They also have a social development role which involves using culture and creativity to improve the quality of life within their locale, and to encourage life-long learning, cultural diversity, social integration and community development. So for both particular and broad public cultural reasons, learning to engage with the public sector and being able to 'speak their language' is a key aspect of understanding and working with the context of creativity.

Historically, there has always been a close relationship between those in power – empire builders of all stripes, states, governments – and the cultural artefacts and spectacles of that era. That is, there have always been *cultural policies* of some kind which have formed part of the context of creativity. The Roman poet Juvenal first coined the term 'bread and circuses', a need to provide the basic material security of the population – the bread – but also the need to provide public cultural entertainment – the circuses. People cannot live by bread alone. The public face of power has always referred to cultural artefacts – courtly rituals, fashions, imagery and festivals – as a demonstration of their authority and legitimacy. There has always been an architecture of leadership and government demonstrated through the building of palaces, castles, temples, monuments and statuary. Outright propaganda, from early folklore to the use of music and theatre, to radio and film, shows another intimate historic link between public government policies and the outcomes of creativity.

But in the developed industrial societies of Western Europe at least, the 19th Century saw the early developments of a concerted *professionalized* cultural policy. Within the context of growing concerns about the negative impacts of the industrial revolution upon the masses, this professionalized cultural policy agenda took on new and urgent priorities. The social and cultural impact of the industrial revolution, linked to new phenomena such as secularization, urbanization and ever growing bureaucratization, has been called the 'de-traditionalization' of cultural patterns of life and the 'sequestration of experience' (Giddens 1991). This cultural disconnection of the new industrial masses from their national cultural heritage was experienced by some as a cultural disenfranchisement, which seemed to some to threaten social cohesion and stability. The successions of revolutions between 1789 and 1917 formed the political cultural backdrop to much of this for regimes throughout Europe at the time. It was becoming increasingly clear through this period of history that the quality of life for new industrial classes was seriously lacking. Much of this was due to squalid living conditions and outright poverty. But this concern quickly took on other cultural dimensions too. It was seen as increasingly necessary for public policy to take on a cultural education role, to promote a living knowledge of the perceived high points of the National Cultural Canon. This was in pursuit of a greater shared knowledge of the National Heritage and a greater integration into a 'civilized society'. In the 18th Century, the role and outputs of creative people still remained rather 'courtly', still something of the preserve of the elites. But by the late 19th Century this view had begun to change, such that now the role of creativity had become more tied to a public culture which could promote a broader acculturation within the everyday lives of the majority.

But this notion of *public cultural value* took on different forms and had within it different emphases. Some early proponents took a rather paternalistic view which centred around providing greater public access to High Art and Culture *for* the masses, which was carried forward by an expression of rather elitist views of public cultural provision as being part of a 'civilizing process'. An alternative expression of public cultural value centred more upon the notion that the public, the masses, the working class – call it what we will – should be encouraged to value *their own cultural voices*. Rather than a top-down, paternalistic, still elitist notion of Culture, public policy should be more about an educational endeavour to foster greater creativity *within* the masses. William Morris, a socialist and an educationalist, is one of the best known proponents of this emphasis, someone who attached greater value to vernacular cultural. Much more egalitarian, much more bottom-up, much more about an *active* creative engagement by the working class, compared to the rather *passive* cultural proposition offered by the paternalists.

And this is still a fundamental distinction within the cultural public sector today, concerning the relative degree to which cultural policy should concentrate upon sponsoring traditional cultural heritages and values, or should support more diverse cultural voices within contemporary society. The relative degree to which the public sector should promote greater participation in High Art and Culture, or should fund more popular forms of creativity. The degree to which public investment should be for conservation and heritage of the past, or look to growing contemporary creative expressions for larger numbers of people from the marginalized sections of society. But back to our main concern. This very brief history is only of use to us if it helps to draw out the public policy facets of the context of creativity, and the practical implications of learning to 'speak public sector'. Cutting to the chase, we can refer to a useful distinction between the *cultural development* emphasis within cultural policy on the one hand, and the *culture and development* emphasis on the other.

The *cultural development* emphasis within the cultural public sector seeks to foster more access to art and culture by providing more 'audience opportunities' to engage with professional creative outputs. It seeks to generate more participation in Official Culture by a wider range of people. And as part of this, it seeks to support newer, diverse, quality and challenging artistic and cultural productions. Its focus is squarely upon the *intrinsic value* of creativity to the public, flowing out of the fundamental idea that such access is a positive contribution to an open and progressive society. The fundamental basis of the *culture and development* emphasis for the cultural public sector is not necessarily at odds with this, but it tends to focus more on the idea that creativity can be a vehicle for *other kinds* of development. As such, its focus is more on its *extrinsic value* of creativity, in terms of how it can contribute to social and economic developments.

And a big part of this is its economic development dimensions. The creative industries are now seen as potential contributors to business start-ups and job creation within creative businesses, and so as a significant aspect of national economic growth. In the context of the new, cultural, 'weightless' and experiential economy, the outputs of the creative industries are seen as a factor in the improved quality of life of a particular locale, and as such as a contribution to its potential for attracting inward investment, developing cultural tourism and so bringing in extra income to the local economy, and as a facet within the 'branding' of the town, city, region or country as part of their broader economic endeavours. This broad economic emphasis is often intimately intertwined with infrastructural development issues. The cultural and creative reputations of a particular locale can often stimulate investments in the development of new cultural facilities, creative buildings and production spaces, better communications networks and the like. This is often tied to material improvements to the physical quality of life within the town/city/region and to more general urban renaissance endeavours.

The social developments which the culture and development emphasis envisages for the role of creativity continue to include stimulating greater social inclusion, minority representation and general social cohesion. Community development generated by the educational role of the arts and culture, leading to greater (re)integration of vulnerable, marginalized and disaffected people, along with those of newly arrived ethnic minorities, are part of this. And on the more individual level, the culture and development emphasis sees a role for creativity in fostering health, well-being and 'therapeutic' initiatives. The growing use of cultural 'prescriptions' by the health professions – prescribing participation in socially engaged arts and cultural projects as a way of dealing with stress and loneliness – is but a new turn in this emphasis. So for all these reasons, in all these multi-faceted ways, over and above the contextual features described by the systems perspective and commercial markets, there is a large, highly significant and very powerful *public* aspect to the broad context of creativity.

But if the context for creativity is made up of these often over-lapping institutional, commercial and public facets, is it time to think about a new and expanded role for creative practice? One which takes into account not just what creativity is to mean for the individual creative person or group as they develop their own creative outcomes, but one which embraces a more public role?

Public dialogue and creativity: a polemic continued

So far within our polemical pieces, we have suggested that the creative milieu of the city cannot be a full account of the overall location of creativity unless it takes into account the informal and hidden aspects of said city. We have also suggested that the informal outsiders who work creatively through the Web have in recent years been forging a new location for creativity on the 'edge', away from the previous, usually Institutional, Centres. There is a kind of cultural geography in much of this. But there is also a cultural politics. Having looked in this chapter at some of the broad contexts against which creativity gets played out, we have identified, in broad contours, the market and the public sector as two key features. And these two features of the contextual landscape have particular relationships with the public. Relationships which are far from benign. So let's take a closer, more critical look at how the broad contexts of creativity, especially the public sector, relate to, underestimate, often misunderstand and sometimes fail to support a more *public conception of creativity* – that is, a creativity which is about a broad public articulation of its collective benefits and values of solidarity and common existence.

The great physicist Richard Feynman (1999) recounts the story of the 'Cargo Cult' phenomena of the South Sea Islands. On seeing the first air planes in the sky, and then their landing to unload a cargo of wondrous things, the islanders started to fashion their own runways so as to encourage other air planes to land, and deliver similarly wonderful things to them. Of course, this did not happen. They had failed to understand the myriad facets of everyday creativity that lay behind the fact of wonderful flying cargoes. The cargo had not come from the 'Gods' but from real people doing real things. Being entranced by the possibility of something and developing a 'policy' in the hope that it happens is not the same as fully understanding what is going on, or working to ensure that it actually happens.

The Cargo Cult is an interesting metaphor for thinking about certain aspects of the broad public context of creativity. There are elements within the cultural system of public sector agencies which seem entranced by the possibilities of achieving the same public mandate as that enjoyed by the health and education sectors, of achieving the same 'scientific respectability' as economics, and using public culture for community development. But this is unlikely to succeed if its institutions suffer from a chronic democratic deficit, if its economics move through the wooden replicas of cultural statistics, and its take on community development is underpinned by an elitist conception of creativity which only really values what the 'professionals' selected by the field do. If the cultural system fails to understand and develop relationships with the myriad sources of creativity within the everyday lives of the outsiders, the hidden and the informal aspects of the city beyond the Institutions of Official Culture, they will never develop things as fully as possible. Building 'runways' of instrumentally conceived, institutionally designed and curatorially programmed 'audience opportunities' will not, in and of themselves, encourage the entrancing wonders of greater public creativity, especially if the public have insufficient resources and capabilities to gain 'take-off velocity' or 'landing permission'. The rather elitist conception of creativity which forms part of the conceptual framework of the public cultural system has become analogous to a Cargo Cult because its closed conversation takes place between the 'runway builders' – the cultural organizations and professionals – on the one hand, and 'the Gods' – the 'cultural leaders', field 'experts' and associated opinion makers – on the other. Other voices are left chronically unheard as pre-set cultural policies and plans take the place of sufficiently nuanced communications with the public.

But, as we will see, a critique of this conceptual framework can suggest some positive things. Cultural organizations, often working in very innovative ways, occupy a central position within the local cultural context. But rather than simply delivering 'audience opportunities' in which other peoples' cultural cargo can be consumed, they hold the potential to do much more to support local, vernacular creativity. By forging more convivial (Illich 1973) relationships with the outsiders, the hidden and the informal, they could do more to stimulate the cultural milieu as the context of creativity for a much broader range of people and communities, for a much richer portfolio of reasons. So, from the outset, we do not offer this polemic to suggest that cultural organizations do not do any of this kind of work. They patently do. But they could do more, given their role as a 'keystone species' within the local creative ecology, to support local, vernacular creativity as a public good. They could operate with a much more developed *public conception of creativity*.

John Holden (2006) discusses the public 'cultural system' as being comprised of all sorts of cultural agencies, government departments and broader cultural governance settings – all the institutions which deal with setting cultural policies and plans. But he also sees the professional cultural organizations which seek to deliver culture as part of this system. The cultural agencies etc. tend to operate according to *instrumental* values – seeking cultural returns from the spending of public money – whilst professional cultural organizations tend to operate according to *institutional* values – seeking efficiency, sustainability and best value within the cultural marketplace. And together, this instrumental–institutional value orientation on the 'inside' of the cultural system forms something like the basic mind-set of all those different cultural organizations charged with shaping and delivering public culture. Individual professionals inside this cultural system are mostly good people pursuing their vocation with energy and commitment. But there are endemic problems with(in) the system itself. One of the most chronic of these is its failure to foster genuine public participation in discussions of how the cultural system finds its basic orientations and shapes its policies and plans. Criticisms of this have been trundling along for many years now (Balfiore 2009; Bennett and Mercer 1998; Gibson 2002; Gray 2007; Holden 2006; Janovich 2011). Debates come and go, and new priorities are discussed. Most recently, the *Report by the Warwick Commission on the Future of Cultural Value* (2015) advocates for many laudable things concerning the broad context of public creativity. However, within the section on 'Creation, Voices and the Creative Workforce', the *Warwick Report* adheres to the old distinction between 'professional' and 'amateur' creativity. This is indicative of a mind-set still wedded to an unhelpful misunderstanding of the nature of creativity, and implies a continued *de facto* public hierarchy. Without wishing to be unkind to the *Report*'s compilers, other facets of its overall approach – its focus upon structural changes within broad cultural governance regimes, and its continued emphasis on economic and business growth – suggest that the *Warwick Report* is still coming from an institutional–instrumental value orientation. Implicit or explicit, it still represents a view of creativity and the cultural milieu which continues to neglect public voices. It seems that the cultural system still only really wants to have a conversation with itself, within the institutional setting between self-selected field 'experts'. Indeed, one could argue that the closed nature of this conversation has become more entrenched given the rise of the 'special advisor' and 'cultural leaders'. The 'expert system' is as alive and well within public cultural policy as it is within public economic and political debates. The technocrats are ubiquitous, and their crises of legitimacy remain a problem.

We have already criticized the idea of the cultural 'expert' capable of making pronouncements about the myriad cultures of other people as elitist and fundamentally facile. Over and above this, however, the closed conversation revolving around instrumental and institutional values in and of itself denotes the view that culture is a system of variables, and can be reduced to institutional 'inputs' and 'outputs' and measurable instrumental impacts. Too often the system of public cultural agencies and policy-making still talks about 'pulling levers' and 'making interventions'. And viewed as a system in this way, the 'experts' have convinced themselves that they can have a consolidated overview of public culture. This already signals two negative consequences. Firstly, it signals a highly reductionist notion of the public context of creativity and the cultural milieu. And so, secondly, it forms part of the conceptual origin of the democratic deficit and consequent crisis of legitimacy facing the public cultural system, because it descends into the cultural elite talking to other members of that self-selecting elite. So within this Official Cultural context, public participation is largely restricted to the 'audience' opportunities offered by professional cultural organizations. However great the individual pieces of creativity on show, the public remains largely passive and the potential for a more open and vital context for public creativity is left under-explored.

The closed nature of this conversation comes not from a casual neglect of informal creative voices so much as from the deep conceptual roots and pre-established frameworks with which the cultural system understands, and we might add, reassures itself. As Holden (2006) has shown, its tenor of the closed conversation and its neglect of the public is *authorized* by its own instrumental values – achieving external cultural and economic outcomes – and its own institutional values – managerial foci upon the internal organizational imperatives – and together this instrumental–institutional values nexus routinely takes precedence within 'defensive' cultural policy-making, planning and delivery (Balfiore 2012). It is easier for cultural professionals to operate according to their own internal values and logic, work with the usual professionals and avoid embracing the more risky and unknown processes of the public creativity of the outsider, the hidden and the 'amateur'.

Much of the relative rise of this instrumental–institutional value orientation, which sets the broadly dismissive tone towards public creativity, has come about due to the overtly political and economic climate of the day. But it is also due to an immaturity at the heart of how the cultural system thinks about, and talks to, itself. As in so many other institutional arenas, the cultural system is characterized by 'one-dimensional' thought and language, which tends towards an *a priori* 'closing' of the discourses at work within the public realm, such that it routinely refers only to its own 'self-validating' logic and language (Marcuse 1964; see also Shorthose 2011). And this one-dimensionality is itself a facet of a broader characteristic of our political culture. Many key social, political and economic institutions, both public and private, are currently facing a profound crisis of legitimacy born of specific instances of ineptitude and/or corruption. The broad context of some many aspects of social and economic life are now characteristic of the *age of illegitimacy*, produced by an overriding malaise within many public institutions which seem to work only to satisfy their own internal needs and agendas. We might diagnose this public malaise as a chronic *institutional aphasia* – a learned language disorder resulting in the loss of the ability to produce and understand written and spoken communications, despite the intelligible nature of such communications. The evidence is everywhere – hospitals, social welfare agencies, police, professional politicians, banks, the church, media companies, corporations of all stripes – all seem unable to understand what is being said to them, incapable of authentically communicating with the world and unwilling to advance the thinking necessary to correct their failings. Whilst the cultural system is by no means the worst offender, it could do more to recognize this particular contextual moment and become part of the solution rather than being representative of the problem. The closed conversation that the cultural 'experts' insist on having with each other affects not just their 'turf', it is more widely perceived as just another facet of a whole world of institutional self-interestedness. If the public cultural system continues to place this instrumental–institutional value orientation at the heart of its conceptual framework, strategic planning and political advocacy, it is unlikely to gain increased legitimacy. And so it will reproduce its own public vulnerability.

Nassim Taleb (2010) recounts the story of Procrustes, who offered a strange kind of hospitality. The guests who stayed with him had to use a specific bed. Those who were too tall had their legs chopped off, whilst those who were too short were stretched. Either way, the guests were expected to change to meet the requirements of the bed. The instrumental–institutional value orientation current within the cultural system works in a similar way, changing its creative citizenry so as to fit the 'bed' of its pre-established policies and plans. The Procrustean Bed of instrumental–institutional values underwrites the conceptual reduction of what public creativity *is*, and where it comes from. As such, it sponsors an insistent measuring agenda and the carrying of 'rulers' and 'axes' which act in ways which echo the Procrustean Bed. Operationally, it is one dimensional in that it only refers to self-validating reductive categories, specific technocratic vocabularies and pre-packaged narratives to perpetuate the view that creativity is delivered only by professional artists whose work is seen within professionally managed and curated programmes. A similarly inauthentic 'hospitality' lies at the heart of the democratic deficit so prevalent within public perceptions of the cultural system, which is nothing more or less than a drift towards the bureaucratization of the cultural milieu itself. And this, in turn, runs the risk of suffering from the standard 'dysfunctions' of bureaucracy – mistaking cultural 'means' for cultural 'ends'; ritualism; goal displacement; and the 'iron cage' of a certain, limited rationality (Merton 1952; Weber 1975). A Cargo Cult indeed.

The over-insistence upon the instrumental–institutional value orientation also affects the way it constructs knowledge about the context it itself works within (Mlodinow 2008;

Ormerod 1998). The 'defensive-ness' (Balfiore 2012) of the instrumental–institutional value orientation threatens one-dimensionality if it insists upon a self-repeating process of relying upon, then authenticating and thus perpetuating, a reductive agenda of research for understanding the public. The instrumental–institutional value orientation tends towards research into its own *presence* – what it 'is', what it has 'delivered' and what impact 'it' has had. Most obviously, this focus upon presences is shown by hearing the voices of those who already participate – as audiences, as stakeholders, as partner organizations and investors. Non-users, non-participants remain chronically un-heard. This is nothing but a chronic neglect of research into *absences* – what the cultural system does not do, who is not participating, whose creative voices go unheard and why. But researching absences is key to becoming a learning organization capable of its own creativity.

And these problems are compounded at the level of research methodology. A research strategy coloured by an over-reliance upon quantitative methods will always mean measurement *from the outside*. Research can only approach authenticity if it includes more thoroughgoing and sustained research into what is already within the creative and cultural lives of the public as *they live them*. More qualitative cultural research is needed. No amount of professional cultural delivery, effective arts management or curating can be a supplement for this. It is remarkable that as macroeconomics, not well known for its methodological sophistication, starts to go through its 'behavioural turn', cultural policy research seems to have turned to the standard economic discourse of consumer spending, multipliers, elasticity of demand, monetization and the rest, all of which means that it pays insufficient attention to ethnographic ways of researching its impact upon public creativity and the cultural milieu. By putting such instrumental–institutional values and economic impact narratives at the heart of its advocacy, the cultural system now finds itself with strategic problems. There have been some understandable historical reasons why advocacy based upon economic impact was taken up. However, despite the intermittent success of such advocacy in recent years, the tap is being turned off in the 'age of austerity'. Over-reliance upon economic impact rhetoric has brought profound 'organisational risk' (Beck 2000) to cultural sustainability. The instrumental value lens has underplayed what cultural organizations are best at in favour of advocacy based upon what they are less good at. To compound things, the methodology of economic impact orientations is just plain shaky, even on its own terms (Shorthose 2004b). Measuring the right thing badly is not a great position to adopt. Measuring the wrong thing well is not much more helpful. But measuring the wrong thing badly is the worst of all worlds. Over-adherence on one way of 'paying the mortgage' at the expense of other more sustainable ways has left the cultural system with a kind of conceptual 'negative equity'. Its rhetoric of job creation and urban regeneration has meant that it has neglected ways of thinking and acting to develop a context for greater public creativity which could have helped it generate the broad public mandate it so sorely needs. But it need not be this way. In previous chapters we have made some specific points about the social nature of creativity, based as it is within relationships. We have raised the notion of the creative ecology, and the idea that creativity is inherently public in that it emerges from open collaborations of myriad kinds. But beyond these rather specific, detailed points, the history of civilization is full of examples of how connections between people have enabled, and simultaneously created, mutual creative and cultural growth. And much of this can be said to lie in a fundamental value of dialogue, or dialogical value, which contrasts markedly with the instrumental–institutional value orientation.

The Caliphate of Cordoba, between 756 and 929, was characterized by a high degree of mutual understanding between Christians, Muslims and Jews, guided by sustained dialogue between and across all groups. Reigning between 1095 and 1154, Roger of Sicily became well known for presiding over *convivencia*, a regime of governance that exhibited similar levels of cross-faith dialogue as the vehicle for mutual respect. And there are many other examples throughout history. The emperor Ashoka in 5th Century bc India, the Islamic Translation Movement of the 8th and 9th Centuries, the Hanseatic League throughout Northern Europe between the 13th and 17th Centuries – they all bear testament to the value of extended and prolonged dialogue as the basis for a broad context of public creativity and cultural growth.

The conceptual roots of dialogical value can be found in the work of Martin Buber (1992). He asserts that 'genuine dialogue' does not speak of 'things' or their 'quantities', but is achieved only if it is an open expression of inter-subjective possibilities between people who fully appreciate each other. Without this, a technical monologue ensues which allows only for inherently hierarchical relationships. In the guise of the scientism, rationalism and individualism, as we discussed in Chapter 2, technical monologues work to broaden and deepen their own internally self-validating logic and language. Within the cultural system, we see this at work as potential cultural encounters between the Institutions of Official Culture and the public are transformed into variables to be measured, opportunities to be operationalized, issues of resources to be monetized. This is the opportunity cost it seems willing to pay for the prolongation of its instrument–institutional value orientation. And as such, its technical monologue with the public remains inauthentic. Carl Rogers takes Buber's philosophy of dialogical value forward by introducing the idea of *congruence*, a notion which contrasts markedly with instrumentalism–institutionalism.

As we have already mentioned, both Rogers' notion of congruence and Ivan Illich's notion of conviviality echoes this theme of establishing dialogical value at the centre of building a more germane context for public creativity. Illich speaks of re-focusing upon *cultural ends*, rather than mistaking *institutional means* as *ends in themselves*, which, as Weber (1975) has already shown, is the source of so many of the negative unintended consequences of bureaucratic instrumentalism. Conviviality articulates the value of embracing a broader panoply of cultural voices as part of the *practical wisdom* within dialogical value, so as to overcome the current self-privileging of the Institutional Centre by the 'cultural expert'. As such, it helps us re-envisage cultural organizations as 'tools for conviviality', as sites which can help enhance what Sen (1999) and Nussbaum (2011) have already called the capabilities necessary for taking creative motivations through to self-determined, concrete and collective creative action. Re-envisaging cultural organizations as tools for public conviviality helps to envisage local creative milieux of any particular locale as a context for locally self-organized *dialogical journeys* as the seat of collective public creativity. This contrasts with the instrumental–institutional defining of 'cultural development' for the public seen as the *arrival* at pre-ordained stages of instrumentally-institutionally authorized outputs. Cultural organizations recast as tools for conviviality helps envisage a new creative milieu as an authentic *creative authorship of local culture*, which could replace rather facile notions of cultural 'ownership'. All this could be part of a new context for public creativity which moves through articulate relationships of cultural immediacy and appropriateness between cultural professionals and the creative outsiders, between the centres and the edge, between the current, rather mechanical way in which the institutions of the cultural system work and the more organic nature of the creative ecology. These changes also suggest a new mind-set, one which seeks to put into the practice of professional cultural organizations the emergent, autopoietic, mythopoietic logics at work within the informal worlds of public creativity, found in the informal, hidden aspects of the creative city. Envisaging dialogical value in terms of these kinds of concrete conversational practices, both Colin Mercer (2002) and Richard Sennett (2013) in their different ways bemoan the tendency of our culture to engage in conversations based on 'silo' thinking and position-taking attitudes. Following Buber, Rogers and Illich, Sennett highlights the 'de-skilling' of dialogical capabilities as a particular facet of our broad cultural context, and argues for a context of greater attentiveness and responsiveness to the other person. Indeed, this genuine inter-subjectivity is the very origin of culture itself for Buber (1992). Genuine dialogue cannot flow simply from being in the same space as someone else and taking turns to state already established positions, least of all those of supposed 'expertise'. Developing concrete dialogical skills rests upon improved capacity for listening rather than making declarative statements from already formed opinions. But the institutions of the cultural system, along with the 'expert' opinions of the field, tend to do just that, to 'listen' from a one-dimensional, internally self-validating position. And this is the fundamental conceptual origin of the current, unsatisfactory nature of the context of public creativity. Whether it is the instrumental–institutional value orientations voiced by the 'experts' of the cultural system as defined by Holden, or the 'opinion formers' of the field as defined by the systems perspective, that is, whether it is the public sector or the market, the context of public creativity is too hierarchical, espouses too many features of the elitist conception of creativity, misunderstands too many features of the emergent creativity at the edges and neglects too many opportunities to provide public support for the public's own creative potentials. Echoing Buber, Rogers and the rest, Bakhtin (1981) argues for dialogical value as the basis for a more open, public creative milieu which is an *on-going cultural process in its own right*. Rather than being the backdrop to various overt 'artistic' outcomes, this notion refers to creativity as a public *end in itself*, that it is in and of itself a public good because it is the basis for a more open and supportive context for the creativity of others and so forms an integral part of a vibrant collective life, a healthy public realm and an ethic of public solidarity. In his history of conversations which the instrumental–institutional nexus has had with various creative realms, Sennett makes a distinction between the top-down 'political' on the one hand, and the ground-up 'social' on the other:

> . . . any think tank filled with policy wonks who speak in bullet-points is heir to the spirit of the old political; any grass-roots organization which embraces different, sometimes conflicting, sometimes incoherent voices, is heir to the spirit of the old social.
>
> (Sennett 2013. p. 45)

The closed, top-down, instrumentally-institutionally oriented cultural system is clearly from the spirit of the 'political'. In their various ways, Buber, Illich, Rogers and Sennett see genuine dialogical value as a necessary return to the social, to the public. For them, it is as much a matter of one's 'social temperament', one's propensity to see, develop and creatively work through creative relationships as opposed to bureaucratic offices or institutional powers. As an exemplar of this kind of creative dialogical attitude in cultural practice,

Sennett highlights the conversational temperament of Saul Alinsky, a Chicago-based community activist working in the second half of the 20th Century:

> His 'method' of organizing was to learn the street of the community, gossip with people, get them together, and hope for the best; he never told people what to do, instead encouraging the shy to speak up, himself providing information in a neutral manner whenever it was requested . . . by getting people together who had never really talked, providing them with facts they did not know, and suggesting further contacts, the Alinsky-style community organizer hopes to sustain dialogical talk.
>
> (Sennett 2013. p. 50)

Is the institutionalized, professionalized cultural system able to grasp this idea of a public sensibility and start such open conversations? Are the 'experts' willing to adopt such a social temperament? Is the closed conversation going to open itself up by embracing and animating the spirit of dialogical value? The politicians and policy-makers at the top of the cultural system have a key role in this. But cultural organizations have an even great potential role in initiating greater dialogical value by stimulating congruent and convivial cultural conversations with(in) their local creative ecologies. Are the cultural professionals and the organizations they run interested in stimulating and sponsoring such on-going public creative conversations as *ends in themselves*?

Clearly, the 'devil' of all this will be in the local details. There can be no universal, prescriptive manifesto for how dialogical value could be translated into concrete action for a cultural milieu more supportive of public creativity. That must continuously emerge from the on-going dialogues themselves. But we can say with certainty that it is time that our 'cultural leaders' and 'experts' initiate more open conversations *about* that context, rather than being satisfied with self-referential conversations *within* their cultural system. Creativity in all its manifestations, and especially the great potential that public creativity holds to stimulate a more creative public, is too important to be left to the politicians, policy-makers and assorted technocratic 'experts'. We have seen public challenges to the technocracy in many arenas of public debate in recent years. Some of these have been rather anti-intellectual, ignorant and under-informed. So there are dangers in such challenges. But when it comes to a challenge to the self-selecting, internally self-validating, often elitist and sometimes just plain smug figure of the 'cultural leader' or 'expert', such dangers are much less pronounced. Not least because we are all 'experts' in our own culture. That is why it is our culture, because we live it. Challenging the idea of the 'expert' will never therefore be to reject that part of the public realm. But it will be to challenge the power of the cultural 'expert' on the basis of their relative lack of legitimacy and the deficit within democratic credentials when it comes to the question of public creativity and the development of a more supportive context for that. As Colin Mercer has put it:

> . . . there needs to be a new compact and relationship between 'local knowledge' and tactics on the one hand, and the larger and strategic prerogatives of cultural policy and service delivery on the other. This is not simply a matter of the adjustment of existing settings but also the production of new forms of knowledge through inclusive and integrated research agendas . . . (*which requires*) a new conceptual paradigm – or at least a theoretical horizon.
>
> (Mercer 2002. p. 170)

So much for the notion that creativity exists within, or against, or is shaped by, some broad contextual features. Indeed, so much for the even broader argument that creativity itself is located in many places far beyond the individual brain, mind or personality. We have explored now several areas which in aggregated form show many, many arguments from multiple perspectives that creativity sits within myriad relationships. And that those relationships exist due to particular places, due to new forms of interactions given the Web, and that broad contextual features also help to shape those relationships. This brings us to one kind of end for this book, an end to the broad conceptual and theoretical discussions about this general *where* of creativity.

But we still have another unfinished task. We said at the beginning of this book that we would try to supplement the conceptual and theoretical with some arguments about the practical. We said we would try to summarize some of the things we have said, sometimes critical and polemical, into something of an 'anatomy' of creativity. We have also said that we would return to the motif running through our thinking, that of the dialectical conception of creativity, as part of that 'anatomical' consideration. So let us now turn to that discussion.

Chapter 7

An anatomy of creativity

. . . the four stages of preparation, incubation, illumination and verification of the final result can generally be distinguished from each other. . . . Our mind is not likely to give us a clear answer unless we set it a clear question, and we are more likely to notice the significance of any new piece of evidence, or new association of ideas, if we have formed a definite conception of a case to be proved or disproved.

(Wallas 1972. p. 15)

We can see from this quotation that George Wallas is among those people who argue that we can identify clear and distinct stages within creativity. But he is far from the only one. We have looked at various debates which help us situate creativity within places far beyond the orthodoxy of the brain, mind or personality, as this helps us understand its characteristics. We now turn, with a little trepidation, to our final chapter, which tries to use these various ideas and schemas to say something about the anatomy of creativity. The trepidation comes from our sense that this brings us uncomfortably close to an argument which 'defines' creativity. As we argued in Chapter 1, we are of the opinion that creativity flows from different sources following different 'logic(s)' for each person each time they do it. And different people experience and develop their particular creativity in their own idiosyncratic ways. We do not believe that creativity can be defined because we do not believe it is a single unified 'thing'. However, we do believe that tentatively outlining an anatomy of creativity might be useful for bringing together the different aspects of the creative person and the interpersonal dynamics of creative relationships into a more manageable and portable shape, as a kind of summary. We will try to alleviate our sense of trepidation by quoting from many different creative practitioners who have themselves reported upon the mindsets, experiences and emotions within each 'stage' of this anatomy. But this notion of 'stages' is in itself also something which adds to our slight sense of unease. The systematic accounts of creativity considered below, along with the general proposition that it has an anatomy, all share the idea that various 'stages' of creativity can be identified. Whilst we accept this to some degree, the notion that clear 'stages' with definite dividing lines separating one from another in a clear cut way is something we are less happy to accept. From our own experience, we know that things are never really that clear cut, and different aspects of creativity are always intersecting one another in dialectical ways. This is why we have until now always put the notion of 'stages' in inverted commas. We still have this concern, but we will drop the inverted commas now as it could become tiresome.

For this reason, the picture we will draw in this chapter will have two fairly distinct shapes to the anatomy of creativity. One offers a kind of straight line, or *linear conception of creativity*. The other will return us to the *dialectical conception of creativity*, and will be a more circular picture. The linear picture is useful because it offers a clear way of appreciating the various ways in which an original creative idea can be developed through to something which can exist in the world and become something which other people can relate to. The circular picture complements this to represent the continually interpenetrating inner dynamics of creativity as it emerges from more iterative and recursive processes. There is a linear path through stages of creativity, but at the same time there are many wheels within wheels as this linear process goes forward.

But systematic accounts of creativity are often resisted. Many prefer to hold onto the idea that creativity is a mysterious process which is inherently ineffable. This view often holds the suspicion that attempts to explain it through systematic accounts will somehow 'kill it'. Many accounts of creativity have emphasized accident, error, luck and other aspects which militate against systematic accounts. The history of creativity does appear to be characterized by accidents that have taken people down wrong turns, requiring re-adjustments to correct mistakes, which have proved to be the key points within their creativity. Such re-adjustments have often forced people to steer in new, less than clear directions beyond their normal navigations, to experiment to find routes to better destinations. As we have seen, creativity is often characterized by serendipitous accidents which get it to its destination without looking, or even sometimes knowing that such a destination was relevant.

Simple blind luck often plays a large part in creative success, which again militates against systematic accounts. We all like to assume that our successes are due to our own innate abilities, and our failures are due to unfair external circumstance. But a different view suggests that a great deal of luck is involved either way – for getting creativity 'off the ground'; getting it selected and well received by the 'experts'; putting it into the right place and time so that it leads to success.

> Academics call the mistaken impression that a random streak (*of success*) is due to extraordinary performance the hot-hand fallacy. . . . In all aspects of our lives we encounter streaks and other peculiar patterns of success and failure. Sometimes success predominates, sometimes failure. Either way it is important in our lives to take the long view and understand that streaks and other patterns that don't appear random can indeed happen by pure chance.
>
> (Mlodinow 2008. p. 63)

So we do need to be careful with overly rational, overly mechanical, overly linear accounts of creativity which underplay the accidental, serendipitous, iterative and recursive nature of creativity. But this should not lead to the blanket rejection of systematic accounts of creativity which characterize some of the more artistic temperaments. But as we have argued above, we do believe that systematic accounts of creativity do have their uses, and are worthy of consideration.

James Webb Young (1965) compares the development of a creative idea to the growth of a South Sea atoll. Both result from the accretion of lots of material underneath the 'surface' (of water or conscious attention), which leads to the growing phenomena breaking through the surface and 'coming out'. It is this process of growth within or behind a conscious idea that Webb Young is keen to draw our attention to, as the fulcrum of his attempt to explain creativity. He argues that we all have the natural capacity for creativity, and his 'systematic account' is offered as a contribution to the 'means of developing it'. His account is one of the first to offer both *clear principles* and *specific methods* to account for where new ideas, as the basis for creativity, come from. He sees this systematic account as being more important for the development of creativity than learning specific items of knowledge which quickly become out of date. And to develop this systematic account, he refers very much to the idea of stages of creativity within an overall process, an idea which, as we will see, has had traction elsewhere too (Bohm 1998; Csíkszentmihályi 1996; Gardner 2011; Roszak 1986; Wallas 1972).

It is perhaps no surprise that another systematic account of creativity is offered by the scientific mind of David Bohm (1998). He argues that it grows through on-going stages which stand in a hierarchy, whereby increasingly higher stages of creative insight and efficacy are based on the foundations of the previous stages. Bohm makes a distinction between occasional insights on the one hand, and on the other hand a deeper sense of new underlying patterns of understanding, established and sustained in more developed ways over a longer period of time. This higher stage of creativity leads to a broader, more generally applicable, more structured and ordered creative application that moves it beyond a simple one-off, free-standing 'bit' of creative work. For Bohm, movement towards the 'perception of a new basic order' means replacing a stage of relative disorder with more self-consciously and self-reflexively ordered creative thinking. As this higher degree of order develops, the contours of the overall creativity become clearer, more graspable, more demonstrable and more applicable. The growing degree of order means that one is able to describe its inner trajectory back to oneself. His point has strong echoes of Erich Harth's (1995) idea of the *creative loop*. As Bohm himself puts it,

> . . . each order can become the basis of a new higher order, to form a continually evolving hierarchy, leading to new structures (*of thought, insight. etc.*) that are generally able to order those of a simpler nature. . . . Thus (*creativity involves*) not merely new structures, but also new orders of structures.
>
> (Bohm 1998. p. 17)

This is a very clear expression of creativity as a linear process which goes through discrete stages and moves towards ever more developed and ordered forms of insight. And this picture makes experiential sense. Creative people often report that the early stages of a project are difficult, confusing and 'messy', but as the particular project develops clarity and order seems to emerge, which in turn helps to suggest further levels of clarity as further developed levels of order emerge. This implies that when thinking about one's creative thinking, or planning one's creative plans, higher levels of self-reflexivity are used to grasp emerging orders of insight as new stages of understanding replace previous ones, which get 'pushed down' the hierarchy. Reflecting back upon the creative process as one goes from lower orders of insight to higher ones is, it seems, something which grows out of an emerging awareness of the process as a whole. Perhaps stages of creativity can only be seen retrospectively, and make sense as discrete 'bits' as one reflects back upon them as parts of an overall process. As we remember how an initial 'flash of inspiration' led to more concerted work to take things onto firmer, sustained creative plans and strategies, we can begin to recall different stages. When we have developed the higher orders of creative reflection which are analogous to a 'filing cabinet', we can better 'file' the wider panoply of experience and research within a clear, structured plan of work. And it is this propensity of higher order stages of thinking which help us to synthesize *information* into something more like *knowledge* (Roszak 1986). It is perhaps something which we are forgetting in the age of the Web, that information, however freely available and accessed, is not knowledge. Something has to be done within information – processing, consolidation, synthesizing and combining with other information – for it to constitute knowledge.

Bohm takes the idea of hierarchical stages of creativity further to suggest that a more *creative* creativity can flow from this. New fundamental distinctions, concepts and insights can flow from the development of new stages when they become genuinely new orders of thinking. He argues that the *quantitative accumulation* of more information can flip to become *qualitative re-conceptualization* taking creativity into wholly new areas of insight.

> Evidently, creation of this kind has been fairly rare. In the whole of human history, perhaps only a few people have achieved it. . . . With this spirit, it is always open to learning what is new, to perceiving differences and new similarities, leading to new orders and structures, rather than always tending to impose familiar orders and structures in the field of what is seen.
>
> (Bohm 1998. p. 21)

And for Bohm, the highest order of creativity seems to require this total immersion:

> This kind of action of the creative state of mind is impossible if one is limited by narrow and petty aims, such as security, furthering of personal ambition, glorification of the individual or the State, getting 'kicks' and other satisfactory experiences out of one's work, and so forth. Although such motives may permit occasional flashes of penetrating insight, they evidently tend to hold the mind a prisoner of its old and familiar structure of thought and perception. Indeed, merely to inquire into what is unknown must inevitably lead one into a situation in which all that is done may well constitute a threat to the successful achievement of those narrow and limited goals.
>
> (Bohm 1998. p. 23)

To be successful in this movement from lower to higher stages of creativity, Bohm suggests the need to consider:

- becoming as aware as possible of one's 'normal way' of doing things, and using that as a route to self-transcendence which can better other perspectives
- being aware of one's normal social self, looking for creative confirmation and using that as a route to greater self-awareness which can better embrace the unknown
- exploring one's potential for creative experimentation, and using that for greater self-renewal which can better appreciate the ever changing nature of things

It is through such deep processes that creativity becomes an expression of the 'implicate order' of things, an expression of how things 'really are', or 'can be', or perhaps 'ought to be'. But Bohm's account is only one example of a broader body of research which expresses creativity as a linear process which moves through various stages. A consolidated account of these various anatomies of creativity can help us add fine detail to Bohm's initial systematic account.

So, as we are beginning to appreciate, many researchers have offered their particular anatomy of creativity. Whilst they are all slightly different, these differences are not pronounced and we can make a consolidated account from them. This includes the following discrete facets.

Preparation

This stage of creativity speaks to the necessity of getting all the information which might be useful for a creative project into one's head. It speaks very much to the idea that creativity comes from the inner workings of the creative person – the brain, the mind, the personality – as the site where information and experiences coming from the world are processed, interpreted and remembered. The preparation stage can be summarized as *gathering raw materials.*

This gathering might come from the relatively simple process of looking around, or it might come from more concerted processes of prolonged research, which as we will see below can have many particular facets to it. It might come from a process of accretion by which we seek to gather information to broaden and deeper our current thinking, or it might entail a more uncomfortable process of re-problematizing everything we thought we could previously take for granted and 'know'. Preparation might be specific, concerned with gathering information on the tools, techniques and other detailed aspects of the actual practice of creativity. Or it might be more general, concerned with gathering information about the history and context within which one is working, and the potential for learning from other traditions of knowledge, and collaborations within the cross-disciplinary process of creativity found within relationships.

Whatever the scope or dynamic of preparation, it appears to be a commonly reported starting point. As athletes often say, 'preparation is everything'. The race is not won on the day of the race, but during the period of preparative training leading up to that day. For example, Csíkszentmihályi argues that a prepared mind is best placed to receive insights. And we can find similar sentiments from creative practitioners. For example, Brancusi talks of how preparing himself to do things is, for him, more difficult than actually doing those things, and for Picasso, inspiration needs to 'find you working'.

The preparation stage, given that it is about gathering raw materials, is closely connected to developing research skills within a *reflective creative practice*, which we will come to later in this chapter.

Digestion

Preparation for creativity is taken forward by a period of digestion, which is characterized by the general mulling over of ideas so as to become familiar with them, or playing with them so that they become part of our 'normal' thinking. For Webb Young, this stage of creativity involves

> . . . masticating (*chewing over*) these (*newly gathered*) materials, as you would food that you are preparing for digestion. . . . What you do is to take the different bits of material which you have gathered and feel them all over, as it were, with the tentacles of the mind. You take one fact, turn it this way and that, look at it in different lights, and feel for the meaning of it.
>
> (Webb Young 1965. p. 57)

And Mozart gives his version of this:

> When I am, as it were, completely myself, entirely alone, and of good cheer – say, traveling in a carriage, or walking after a good meal, or during the night when I cannot sleep; it is on such occasions that my ideas flow best and most abundantly. Whence and how

they come I know not; nor can I force them. Those pleasures that please me I retain in memory, and am accustomed, as I have been told, to hum them to myself. If I continue in this way, it soon occurs to me how I may turn this or that morsel to account . . .

(quoted in Cropley 1972. p. 65)

Many artists and scientists report this digestion stage as a favourite part of the overall creative process. It is the experimental stage which involves trying out tentative new ideas for no clear reason, playing with new thoughts just for the pleasure of playing, and the general envisioning of things to see if and how they 'fit together', or are 'going somewhere'.

For Bohm, this spirit, or indeed 'logic', of playful experimentation is central to creativity, as shown in Chapter 1. And many famously creative people have reported such a 'logic' of playful, pleasurable experimentation. For example, Charles Darwin declared his love of 'fools' experiments'. Carl Jung thought that the play instinct was more important for creativity than the serious intellect. Isaac Newton spoke of how he imagined himself as a boy playing on a seashore, whilst the great ocean of truth lay undiscovered before him.

This notion of playful experimentation as central to the digestion stage echoes certain aspects of the more dialectical picture we touched upon in Chapter 1, and to which we will return to later in this chapter. It echoes the interpenetrating opposites of working and not working, of being serious and playful, as part of the inner dynamic of creativity.

Incubation

This stage of creativity seems to be the stage that the mind, as it were, 'does for itself'. Incubation seems to allow the mind 'time off' to generate unconscious and/or pre-conscious thoughts that are capable of becoming consciously known creative solutions. We could get into conceptual tussles here about the existence of the unconscious aspects of the mind, and the degree to which we accept a Freudian position in psychology (a debate which has been running for many, many years). But instead, let's perhaps recognize that even the most mainstream, 'scientific' psychological perspective, the one most implacably opposed to psychoanalysis, that is, cognitive psychology, accepts that something like 80% of our behaviour is affected by unconscious influences (Brookes 2011).

Moreover, recent neurological research is confirming what creative people have always known, that the preparation-digestion aspects of creativity often need to be followed by a period of seeming inactivity. It appears that this allows the mind the time to process the raw materials and make the playful experiments in order to develop novel ideas for particular creative objectives. It appears that this incubation period works best if we divert our attention with something mundane – going for a walk, driving the car, taking a shower are often reported by creative people as a useful part of their creative routine. It is important to note that for good incubation, complete mental inactivity seems to be almost as bad as trying to force our attention. Some activity, but activity not directed onto what has been prepared and digested, appears to be what the mind needs to allow new ideas and insights to form.

. . . a physiologist watching an experiment, or a business man going through his morning letters, may at the same time be 'incubating' on a problem which he posed to himself a few days ago, be accumulating knowledge in 'preparation' for a second problem, and be 'verifying' his conclusion on a third problem. Even in exploring the

> same problem, the mind may be unconsciously incubating on one aspect of it, while it is consciously employed in preparing for or verifying another aspect.
>
> (Wallas 1972. p. 43)

And this notion of seeming inactivity, or at least mundane activity, relates to the significance of daily routines and rituals which many people report as an aid to their creativity. Again there is a dialectic here between focused action and relaxed semi-action. In his book *Daily Rituals*, Mason Curry (2013) implies this dialectic within his survey of the daily working patterns of many creative people. Although there appears no discernible, universal daily pattern of creativity across all his subjects, Curry's survey implies a common interpenetration between working and not working within many creative careers. The only regular feature within these daily creative routines appears to be a four-to-five-hour work day, but his subjects report that these working hours occur at many different times of the day. Daily working hours may sometimes occur early in the morning to become the precursor to a period of relaxation and reflection during the rest of the day. Or they may take place throughout the night, and follow a day's reflection. But whatever the daily routine, we can take from Curry's survey that incubation is taking place within regularized daily periods of non-work, and is for many a necessary and important part of their daily routine. It seems that such daily routines allowing for reflective incubation are a general feature of a creative life, despite the idiosyncratic daily patterns of specific individuals. For Aristotle, creative excellence came from habit more than from specific one-off acts. The poet Stephen Spender has spoken of the importance of habits and rituals, often involving lots of coffee and cigarettes, for his creative practice.

This incubation stage seems to underpin the finding of creativity when we are least looking for it. It seems to be connected to the mental state required for non-deliberate creative wanderings which can lead to unexpected, serendipitous avenues for finding solutions to problems, or even problems for solutions. Creative people also report the value of *obliquity*, allowing one's self the time for oblique creative approaches to develop, rather than always trying to bash away at things head-on before the incubation period has been gone through.

> The direct decision maker perceives a direct connection between intentions and outcomes; the oblique decision maker believes intention is neither necessary nor sufficient to secure the outcome. The direct problem solver reviews all possible outcomes; the oblique problem solver chooses from a much more limited set. The direct problem solver assembles all available information; the oblique decision maker recognizes the limits of his or her knowledge. The direct decision maker maximizes his or her objectives; the oblique decision maker is continuously adaptive.
>
> (Kay 2011. p. 44)

It appears that the incubation stage is a necessary precursor for the aforementioned *divergent thinking*. Again, this echoes certain aspects of the dialectical picture, whereby the interpenetrating opposites of continuous and discontinuous working form a part of the inner dynamic of creativity.

Illumination

Perhaps the most common myth about creativity is the view that the illumination stage – those 'aha' moments, those flashes of inspiration, those moments when everything becomes clear and we can see our creativity as a unified whole – that this experience *is* creativity.

This myth holds that creativity just 'comes from nowhere'. It also implies that it either 'just comes' or it doesn't, which is perhaps its most unsatisfactory element. It also underpins the elitist conception that some people just have these abilities and other just don't. Of course these flashes of illumination do often come, and many creative people report such experiences, but as the stages of preparation, digestion and incubation have already implied, they do not come from 'nowhere'. Work has already happened before the flash of illumination is experienced. As Wallas puts it, 'the final "flash", or "click", is the culmination of a successful train of associations, which may have lasted for an appreciable time, and which has probably been preceded by a series of tentative and unsuccessful trains' (Wallas 1972. p. 58).

And such illuminations come in different shapes and sizes. They can be very fleeting, or might stay with us for the rest of our lives; they can be very personal and idiosyncratic, or can re-confirm widely shared beliefs, they can be rather trivial, or can radically change previously held beliefs. But many creative people report some sense of creative illumination which has changed the way they see the world and their work within it. They often make a distinction between their work before illumination and after it as a key characteristic of the overall anatomy of their creativity. It is the illuminating flash of inspiration itself which is often reported to be the defining experience of a creative life. Perhaps one of the world's most famous reports of such a life-changing flash of illumination is that reported by Alfred Russell Wallace (1901). Being forced to rest due to a period of intermittent fever, Russell Wallace could do nothing other than 'think over any subject that interested' him. Having read the ideas of Malthus twelve years earlier, and vaguely thinking about the constant destruction of life which that implied, a new formulation of his questions occurred to him – 'Why do some die and some live?'. And he reports that in a 'sudden flash' the answer occurred to him, that the whole self-acting process was behind why some members of a species survived and some died. It was this 'sudden flash' which, for Russell Wallace, enabled him to see for the first time his version of the theory of the origin of the species.

Illuminations such as the one felt by Russell Wallace are keenly awaited by creative people, are welcome when they arrive and are often seen as the very definition of creativity. But let us not forget what has gone before. Without the preparation, digestion and incubation stages, it is unlikely that his illumination would have come to him. Russell Wallace had done many years of rather mundane research, had read Malthus twelve years earlier and was only 'vaguely thinking' when his illumination came to him. To see such illumination *as itself* creativity is analogous to suggesting that the individuals' minds are the sole location of creativity just because individual minds are involved. Secondly, many examples of creative work exist without these flashes of illumination as their defining feature. And thirdly, illuminations need to be developed, tried out, worked upon and made into something real for other people if they are to become something which we could reasonably call a work of creativity. Sometimes, as the saying goes, creativity is '99% perspiration and only 1% inspiration'. So it is these other, less dramatic stages of creativity, those which require 'perspiration', to which we now turn.

Elaboration and extension

As those engaged in prolonged and serious creative work know only too well, illumination only really fires the starting gun for a lot of hard work. If illumination is to actually lead somewhere, then it has to be elaborated upon to find its form of expression, its inner details and its technical articulation. Illumination must be followed by the kind of creativity which broadens and deepens the idea, so it can come to have a real life leading to actual creative outcomes which can be appreciated by others. Creative illuminations must be extended, and so in many ways the elaboration and extension stage is at the very epicentre of creativity. It is the place where many of the emotions and experiences we have referred to in Chapter 2 as the creative attitude take place. It is the place where many of the contradictory aspects of the 'logic' of creativity found in the dialectical picture get played out.

For Theodore Roszak (1986), the 'true art of thinking' elaborates and extends initial 'bits' of illuminations into broader and deeper knowledge through a process of *analysis* – understanding the meaning of each 'bit' – and *synthesis* – fitting them together into a more coherent whole. And such elaborations and extensions can come in different shapes:

- finding new interplays between the various 'bits' of meanings found within new pieces of information
- forging new perspectives by enlarging interpretations and/or elaborating a new focus
- developing applications, adaptations or uses for these interplays and new perspectives

As we saw above, for Webb Young (1965) there are clear *principles* and specific *methods* which can account for where newly elaborated ideas come from. His first principle of elaboration and extension refers us back to the combinatorial idea of creativity – finding a new combination of old ideas. His second principle of elaboration and extension is the *ability to see relationships*. For Webb Young, some people tend to see 'bits' of information as separate facts about the world, whereas others tend to see 'bits' of information as links in potential chains of knowledge. Such people tend to see patterns across 'bits' of thinking, and find illustration therein of ideas which have more general applicability.

These two elaboration and extension principles chime with Roszak's (1986) anatomy of 'the true art of thinking' – 'bits' of information must be defined, contained, evaluated and judged as to their worth against all the other myriad 'bits' of information within any field of creativity. Then comes the synthesis which seeks to 'do something' with illuminating 'bits' of information if it is to become knowledge which has some kind of 'shape'. Without connecting illuminations into new combinations, and finding new relationships with(in) broader chains of knowledge, any illuminations will have little or no location and will only ever be free-floating experiences. For Roszak, the 'true art of thinking' produces knowledge through elaboration and extension because that is what gives creativity its broader meaning, its more focused context, its greater interpretative potential, its extended prospects for further adaptation and, ultimately, its use in the real world beyond the mind doing that thinking. As we saw above, Mozart described his creative method as involving a certain kind of digestion of 'bits' of creativity, but he also he referred to the idea of taking each 'bit' and 'turning it to account', which also expresses his need for 'enlarging', 'methodizing' and 'surveying':

> . . . it soon occurs to me how I may turn this or that morsel to account. . . . All this fires my soul, and, provided I am not disturbed, my subject enlarges itself, becomes methodized and defined, and the whole, though it be long, stands almost complete and finished in my mind, so that I can survey it. . . . When I proceed to write down my ideas, I take out of the bag of memory, if I may use that phrase, what has been previously collected into it the way I mentioned.
>
> (quoted in Cropley 1972. p. 65)

But this stage of creativity is often experienced as the more difficult and 'thorny' part of the overall process. It is the stage of creativity where a different creative attitude is often needed, one which is less playful and experimental and characterized by a new urgency. There is often a very different emotional cadence to the elaboration and extension of creativity. For instance, a sense of *seriousness* is also often reported by creative people. There is also the experience of a visceral need among creative people for their creativity to 'come out' in some way. For example, Beethoven declares how he never wrote to increase his reputation, but only so that what was in his heart could come out. Miro saw his painting as being akin to stripping his soul naked, as a total embrace where caution was thrown to the winds and nothing was held back.

And this can bring with it a sense of *momentum*. According to physicists, an object which is not moving needs some initial external energy to start *because* it is not moving. A moving object has the energy to overcome inertia and friction *because* it is moving. Momentum is the added impetus gained by a moving object by the very fact of its movement, and is analogous to experience reported by many creative people. It may take an extra exertion to get a creative project out of inertia and set it moving towards elaboration and extension. But often, once it is moving, it seems to have its own energy, seems to move under 'its own steam'. Because of this, many creative people report paying specific attention to creative momentum. Once the extra energy to overcome creative inertia has been applied, they are keen to 'keeping things going' at all costs, because they know what the reappearance of inertia can mean. For example, Michael Korda always sought greater goals as a self-conscious way of keeping his creative momentum high. Annie Lennox talked of how, for her, success seemed to bring its own creative momentum, to the extent that she could sometimes not tell if she was creating the momentum or if that very momentum was creating her!

Seriousness and momentum are connected to the higher than usual levels of creative motivation we have touched on above, and dovetail with heightened levels of *involvement* many creative people have with their work. We all become subject to heightened involvement in achieving something towards an external end from time to time – finishing the shopping in time to pick up the kids; filling the car with petrol because we have to go somewhere. This is basic *goal-oriented behaviour*. But creativity seems to bring a different quality of involvement, one located within and focused on the 'thing' itself, rather than outcomes geared towards external demands or rewards. Such involvement is often expressed in becoming 'totally immersed', not being able to 'leave it alone', 'having to get it finished'. And this type of involvement differs from basic goal-oriented behaviour in that it is, as we have already noted, *autotelic behaviour*. The elaboration and extension stage is intimately intertwined with the sense of involvement which comes from within the creative activity itself, as opposed to an external goal or motivation. This autotelic character is often what gives creative elaboration and extension its great energy, especially when creative flow is experienced. And this is often reported as an emotional experience connected with various senses of *audacity* – taking risks, having the courage to step into the unknown territories, being willing to be mocked, being happy to be an outsider. For the philosopher John Dewey, an audacity of the imagination has been behind every new scientific advance.

But some degree of creative *disorientation* also seems to be a necessary emotional component if new perspectives are to be elaborated from initial illumination. Reflecting back on the creative process as it is developed and put into action, what has been called *reflective practice*, may require the active embrace of uncertainties about what 'it is', where 'you are' and how it all 'fits together'.

And this often brings the tensions and sufferings we have already noted above. Creative people often talk about how they have 'suffered for their art', how it brought many internal tensions and even bordered on madness. There may be a degree of hyperbole in this, but nevertheless creative elaborations and extensions are often motivated by strange dialectical interplays between visceral need, unclear and complicated ideas, and pleasurable experiences of flow and many other contradictory emotions. Sometimes it is the suffering already there in our lives which stimulates a burst of creative expression. Creativity to suffering or suffering to creativity – either way, they are often intertwined. For example, Florence Welch has talked of how being heartbroken has led her to her most creative moments, where she has tried to channel her energies into things beyond the heartbreak itself. For her, contentment is a 'creativity killer'.

And as such, creativity often needs a great *resilience* to deal with disorientation and suffering. Sometimes creativity requires that we accept these times and just keep going. For Andre Gide, all great art begins with resistance to the prevailing times, and proceeds through 'great labour'.

It is these thornier facets of creativity within the elaboration and extension stage, the question of multi-faceted 'logic' behind it briefly explored in Chapter 1, and the emotional contents of the creative attitude briefly explored in Chapter 2 which seem to sometimes give creative work its great sense of *purpose*. And the quest to make these elaborated and extended creative expressions to the world and its people seems to be intimately intertwined with finding ourselves in and through this sense of purpose. Another dialectical interplay between purported opposites, perhaps the most profound one, is developing a greater subjective sense of self out of making expressions to the objective world beyond, and consequently developing those very expressions to the world beyond the self so as to enable the self to hear its own voice. The elaboration and extension stage of creativity seems to be the stage where the inner world of preparation, digestion, incubation and illumination starts to look outwards to the world beyond, starts to think about making things seen, heard and understood by others. And this requires testing and dissemination.

Testing and dissemination

After all the perspiration, all the thorny difficulties, all the less than happy emotions which seem to be located within the elaboration and extension stage of creativity, testing is necessary. If creativity is to come to fruition, it requires that we test the elaborated and extended ideas to see if they really do work, and disseminate them to the public. And this involves a more cold-eyed, objective approach. But when it comes to testing creative elaborations and extensions, this objective approach is improved if a counter-intuitive piece of logic is born in mind – falsification.

Understandably we get great personal satisfaction from evidence which confirms we were on the right creative track. The problem is, we can always find such evidence if and when we look for it. We are all potentially prey to this *confirmation bias*, as we pay attention to what confirms our work, and ignore what contradicts it. But confirmation bias is the enemy of creativity. It is better to reject confirmation, or, as Karl Popper has called it, *verificationism*, and turn to *falsificationism* to test creative elaborations. That is, it is better to try to disprove one's creative plans rather than prove them, and if they remain 'un-disproven', then they are probably good ideas, plans, elaborations or extensions. Such a method is often used within the testing stage of creativity, if only implicitly. For instance:

- Falsificationism is central to the scientific method, which sees 'truths' as only contingent until they get disproved.
- Engineers and designers routinely talk of 'testing things to destruction' so that they know what is 'wrong' as well as what is 'right' with their plans.
- Creative writers often recognize that well-loved characters whose presence in the emerging narrative cloud the story, need to be removed. They refer to this as 'killing one's darlings'.

For Popper (2002), it is the extent to which an idea can be potentially falsified, whilst still holding up to scrutiny, that is the hallmark of true creative thinking and progress. The testing stage is based upon actively seeking criticisms. And this means that it is disseminated to the public in some way. This often requires a more methodical, patient, practical mind-set capable of hearing frustrating, negative responses and still dealing with the often boring aspects of actually getting it done and 'out there'.

> (This) might be called the cold, grey dawn of the morning after . . . (when you) take your little new-born idea out into the world of reality . . . do not make the mistake of holding your ideas close to your chest at this stage. Submit it to the criticism of the judicious. When you do, a surprising thing will happen. You will find that a good idea has, as it were, self-expanding qualities. It stimulates those who see it to add to it.
> (Webb Young 1965. p. 71)

And dissemination requires particular skills. Between elaboration and dissemination, many creative projects suffer from a lack of *clarity*. Artists, scientists and associated academics are some of the worst communicators in the world, referring as they often do to self-referential jargon and tortuous self-repeating mystifications. As the saying goes – if you cannot explain your creativity clearly to someone not schooled in your discipline, it probably means that you do not really understand things all that well yourself. For creativity to come alive it needs an audience, and the audience needs to know what you are trying to say. So a conscious and deliberate clarity of expression is a necessary stage within an overall creative process. When thinking about skills in rhetoric for effective self-expression, Aristotle suggested that we should consider:

- Pathos – how one and one's ideas connect with the broader events of the one's time
- Logos – the internal consistency of one's argument
- Ethos – the colour, flavour or 'personality' of one's expressions

Around 2,500 years later, George Orwell suggested that one should:

- clarify your argument before you attempt to express it
- avoid 'ugliness' in one's expressions
- always use the fewest words possible
- choose simple expressions rather than the overblown, flowery or unnecessarily poetic

Such clarity of expression within the dissemination stage should never be an add-on. Issues of clarity of expression should not be approached as something to think about after the creative elaboration and extension. It is a more central part of the creativity itself, when at its best. Practising clarity of expression for effective dissemination is almost the same thing as practising the creativity itself. Often the process of explaining your creativity to others is the same as explaining it to yourself, which enables you to explain it to others. And there is a dialectical interplay between speaking to oneself and speaking to the world within the movement from elaboration and extension on the one hand, and testing and dissemination on the other. Similarly, testing and dissemination often entails going back to a new phase of elaboration and extension. There are many potential feedback loops and circular interactions within the various stages of creativity because it is recursive and iterative.

Recursive iterations

Creative work often takes in influences from many strands as it emerges. It often grows out of itself, as feedback loops from mid-points in the project send you back to a new beginning, to fresh outlooks. It needs to be gone over again and again. That is, creativity is *recursive*.

> . . . the creative process is less linear than recursive. How many iterations it goes through, how many loops are involved, how many insights are needed, depends on the depth and breadth of the issues dealt with.
>
> (Csíkszentmihályi 1996. p. 71)

That is, it is *iterative*. For example, the scientist James Lovelock never considers the truth as something he can conclusively arrive at. Rather he argues that his science is an activity which he hopes will simply lead him a little bit closer to the truth each time he does it. As he declares, he 'iterates' towards the truth within his work.

Enlargement and generalization

And the various iterations of elaboration, extension, testing and dissemination then seem to require that creativity *enlarges* itself, so as to make more *general* statements about the world, to the world. Enlargement and generalization might be about:

- expressing continuity and coherence between one's own creative work and the creative domain one is working within
- expressing some underlying pattern within which it chimes with work coming from other creative domains
- articulating broader overviews or 'conclusions' about the world as a whole

The result of these over-lapping processes is a general aspect of creativity which stems from the imaginative (re)combining of 'bits' of information into broad insights that are not already found within those 'bits' of information themselves. Enlargement and generalization often come from reflecting back upon the creative process as one goes through it, to become more aware of its inner trajectory. Being able to spot new potential combinations by critiquing, deconstructing and re-forming enlarged versions of the creative idea might be called a *creative mindfulness*. This comes from developing the propensity to be able to deal with the inner details of the creative work, whilst at the same time being able to 'stand back' from those details and seek more general ideas. It is this process of critical self-reflection which is at the heart of what Gray and Malins call 'reflective practice':

> There are many parallels between the construction of an art/design work and the construction of a research argument, not least is the way that the form is proposed, critiqued, deconstructed, remodelled and resolved. Much of this process is evaluative and analytical, reflective and deconstructive, creative and synthetic. As practitioners we engage in these activities constantly and most of the time unconsciously. As reflective researchers we must make these activities explicit and accessible . . .
>
> (Gray and Malins 2007. p. 65)

But generalizations can have different shapes and scopes. Cautious generalizations come from a close reading of details of one's creative work, but which are careful about saying too much, too quickly, too stridently. For the painter George Braque, his art does not come from knowing how to continually extend it, but from knowing its limits. Riskier generalizations flow from those guesses, hunches and feelings that become part of the 'buzz' of creativity, and often give it its audacity and sense of momentum. Hazardous generalizations are those large, sweeping statements that we all make about the world, which turn out to be embarrassingly reckless cases of 'overdoing it', but are nevertheless sometimes a vital stage of creativity. For Scott Adams, creativity is squarely located in the permission he gives himself to make mistakes, whilst his art comes from knowing which mistakes to keep! Such variations in the scope and scale of generalization are summed up by Arthur Koestler, in his famous book *The Creative Act*:

> The limitations and peculiarities of his medium force the artist at each step to make choices, consciously or unconsciously; to select for representation those features or aspects which he considers to be relevant, and to discard those which he considers irrelevant. . . . Thus we meet again the trinity of selection, exaggeration and simplification.
>
> (Koestler 1989. p. 90)

For Roszak, working with such generalizations to bring things to some kind of fruition then requires two more steps within our anatomy of creativity. Firstly, he talks of *integration* – the process whereby various ideas are formed into patterns which start to satisfy our minds, start to feel like viable and coherent answers to the creative questions we have asked. Integration is the start of the process whereby answers to questions such as 'What does this mean?' or 'How do I make sense of this?' can begin to be fully addressed. Roszak raises the notion of the 'master ideas', by which he means those big ideas that tend to shape and colour the underlying expectations we have of the creativity we are engaged in. These master ideas might come from our general cultural attitudes and form the stage upon which the creative process is played out. For Roszak, they are born out of the three interrelated aspects of the essential nature of the creative person we explored in Chapter 2, namely *experience, memory* and *insight*.

For Roszak, experience is much broader than simply our habitual responses to everyday life. His notion of experience is one which echoes the cognitive psychological notion of the creative mind as itself an open and creative process whereby we actively choose and shape such responses:

> . . . we ordinarily take in the flow of events as life presents it – unplanned, unstructured, fragmentary, dissonant. The turbulent stream passes into memory where it settles out into things vividly remembered, half remembered, mixed, mingled, compounded.
>
> (Roszak 1986. p. 97)

As we have already noted, such an idea of experience is an important component of the creative attitude or 'logic', because it enables us to know what works and what doesn't. We have already noted above that in recent years the 10,000 Hours Rule has become well known. Just putting the hours in will not, however, in itself guarantee success. Creativity flows from other kinds of experiences too. And for Roszak, the role of memory is a second key dimension of his broader notion of generalization.

Roszak refers to memory as a register of our experiences which becomes shaped by the daily flow of life into signposts and standards which order our everyday conduct (Roszak 1986). As with the way we process experiences, so with the role of memory. We actively shape, select and mould our memories, just as we experience our experiences that flow as a result. We actively choose what our memories are to be on the basis of importance, usefulness, warmth, fear and all the other emotions that make us what we are. We can liken memory more to a stew of unexpected ingredients than to a filing system. It is

> . . . fluid rather than granular, more like a wave than a particle. Like a wave, it spreads through the mind, puddling up here and there in odd personal associations that may be of the most inexplicable kind. It flows not only through the mind, but through the emotions, the senses, the body.
>
> (Roszak 1986. p. 117)

As such, it is the process which 'edits' the words and imagery of our experiences, or perhaps now 'compresses' what is filed away from experience. As we have already touched upon above concerning illuminations, these constant interplays between memory and experience often produce creative insights because they shape what is to be deemed important for generalization. Memory shapes these *insights into importance*, which can be very fleeting, or they can stay with us for the rest of our lives; might be very personal and idiosyncratic, or might confirm what turns out to be very widely shared beliefs; or might radically change our previously held beliefs. But the active shaping and deliberate use of such insights into importance seem to be at the very heart of the curiosity, novelty, imagination, thirst, experimentation and self-challenging that drive creativity forward as an un-ignorable and unavoidable aspect of what is to be enlarged and generalized out of a creative life.

> Perhaps this volatility of mind is what saves human society from the changeless rigidity of the other social animals, the ants, the bees, the beasts of the pack and the herd. We are gifted as a species with the crowning tangle of electrochemical cells which has become an idea-maker. So spontaneously does this brain of ours make ideas and play with ideas that we cannot say much more about them then that they are there, shaping our perceptions, opening up possibilities. From moment to moment, human beings find new things to think and do and be: ideas that erupt seemingly out of nowhere.
>
> (Roszak 1986. p. 119)

And these myriad interplays within the enlargement and generalization often involve the creative ability to see questions afresh by using divergent thinking to loosen up one's approach, by stepping 'sideways' so as to approach the question in new and more effective ways, by adopting what Edward de Bono (1992) has called 'lateral thinking', which is recasting the question to bring in concepts and tool from the 'outside' of it. Such a creative stage has been called various things, but they all amount in the end to *de-framing* one's frame of reference.

Self-questioning, de-framing and movement

Self-questioning may be a stage of creativity where practitioners intermittently stop in their creative tracks to question the way things are going, press the 'refresh' button, assess progress so far and look 'sideways' for other possible routes for progress. Or it might simply be a fundamental part of the creative attitude we have discussed in Chapter 2, the basis for divergent thinking and all the other features of that attitude. But either way, it appears to be a necessary component of an overall anatomy of creativity, and is mentioned, in many different forms, within many accounts of creative thinking. Self-questioning for creativity can come in many guises.

In his book *Black Swans*, Nassim Taleb (2007) explores our tendency to adhere too often to pre-established, fixed perspectives. Whilst adherents to any one perspective like to call their own views 'rational' or 'obvious' or 'common sense', there is often little or no hard and fast evidence for such views, or at least other possible views are just as rational, obvious or commonsensical. This fixity of perspective is one of our main, self-imposed barriers to creative thinking. It squeezes the world into the pre-set models, already established ways of thinking and mental reductions. We then become wedded to maintaining such views because we have invested our time, energy and perhaps reputation in them, such that we *actively choose* to avoid other possible sources of creative thinking. We all need some kind of initial frames of reference to make personal judgements – indeed, to mentally exist in an ever complex world. But if we over-refer to them, over-invest in them to the extent that we avoid other possible views, then such frames quickly become counter-productive. De-framing is as necessary for creativity as developing our initial creative attitude and 'logic'.

Following Gregory Bateson (1987), let's use the basic rules of spelling as a metaphor for understanding how framing can impact upon creativity. If I choose to write down the letter 'F', I have by that very act closed down my options for the next letter, because only certain letters can follow an 'F'. And if I choose next to write the letter 'R', then my choice for the third letter are even more limited. It is going to have to be a vowel, and there are only five of them to choose from! This is only a little game, but it shows something of how the frame within which we conceive creativity can close down options for our next move. Economists use the concept of *opportunity cost* to talk of how the very act of making an economic choice incurs the cost of therefore not being able to choose the alternative. You can only spend your money once, right? So the frame of reference given to us by the simple rules of spelling gives us a context in which to work. And other such frames can be good if they help to 'structure' creative thinking. But because we inevitably make a frame every time we make creative choices, we inevitably suffer from a kind of *creative opportunity cost*. So de-framing is also sometimes needed. Framing and de-framing stand in a delicate balance. For R. D. Laing (1999), our actions and thoughts are in part shaped by what we fail to notice. But moreover, because we fail to notice that we are failing to notice, there is little we can do to change this failure. For him, creativity is in part, counter-intuitively, located in noticing how this failure to notice limits our actions and thoughts. In this way he echoes the more specific points made by de Bono (1992) concerning lateral thinking as the locus of creativity. Richard Feynman (1999) echoes this too, when he discusses the difference between knowing the name for things and actually knowing those things in the real world. In their different ways, all these ideas refer to how established frames of reference can be self-limiting, and how finding ways to de-frame our thinking can be a spur to creativity.

Perhaps the best know example of de-framing is that discussed by Thomas Kuhn in his account of the structure of scientific revolutions (1970). If Kuhn's notion of a paradigm is an example of a frame of reference which shapes and colours the whole nexus of its adherents, then scientific 'revolutions' on the basis of a paradigm shift is an example of a broad de-framing. Although Kuhn's notion of paradigm shifts is sometimes less than clear because it has varying 'restricted' or 'expanded' meanings, we can still use the idea of de-framing for creative thinking within the movement from one paradigm to another. Kuhn's account hinges upon the way one paradigm (frame) is replaced by another more effective paradigm as its inner dynamic becomes discredited and it fails to adequately deal with anomalies through reference to its established inner 'logic'. Paradigms are not rejected when it appears that more work, what Kuhn calls 'normal science', within the established framework is needed. Rather, paradigms are rejected when it becomes apparent that it is the framework itself which is the problem, the barrier to new avenues of thinking, the thing which is preventing new *types* of questions being asked. Although not a point that Kuhn himself makes, we could take from this the idea that fixed frames of reference, fixed perspectives on the world, are always eventually going to be a barrier to creativity. Perhaps with something as potentially open as creativity, no one perspective should be adopted for any length of time beyond their practical, strategic usefulness. A more radical take on de-framing suggests that the absence of a frame or paradigm *per se* is a useful springboard for creativity. Taleb certainly adopts this view:

> By setting oneself totally free of constraints, free of thoughts, free of this debilitating activity called work, free of effort, elements hidden in the texture of reality start staring at you, then mysteries that you never thought existed emerge in front of your eye.
> (Taleb 2007. p. 47)

De-framing allows for the creative attitudes of innocence, play and release we have discussed in Chapter 2 to be part of creativity. Too much regular style, too much experience, too much judgement based upon the 'normal' ways of doing things risks creative dullness if it restricts the imagination. As we have already argued, innocence is the kind of creativity found in the imaginative play of children. Because they do not know the orthodox opinion, the common perception, the professional approach, they are free from inhibition to think whatever they want and so are often much more creative. Children know they are children, and so they know that they have a lot to learn. And so, they are often able to see much further than adults. As Antoine de Saint Exupery has the Little Prince say, 'Grownups never understand anything for themselves, and it is tiresome for children to be always and forever explaining things to them'. And as Edward de Bono puts it,

> Innocence is the classic creativity of children. If you do not know the usual approach, the usual solution, the usual concepts involved, then you may come up with a fresh

approach. Also, if you are not inhibited by knowing the constraints and knowing what cannot be done, then you are freer to suggest a novel approach.

(de Bono 1992. p. 38)

De-framing also fosters the more open divergent thinking or ideational fluency we discussed in Chapter 1 as part of the 'logic' of creativity. Convergent thinking, the opposite of divergent thinking, tends to be about working along set trams lines to arrive as efficiently as possible at the solution. Divergent thinking puts more value in imaginative wanderings and other playful explorations to take thinking beyond the claims of 'rationality' which we all tend to use to justify our own particular perspective on things. Divergent thinking starts with 'what if' types of questions, and a 'let's see what happens' outlook. It is more about *enjoying the journey* than seeking efficient arrival at any one particular 'answer'. This is another way of saying that creativity is often as much about the process of de-framing our views of the world as arriving at a conclusive outcome. For the philosopher Martin Heidegger, the real act of thinking begins only when we overcome the 'stiff-necked' nature of formal rationality. George Bernard Shaw has argued that people only 'think', in the truest sense of the word, very intermittently. He felt that his creative reputation came from the relatively simple act of finding truly de-framed ways of thinking slightly more often than that. So de-framing may be a necessary stage which creativity needs to go through to avoid the opportunity costs of retaining too strong an adherence to one view of the world. If creativity is recursive and iterative, if it often requires greater self-awareness and a reflective practice, then the constant checking of one frame of reference, the constant questioning of one's questions, will be a necessary component of any sustained creative effort.

And it is all of these facets which underpin the *constant movement* upon which creativity depends. There are many ideas which we could call upon to elucidate the necessity of movement of thought and action for the self-questioning at the heart of creativity, but they come with something of a health warning – they are metaphors. They should not be taken too literally, but rather applied to thinking about the details of one's own creative movement.

In 1828, Robert Brown first described *Brownian Motion* as the constant, random movements of particles suspended in a fluid medium. Brownian Motion is not propelled by movements of the fluid medium, but by the random collisions between the particles themselves. In scientific terms, Brownian Motion became a key concept for the burgeoning scientific study of molecules. But for us, it presents a metaphor with which to think about how creative thinking similarly brings its own internal random movement as discrete creative 'bits' swirl and collide given that they exist within the fluid medium of the creative life as a whole, if we are self-reflective enough to become aware of it. A creative Brownian Motion.

As we began to see in Chapter 1 with reference to the ideas of Krishnamurti, Eastern psychological philosophies such as Buddhism, Hinduism, Jainism and Daoism all share a focus on mindfulness, which encourages us to better understand our understandings and more consciously develop our development. As such, they all in their different ways articulate the benefits of overcoming mental fixations and embracing the ever changing movement which comes with self-questioning. Their focus upon movement asks us to accept that the only thing that stays constant is change, the only thing we can rely on is uncertainty. They ask us to overcome our desires for certainty, our attachments to (self-)illusions, our sense of aversion we tend to feel for the unknown and our consequent ignorance thereof. Dealing with the ever changing world with this spirit and allowing our creative self-questioning to gently move and change without fear or hostility can be seen as one of the simple pleasures of a creative life.

But the focus upon self-questioning can also help to appreciate more specific and 'tactical' movements to take us to where new creative avenues might lie. As we have discussed above, if the creative person is analogous to Stuart Kauffman's (1996) idea of the 'autonomous agent' – the biological organism adapting to the world – then the creative ecology we discussed in Chapter 3 is analogous to his idea of the 'biosphere' – the environment in which this happens. For Kauffman, life is so creative and fertile because autonomous agents respond to *adjacent possibles* offered by the biosphere. As we referred to in Chapter 4, understanding Kauffman's idea of the adjacent possible asks us to imagine a palace with an ever expanding number of connected rooms, each with several doors connecting to other such rooms. Being in the first room gives the possibility of movement into several different rooms next. Being in one of these second rooms allows new choices about the third set of adjacent possible rooms. Maybe room 2 was uninteresting, but it allowed the movement from room 1 to room 3, which contained stuff we were looking for. It also brings access to room 4, and that holds the promise of a choice of room 5. And connecting to possible choices offered by what is adjacent in itself means that further movement and choice opens up.

This adjacent possible metaphor suggests that creativity can come from opening unexpected doors so as to travel to other adjacent possible rooms of creativity. And if we see enough adjacent possibles, we have a palace of creativity. This metaphor also allows an overview of the whole palace beyond the particularities of each room, so articulating whole creative journeys of possible 'nexts'. As the Buddha is purported to have said, 'There are only two mistakes one can make along the road to truth; not going all the way, and not starting'. A dialectic of self-questioning to stimulate movement, and movement to allow for better (self-)questions, is central to this view of creativity. But questioning and movement need to be confined to an individual conception of creativity. As we discussed in Chapter 3, using relationships to help with navigation between and across different creative rooms is often a key source of creativity.

Collaboration and aggregation

Much of the above could be read as being an anatomy of individual creativity. But as we have been at pains to emphasize during the whole of this book, it is our strong belief that creativity is more firmly located within all the relationships we have been discussing. So it would be strange to say the least if we did not figure the notion of collaboration within our anatomy of creativity. Sawyer (2007) has offered us just such an anatomy, within which he identifies seven features of effective creative collaboration. These are:

- **Innovation emerges over time** – whilst no one person within a creative collaboration has the full picture, the aggregated creativity emerges as the dialogue of relationships grow and understanding ripples throughout the group. Time is often needed.
- **Successful collaborative teams practise deep listening** – a delicate balancing act between pursing one's own creative skills and agendas on the one hand, and listening

to what others in the group are saying and doing on the other is necessary. A dialectic of speaking and listening is central.

- **Teams build on their collaborators' ideas** – as each new idea within the group emerges from that very group, the more that every other member had to go on, to develop, to work with. Self-organizing groups develop their own creative synergy, as developments lead to ever newer developments.
- **Only afterwards does the meaning of each idea become clear** – each individual idea cannot, nor need not, be attributed to any one individual, and the aggregated process becomes something which can only be appreciated after it has made its progress. A 'logic' very similar to swarm intelligence is at work here.
- **Surprising questions emerge** – as the collaborative group develops its aggregated creativity, new creative avenues also emerge. De-framing, creative movement and lateral thinking are natural consequences of group creativity.
- **Innovation is efficient** – collaborative group creativity can be characterized by obliquity and serendipity, can take time and may result in creative 'dead ends'. But it has a self-organized sense of self-evaluation built into it, and often leads to greater innovations more efficiently due to this. It has testing inherent within it, because it is based upon relationships.
- **Innovations emerge from the bottom up** – collaborative group creativity is able to self-organize due to the actions and motivations of the very people engaged in it. As such, its creative 'logic' is inherently emergent and aggregated.

And for Sawyer, these effective features of collaborative group creativity are most present when the said group has the following features:

- a shared and recognized goal based around common problem-solving or solution-spotting agendas
- an ability for close and effective co-listening
- complete concentration
- an ability to blend creative egos, or at least overcome ego clashes
- a culture of equal and open participation by all
- a degree of familiarity across all the group members
- a culture of good, effective communication throughout the group
- an ability to move things forward towards elaborations and extensions
- an ability to think about things for the future as well as the present

Such features all tend to imply that creativity is focused upon the possible on the one hand, but also focused upon the new and innovative on the other. So as well as implying a constant dialectic between the creativity of the one individual, and that of their 'others', it also implies a dialectic between the present and the absent, and the value of movements *away from certainty towards uncertainty*, so as to enable things to make newer things more certain. This implies a movement away from the linear picture of the anatomy of creativity, one focused on stages like the one above, back towards the more dialectical conception which we laid out in detail within Chapter 1, and which we have been highlighting throughout the various chapters since then.

From his systems perspective on creativity, which situates it against broader contexts, Gardner (2011) not surprisingly brings those broad contextual features into his ideas concerning the anatomy of aggregated creativity. For him, the anatomy of creativity involves:

- **The subpersonal** – the neuroscientific, genetic and evolutionary features of our human existence which, whilst we might not be consciously aware of them, have an impact upon the nature, scale and scope of creativity
- **The personal** – the cognitive, conscious aspects of creativity of which the individual is fully aware, which forms the sustained part of their practice
- **The impersonal** – the impact of those contextual features beyond the specific creative person, which shape what gets created, what gets selected, what gets rejected or ignored, and sometimes determines how and why creative people do what they do
- **The multipersonal** – the institutional context within which creativity resides

For Gardner, 'The full-blown study of creativity can best proceed . . . through examination of creative phenomena for multiple perspectives of the neurobiologist, the psychologist, the domain expert, and the sociologically oriented student of the field' (Gardner 2011. p. 36).

Strange shapes, and back to dialectics

We first explored the dialectical conception of creativity in Chapter 1, and suggested that it lies in understanding how different, contradictory aspects of creativity interpenetrate each other to give it its movement and flux. This gives us a picture of creativity which is more circular. Before we explore this in fine detail, let's continue thinking about some other strange metaphorical shapes, because they will help to take us to the quite complex, rather counter-intuitive nature of dialectics in a gentle way.

For Ilya Prigogine (1984), *dissipative structures* are dynamic systems which constantly veer away from internal equilibrium, but which nevertheless maintain structured integrity over time. They 'stay the same' all the time that they are changing, and constantly change so as to stay the same! The human body is a dissipative structure – as cells divide and/or replace themselves on the basis of resources taken in from the outside world, the body is constantly becoming something made out of wholly new 'stuff'. But at the same time, it self-organizes to maintain its structural integrity and sustained 'identity'. For Prigogine, such dissipative structures are a defining feature of the natural world and are to be found everywhere. Within the context of our consideration of the anatomy of creativity in general, and the question of creative movement in particular, dissipative structures are a great metaphor. It helps us to think about how creativity is constantly changing whilst remaining focused, constantly innovating whilst remaining 'on target'. Points of creative choice and decision, what Prigogine would call *bifurcation*, within dissipative creative structures help to explain the process of constant change within a regular creative practice over time.

But this also shows that there is a dialectical interplay between regularity and change, between experience and disorientation, between the creative self and the relationships we have with others, and all the other points of creative contradictions we have looked at so far, within dissipative structures. And the way that dissipative structures go through their own internal dynamic is also best understood as a dialectical process of flux – inner change within regularity creates new dynamic processes which emerge out of the inner dynamics of previous incarnations, which in turn lead to ever new interrelationships between new phases of regularity and change.

This is all potentially confusing. It is very counter-intuitive, especially for people of a Western background, to accept that we can understand things in terms of what they are not, in terms of the opposite. Perhaps a less abstract metaphor will help us to pin down the dialectical conception of creativity a little more. The musical idea of *counterpoint* refers to the way sounds can form pleasing contrasts, create mutually informative relationships or otherwise become 'harmonious' when placed next to other sounds, even though each one is rhythmically independent. Counterpoint forms a dynamic context for each component to have its own place whilst simultaneously encouraging the emergence of novel combinations within the mutual space as a whole. Each sound has its own identity, but this is in part created by its relationships to what it is not, the other sounds, which combines to form a whole which is greater than the sum of its parts. Counterpoint as used in music is a form of synergy and as such is analogous to more abstract ideas about the dialectical conception of creativity we are developing here. Independent 'bits' of creativity often find their location, their meaning and their (dis)harmony when they get to play against other independent 'bits'. 'Bit' A helps 'bit' B to come to life, just as 'bit' B is returning the favour. Creative thinking often comes from the colliding mergers of the independent and interdependent 'bits' within a broader moving whole, and it is this whole which in part allows the novel idea or insight to emerge out of its own internal interplay with its opposites. Musical counterpoint speaks of interesting contrasts even though each musical act has its own rhythm or logic. Think of how imagery and music play across each other in a film. But sometimes counterpoint can be a much broader thing played out across different types of creative trajectory, relationships, place, medias and contexts. Creativity stands in, moves through and emerges out of dialectical interrelationships across all these locations.

Another interesting metaphor for discussing another facet of the anatomy of creativity is found in the notion of *fractals*. This refers to the way natural structures are often self-repeating across the different scales at which we can look at them. Zoom in from the branches of the tree to the twigs on the branch, to the leaves of the twig, to the veins in the leaf – and you see the same shapes and structures. Zoom out from the pebbles on the tide's edge, to the rocks along the beach, to the headlands and bays along the coast line, to the shape of the whole island – and you will see the same shapes. *Fractality* involves the idea of *self-affinity*, an idea which describes how systems refer to and repeat broad patterns at the levels of fine detail. Such self-affinity is often a feature of creative thinking, and fractality is a useful metaphor with which to grasp interrelationships between different levels of creativity, whilst still seeing the overall pattern or structure. As well as being a dissipative structure, or perhaps because of being a dissipative structure, creativity is also fractal. It tends to have a similar impetus, similar inner patterns, shapes and dynamics regardless of what level of detail one looks at it from. The broad scale trajectories will inform the fine detail, and vice versa.

> Visual arts: Most computer-generated objects are now based on some version of the Mandelbrotian fractal. We can also see fractals in architecture, paintings, and many works of visual art – of course, not consciously incorporated by the work's creator.
>
> Music: Slowly hum the four-note opening of Beethoven's Fifth Symphony: ta-ta-ta-ta. Then replace each note with the same four-note opening, so that you end up with a measure of sixteen notes. You will see (or, rather, hear) that each smaller wave resembles the original larger one. Bach and Mahler, for instance, wrote sub movements that resemble the larger movement of which they are part.

Poetry: Emily Dickinson's poetry, for instance, is fractal: the large resembles the small. It has, according to a commentator, 'a consciously made assemblage of fictions, metres, rhetorics, gestures, and tones'.

(Taleb 2010. p. 82)

The creativity of the individual person stands in dialectical relationships to others, with their place, with their media and with broader contexts. Their creativity will in part be expressed within these other sites, and at the same time the impacts of these other sites will be expressed within the creativity of each person. As we have seen, Bohm sees scientific creativity as a 'puzzle-solving' activity which is ultimately motivated by the enjoyment we get from the feeling of discovering something new and stepping into the unknown, even if it is only new and unknown to us. We seem to value the feeling of contributing to the greater understanding of something. Many philosophers have connected this to a felt need to express our innate qualities through an engagement with the world, to express our ability to become more than we currently are, to become part of something bigger than our current self. We seem to place great value upon such connections between the self and the world because we experience ourselves more fully if we demonstrate a 'oneness' with the world in these ways. This seems to involve an inevitable self-reflection, and therefore greater self-awareness through these aspects of a creative life. And for Bohm, it is through such behaviour, which navigates across the dialectic of our self and the world beyond, that we become part of what he calls the *Implicate Order* – an ever moving but recurring expression of Nature which we find within ourselves and our place within it.

And these moving dialectical interplays between creative 'structures' and inner processes suggested by the metaphors of dissipative structures and fractality, by the myriad interplays between the creative self and the world of other people, places, media and broad contexts, are mirrored within more detailed stages of creativity. For instance, within the elaboration/extension and enlargement/generalization stages, there is often a strange, two-way interrelationship between creative problems stimulated by illumination and creative solutions deemed to be satisfactory by the generalization stage. The orthodox view of the relationship between problems and solutions tends to see the linear picture – we have a problem and we look for a solution. But just as often creativity lies in spotting a pre-existing 'solution' looking for a problem, such that the 'solution-ness' is only made apparent when the problem is added to the particular mix. The dialectical nature of this facet of the anatomy of creativity is also seen when the existence of the solution gives the problem its 'problem-ness', when we become aware things could be done better, more creatively. The world of technology calls the creativity of putting pre-existing solutions next to problems the discovery of 'killer app(lication)s'. But for our purposes, we can see the relationships between problems and solutions as a kind of case-study of the broader notion of the circular, ever moving dialectical shape of creativity. The businessman Paul Rand has described how he starts with a problem, and then forgets that problem, so that the problem can better reveal itself. For him this leads to solutions and the possibilities of re-evaluations also revealing themselves. For the artist Piet Hein, art is akin to solving problems that cannot be grasped until the emergent solutions start to become apparent. The way he shapes his 'questions' are simultaneously part of his 'answers'. Within the anatomy of creativity, questions and answers, problems and solutions, also stand in a dialectical relationship.

Western philosophy has routinely progressed through its *analytical spirit* which seeks to understand things by breaking them down into their constituent parts. Since the dawn of time, material production has proceeded through *subtractive production*, producing what it needed by breaking things away from their original location – digging stuff out of the ground, chopping down forests to use trees as wood, cutting out and reusing pieces of metal. Creativity of all sorts has been about subtracting things one from another, eliminating certain aspects and reusing others in different combinations. The economist Joseph Schumpeter famously coined the term *creative destruction* to describe the necessity of breaking apart or breaking away from the equilibrium so as to find innovation.

But we have entered a new phase of *additive production*, characterized by adding things together into new creative syntheses. Bio-tech creativity joins together new combinations of the biological and the technological. 3-D printing is a new industrial technique which works by adding together successive layers rather than cutting out wood, stone or metals. The technological hardware of this new additive phase produces and is simultaneously produced by a new *additive attitude* which seeks creativity in new ways of joining things together.

This kind of creativity seeks to move across what were previously seen as boundaries, in search of news types of addition. It seeks new ways of bringing together what were previously seen as opposite. So the anatomy of this additive attitude is increasingly characterized by recognizing the interpenetration of opposites as a way of finding its inner drive, movement and 'logic'. A dialectical conception is at the heart of its inner dynamic. In Chapter 1 we confessed that, when we ask the question 'What is creativity?', we quickly come to realize that a better question was 'Where is creativity?' because it clearly resides in the interplays between the many places we have discussed – the individual creative person; the relationships they have with others; the places they exist within; the media and technologies they use; and the broad social, economic and historical contexts they exist within. And we argued that when we approached the question of creativity in this way, we saw that a dialectical conception was a better approach, because it promised a way of developing a 'moving picture' of creativity, one which shows all of its ever changing and complex nature. Let's remind ourselves of the many dialectic relationships found within creativity which we suggested in Chapter 1:

- **Your brain and you** – the way your brain functions to take in information whilst simultaneously reflecting back upon its own brain-ness. This process selects certain ideas and information in terms of what is important to this thing you call 'You'. Being aware of this selection process is a good way of getting better at doing it. Being good at creativity entails being good at self-awareness.
- **You and others** – the way this thing called 'You' – your personality, experiences, motivations and skills – are shaped by the relationships you have with everything that is 'Not-You', that is everyone else. And then the way this 'Not-You' of everyone you meet is shaped in turn by their experiences of you. 'You' *are* 'Not-You', and 'Not-You' *is* 'You'. Being good at creativity often entails being good at relationships.
- **Now and the past** – the way that you are working on 'Now' is the culmination of a long series of 'Not-Now' events from your past, which have formed your current perceptions of 'Now'. The present is a culmination of the past, and your sense of creativity for the future is made from the idea you have of the present. Being good at creativity entails being good at the history of you and your creativity.
- **What you do and what you don't do** – the way you define what your creativity 'does' against ideas of what you 'don't do'. The 'presence' of your creativity is made

up partly from what you have decided should be 'absent'. Connecting the interplays between these 'presences' to 'absences' is what sometimes makes new bits of creativity move. Being good at creativity sometimes entails knowing about what you 'don't do', so that you can then 'do it'.

- **Your imagination and the real world** – the way your inner, subjective experiences are shaped by the objective social, political and economic realities of the World, which you then in turn shape to imagine other possible Worlds, and so seek to change things. The 'outer' shapes the 'inner', so that the 'inner' can then seek to re-shape the 'outer'. Being good at creativity often entails being good at thinking about 'what is' so as to think about 'what ought to be'.

- **Working and not-working** – the way creativity involves researching, thinking and planning something so that you can forget about it, go for a walk, do something else, get drunk, so that you can arrive at a solution without appearing to have thought about it. Many creative people report that the flash of inspiration comes when they are relaxed, comfortable, taking time away from work. Being good at creative work often entails taking a bath.

- **Person and city** – the way that creative people and groups have shaped cities, and indeed for some the way they have actually created city life, just as the greater social contact offered by cities have shaped the work of creative people and groups. Being good at creativity often entails going 'into town'.

- **Person and culture** – the way the creative individual generates new ideas which impact upon the broader culture, just as the broader culture shapes what 'counts' as creativity, selects which bits are to be celebrated and decides how the creative individual is doing in terms of cultural 'success'. Being good at creativity often entails finding happy compromises between what *you* want and what *they* want.

- **Focused action and relaxed semi-action** – the way in which creative focus often comes from a period of relaxed semi-action, just as the relaxed semi-action stimulates the creative person into focused action. Being good at creativity often entails knowing when it is 'not working' and when to do something else. It is important that this is actually 'something' else, to keep your mind active but not too focused. Doing nothing at all doesn't seem to work so well.

- **Worldliness and naivety** – the way a smart creative interaction with the world often stems from asking fairly naïve and childlike questions, just as that very naivety spurs the creative person to develop more insightful questions. Being good at creativity often entails choosing the right question at the right time within the lifetime of the project, as it emerges out of itself.

- **Complexity and simplicity** – the way creativity requires drawing together multiple, often competing, sometimes contradictory ideas so they can be corralled into more simple statements, just as blindingly simple statements, images and designs can then sometimes convey a whole world of complexity and nuance. Being good at creativity often entails being good at navigation between 'levels' of meaning.

- **Deliberate and non-deliberate** – the way that deliberately 'paying attention' is often supplemented by more unconscious or playful spheres of non-attention, just as these attentions can then become re-forgotten and 'embodied' parts of creative flow. Being good at creativity often entails skilful navigation between non-deliberate remembering and deliberate forgetting.

- **Continuous and discontinuous** – the way that creative processes carried out in a continuous way are often refreshed by a break, just as the break carries within it the new creative insights developed through our daily concerted efforts. Being good at creativity often entails mixing a holiday from work with a working holiday.
- **Goal-defined and non-goal-defined** – the way that the attention paid to specific things for specific reasons to achieve a specific goal is sometimes informed by those more open-ended activities we engage in for no specific thing, reason or goal, just as the non-goal oriented thoughts are given a creative 'home' by goal-specific needs. Being good at creativity often entails not trying too hard, so that we can try hard.
- **Discipline and playfulness** – the way creative processes require the shelving of play if it is to come to full fruition, just as that very playfulness is the wellspring of the fruitful thing to be disciplined about. Being good at creativity often entails being a grown-up child, or a childlike adult.
- **Extroversion and introversion** – the way many creative people exhibit an extrovert eagerness to engage with the world by overcoming a nervous shyness about their work, just as that shy introversion gives them time and space to develop better articulations of their creative self to the outside world. Being good at creativity often entails choosing the right identity for the right occasion.
- **Pride and humility** – the way creative people exhibit a proud declaration about their achievements, which itself emanates from a humble recognition that they are building upon the work of others and can never really fulfil their dreams for their ambitions. Being good at creativity often entails knowing when to shout and when to be quiet.
- **Tradition and rebellion** – the way that creative traditions can give location to work and educate us into themes and techniques, just as we challenge and push these 'locations' to shine light on new directions and possibilities. Being good at creativity often entails finding a good balance between learning one's craft from previous masters and challenging their authority.
- **Objectivity and passion** – the way that one's creativity requires an objective sense of what will and will not work, just as that very work flows from an innate passion for something that you put your heart and soul into, and will defend to the end, come what may. Being good at creativity often entails working to create your 'creative baby' so as to let it die away, to be reborn at another time.
- **Difficult tensions and great pleasures** – the way that grappling with the tensions, sufferings and difficulties of creativity gives us great pleasure, just as those pleasures remind us of the great tensions to come. Being good at creativity often entails accepting the pain because we know of the great joy to come.

There are no doubt lots of other interpenetrating opposites that form the dialectical flux of creativity, but the point is made: a dialectical conception adds immeasurably to anatomy, and overcomes the potential shortcomings of the rather mechanical picture offered by the linear account of stages.

In this final chapter, we have tried to suggest some ideas which might be useful for a systematic account of creativity which lays out some of its stages, so that perhaps we can start to see something of an anatomy of creativity. But as we said at the start of this endeavour, we did so with some hesitancy because we do not accept that creativity happens in this linear, mechanical, stage-based way. Throughout this chapter, indeed throughout this book, we have addressed the underlying question of situating creativity, and this has entailed that we take one thing at a time. Most books do! But we are convinced that the reality of things, most things and certainly creativity, is much more a case of intimately intertwined factors which are constantly exerting a mutual impact upon each other. On the one hand, we have in this chapter suggested that creativity goes through the stages of *preparation; digestion; incubation; illumination; elaboration and extension; testing and dissemination; recursive iterations; enlargement and generalization;* and *self-questioning, de-framing and movement,* all of which implies that it has a linear shape and that different facets of creativity are to be found within each of the 'stages' along this line. We think there is some merit to this view. On the other hand, however, we have suggested, through reference to the metaphors of *Brownian Motion, adjacent possibles, dissipative structures, fractality* and the *Implicate Order,* that creativity has a more circular shape with myriad moving interrelationships, feedback loops, levels of iteration and repeating patterns within it. We think this circular picture also holds some veracity and is useful in a different way, because it draws our attention to the value of thinking about creativity through the lens of a dialectical logic, so as to bring out its inherently complex, emergent and ever moving character.

Throughout the book as a whole we have explored ideas concerning the creative person in some detail; we have explored a more social conception of creativity premised on the view that all individuals exist within interrelationships which shape creativity; we have suggested that those interrelationships also exist within specific places which have their own particular effects; that the new media landscape has opened up even newer ways of interacting and being influenced by the world beyond the creative subject itself; and, most broadly of all, that interrelationships with social, political, economic and cultural contexts also shape what creativity is and how it is received. We have tried to explore all these features in a way which outlines some of the key debates, but is also cognizant of the dialectical spirit. The linear conception of the anatomy of creativity discussed at length in this chapter notwithstanding, we ultimately see this dialectical conception of creativity as more persuasive, because it draws out attention to the myriad interplays, the mutually impactful interrelationships between all the facets we have discussed. And as such it allows us to recognize that the true nature of creativity lies in the spaces – mental, social, spatial, technological and economic – between rather than within any particular location. In the end, our answer to the question 'Where is creativity' is just that: it is in the interactions between us all, and within the structures which we both make and occupy together.

In the end, we are happy to repeat Howard Becker – if psychology is the study of what people do, and sociology is the study of what people do together, then the study of creativity is about what people do better together, for each other, to make their world, the world of others, our common world anew. It does not reside just in our individual heads, brains, minds or personalities. These factors are obviously involved. But the true essence of creativity lies in two-way, mutually impactful relationships which everyone and everything has with everyone and everything around them. The true essence of creativity is dialectical.

References

Ackroyd, P. (2001) *London: The Biography*. London: Vintage.

Augé, M. (2008) *Non-Places*. London: Verso.

Bakhtin, M. (1981) *The Dialogical Imagination*. Austin: University of Texas Press.

Balfiore, E. (2009) On Bullshit in Cultural Policy Practice and Research: Notes from the British Case. *International Journal of Cultural Policy*. Vol. 15: Issue 3, pp. 343–59.

Balfiore, E. (2012) Defensive Instrumentalism and the Legacy of New Labour's Cultural Policies. *Cultural Trends*. Vol. 21: Issue 2, pp. 103–11.

Bateson, G. (1987) *Steps to an Ecology of Mind*. London: Aronson.

Beck, U. (2000) *The Risk Society and beyond: Critical Issues for Social Theory*. London: Sage.

Begley, S. (2009) *The Plastic Mind: New Science Reveals Our Extraordinary Potential to Transform Our Lives*. London: Constable.

Benkler, Y. (2006) *The Wealth of Networks: How Social Production Transforms Markets and Freedoms*. New Haven and London: Yale University Press.

Bennett, T. and Mercer, C. (1998) *Improving Research and International Cooperation for Cultural Policy*. Paris: UNESCO. Authors' own copy. Available at http://citeseerx.ist.psu.edu/viewdoc/summary?doi= 10.1.1.127.2707.

Berger, P. L. and Luckmann, T. (1967) *The Social Construction of Reality: A Treatise in the Sociology of Knowledge*. Harmondsworth: Penguin.

Bey, H. (2003) *TAZ: The Temporary Autonomous Zone, Ontological Anarchy, Poetic Terrorism*. New York: Autonomedia.

Boden, M. (1990) *The Creative Mind: Myths and Mechanisms*. London: Weidenfeld and Nicholson.

Bohm, D. (1998) *On Creativity*. London: Routledge.

Braverman, H. (1974) *Labour and Monopoly Capital: The Degradation of Work in the Twentieth Century*. New York: Monthly Review Press.

Brookes, D. (2011) *The Social Animal: A Story of How Success Happens*. London: Short Books.

Buber, M. (1992) *On Inter-subjectivity and Cultural Creativity*. Chicago: University of Chicago Press.

Buber, M. (2004) *I and Thou*. London: Continuum.

Calvino, I. (2002) *Invisible Cities*. London: Vintage.

Carey, J. (2006) *What Good Are the Arts?* London: Faber.

Chesborough, H. (2008) *Open Innovation: Researching a New Paradigm*. Oxford: Oxford University Press.

Coyle, D. and Quah, D. (2005) *Getting the Measure of the New Economy*. In The Creative Industries by John Hartley (ed.). Oxford: Blackwell.

Cropley, A. J. (1972) *S-R Psychology and Cognitive Psychology*. In Creativity by P. E. Vernon (ed.). London: Penguin.

Csíkszentmihályi, M. (1990) *Flow: The Psychology of Optimal Experience*. New York: Harper Perennial.

Csíkszentmihályi, M. (1996) *Creativity: Flow and the Psychology of Discovery and Invention*. New York: Harper Collins.

Csíkszentmihályi, M. (1997) *Finding Flow: The Psychology of Engagements with Everyday Life*. London: Basic Books.

Curry, M. (2013) *Daily Rituals: How Great Minds Make Time, Find Inspiration and Get to Work*. London: Picador.

D'Amasio, A. (2012) *Self Comes to Mind: Constructing the Conscious Brain*. London: Vintage.

Dawkins, R. (1989) *The Selfish Gene*. Oxford: Oxford University Press.

de Bono, E. (1992) *Serious Creativity: Using the Power of Lateral Thinking to Create New Ideas*. London: Harper Collins.

de Guy, Paul. (2002) *Cultural Economy: Cultural Analysis and Commercial Life*. London: Sage.

Dennett, D. (1993) *Consciousness Explained*. London: Penguin.

Dissanayake, E. (1995) *Homo Aestheticus: Where Art Comes from and Why*. London: University of Washington Press.

Eco, U. (1989) *The Open Work*. Cambridge, MA: Harvard University Press.

Elias, N. (1965) *The Established and the Outsider: A Sociological Enquiry into Community Problems*. London: Cass.

Ellis, M. (2004) *The Coffee-House: A Cultural History*. London: Phoenix.

Feyerabend, P. (1993) *Against Method*. London: Verso.

Feynman, R. (1999) *The Pleasure of Findings Things Out: The Best Short Works of Richard Feynman*. New York: Basic Books.

Flew, T. (2005) *The Cultural Economy*. In The Creative Industries by John Hartley (ed.). Oxford: Blackwell.

Frazer, J. G. (1998) *The Golden Bough: A Study in Magic and Religion*. Oxford: Oxford University Press.

Freud, S. (1972) *Creative Writers and Day-dreaming*. In Creativity by P. E. Vernon (ed.). London: Penguin.

Freud, S. (1986) *On Creativity and the Unconsciousness: The Psychology of Art, Literature, Love and Religion*. New York: Harper Perennial.

Freud, S. (1991) *Group Psychology and the Analysis of the Ego: Civilization, Society and Religion*. London: Penguin.

Fromm, E. (1976) *To Have or to Be*. London: Continuum.

Garcia, D. et al. (2007) *(Un)Common Ground: Creative Encounters across Sectors and Disciplines*. Amsterdam: BIS Publishers.

Gardner, H. (1985) *The Mind's New Science: A History of the Cognitive Revolution*. New York: Basic Books.

Gardner, H. (2011) *Creating Minds: An Anatomy of Creativity Seen through the Lives of Freud, Einstein, Picasso, Stravinsky, Eliot, Graham and Gandhi*. New York: Basic Books.

Gell, A. (1998) *Art and Agency: An Anthropological Theory*. Oxford: Oxford University Press.

Gibson, L. (2002) Creative Industries and Cultural Development: Still a Janus Face? *Media International Australia Incorporating Cultural Policy*. Vol. 102, pp. 25–34.

Giddens, A. (1991) *Modernity and Self-Identity: Self and Society in the Late Modern Age*. Cambridge: Polity Press.

Gladwell, M. (2008) *Outliers: The Story of Success*. New York: Little Brown and Company.

Goffman, E. (1971) *Presentation of the Self in Everyday Life*. Harmondsworth: Penguin.

Goldmann, L. (1973) *The Philosophy of the Enlightenment*. London: Routledge and Kegan Paul.

Gorz, A. (1982) *Farewell to the Working Class: Essays on Post-Industrial Socialism*. London: Pluto Press.

Gorz, A. (1983) *Ecology as Politics*. London: Verso.

Gould, S. J. (2002) *The Structure of Evolutionary Theory*. London: Belknap Press.

Gray, C. (2007) Commodification and Instrumentality in Cultural Policy. *International Journal of Cultural Policy*. Vol. 13: Issue 2, pp. 203–15.

Gray, C. and Malins, J. (2007) *Visualizing Research: A Guide to the Research Process in Art and Design*. London: Ashgate.

Hall, P. (1991) *Cities in Civilization: Culture, Innovation and the Urban Order*. London: Phoenix Giant.

Harth, E. (1995) *The Creative Loop: How the Brain Makes a Mind*. London: Penguin.

Hartley, J. (ed.). (2005) *The Creative Industries*. Oxford: Blackwell.

Hesmondhalgh, D. and Baker, S. (2010) *Creative Labour: Media Work in Three Cultural Industries*. London: Routledge.

Holden, J. (2006) *Cultural Value and the Crisis of Legitimacy*. Author's own copy. Available at www.demos. co.uk/publications.

Hyde, L. (2006) *The Gift: How the Creative Spirit Transforms the World*. London: McMillan.

Illich, I. (1973) *Tools for Conviviality*. London: Harper Collins.

Illich, I. (1976) *Celebration of Awareness: A Call for Institutional Reform*. Harmondsworth: Penguin.

Illich, I. (1981) *Shadow Work*. London: Boyars.

Janis, I. L. (1982) *Groupthink: Psychological Studies of Policy Decisions and Fiascos*. Boston: Houghton Mifflin.

Janovich, L. (2011) Great Art for Everyone: Engagement and Participation Policy in the Arts. *Cultural Trends*. Vol. 20: Issue 3–4, pp. 271–9.

Johnson, S. (2002) *Emergence: The Connected Lives of Ants, Brains and Cities*. London: Penguin.

Johnson, S. (2010) *Where Good Ideas Come From: A Natural History of Innovation*. London: Allen Lane.

Kane, P. (2005) *The Play Ethic: A Manifesto for a Different Way of Living*. London: Pan Books.

Kauffman, S. (1996) *At Home in the Universe: The Search for Laws of Self-organization and Complexity*. London: Penguin.

Kay, J. (2011) *Obliquity: Why Our Goals Are Best Achieved Indirectly*. London: Profile Books.

Koestler, A. (1989) *The Act of Creation*. London: Arkana.

Krishnamurti, J. (1996) *Total Freedom: The Essential Krishnamurti*. San Francisco: Harper.

Kuhn, T. (1970) *The Structure of Scientific Revolutions*. Chicago: University of Chicago Press.

Laing, R. D. (1967) *The Politics of Experience and the Bird of Paradise*. Harmondsworth: Penguin.

Laing, R. D. (1997) *Knots*. London: Routledge.

Laing, R. D. (1999) *Self and Others*. London: Routledge.

Landry, C. (2000) *The Creative City: A Toolkit for Urban Innovators*. London: Earthscan.

Leadbeater, C. (2008) *We-Think: Mass Innovation Not Mass Production*. London: Profile Books.

Lehrer, J. (2007) *Proust Was a Neuroscientist*. London: Canongate.

Lessig, L. (2002) *The Future of Ideas: The Fate of the Commons in a Connected World*. New York: Vintage Books.

Lessig, L. (2004) *Free Culture: The Nature and Future of Creativity*. New York: Penguin.

Lovelock, J. (1995) *Gaia: A New Look at Life on Earth*. London: Nature Publishing Group.

Lovnik, G. (2004) *Uncanny Networks: Dialogue with the Virtual Intelligentsia*. London: MIT Press.

Lukes, S. (2005) *Power: A Radical View*. New York: Palgrave McMillan.

Lunenfeld, P. (2000) *The Digital Dialectic: New Essays on New Media*. London: MIT Press.

Lynch, K. (1960) *The Image of the City*. Cambridge, MA: MIT Press.

Marcuse, H. (1964) *One Dimensional Man: Studies in the Ideology of Advanced Industrial Societies*. London: Routledge and Kegan Paul.

Marcuse, H. (1969) *An Essay on Liberation*. Boston: Beacon Press.

Margulis, L. (1992) *Environmental Evolution: Effects of the Origin and Evolution of Life on Planet Earth*. London: MIT Press.

Mauss, M. (2002) *The Gift: The Forms and Reasons for Exchange in Archaic Societies*. London: Routledge.

McIntosh, A. (2001) *Soil and Soul: People Versus Corporate Power*. London: Aurum.

Mercer, C. (2002) *Towards Cultural Citizenship: Tools for Cultural Policy and Development*. Stockholm: Girlunds Forlag.

Merton, R. (1952) Bureaucratic Structure and Personality. In *Reader in Bureaucracy*. R. Merton et al. (eds.). London: Collier MacMillan.

Miller, P. (2010) *Smart Swarm: Using Animal Behaviour to Change Our World*. London: Collins.

Mlodinow, L. (2008) *The Drunkard's Walk: How Randomness Rules Our Lives*. London: Allen Lane.

Moore, H. (18th August 1937) The Sculptor Speaks. *Listener Magazine*, pp. 338–40.

Mumford, L. (1966) *The City in History: Its Origins, Its Transformations and Its Prospects*. Harmondsworth: Penguin.

Nussbaum, M. (2011) *Creating Capabilities: The Human Development Approach*. Cambridge, MA: Belknap Press.

Ormerod, P. (1998) *Butterfly Economics: A New General Theory of Social and Economic Behaviour*. London: Faber and Faber.

Penrose, R. (2005) *Shadows of the Mind: A Search for the Missing Science of Consciousness*. London: Vintage Books.

Perelman, M. (2000) *Transcending the Economy: On the Potential of Passionate Labour and the Waste of the Market*. London: MacMillan.

Policastro, P. and Gardner, H. (1999) From Case Studies to Robust Generalization. In *Handbook of Creativity* by R. J. Sternberg (ed.). London: Cambridge University Press.

Popper, K. (2002) *The Logic of Scientific Discovery*. London: Routledge.

Prigogine, I. (1984) *Order Out of Chaos: Man's New Dialogue with Nature*. London: Heinemann.

Putnam, R. (2000) *Bowling Alone: The Collapse and Revival of American Community*. London: Simon and Schuster.

Roethlisberger, F. L. and Dickson, W. J. (2003) *Management and the Worker*. London: Routledge.

Rogers, C. (1978) *Towards a Theory of Creativity*. In *Creativity*. P. E. Vernon (ed.). Harmondsworth: Penguin.

Rogers, C. (1980) *A Way of Being*. Boston: Houghton Mifflin.

Roszak, T. (1981) *Person/Planet: The Creative Destruction of Industrial Society*. London: Granada.

Roszak, T. (1986) *The Cult of Information: The Folklore of Computers and the True Art of Thinking*. Cambridge: Lutterworth Press.

Russell, B. (1960). *In Praise of Idleness and Other Essays*. London: Unwin Books.

Russell, B. (1961) *The History of Western Philosophy*. London: Allen and Unwin.

Sawyer, K. (2007) *Group Genius: The Creative Power of Collaboration*. London: Basic Books.

Sen, A. (1999) *Development as Freedom*. Oxford: Oxford University Press.

Sen, A. (2009) *The Idea of Justice*. London: Harvard University Press.

Sennett, R. (2008) *The Craftsman*. London: Penguin.

Sennett, R. (2013) *Together: The Rituals, Pleasures and Politics of Cooperation*. London: Penguin.

Shirky, C. (2010) *Cognitive Surplus: Creativity and Generosity in a Connected Age*. London: Penguin.

Shorthose, J. (2004a) The Engineered and the Vernacular in Cultural Quarter Development. *Capital and Class*. Vol. 84, pp. 159–78.

Shorthose, J. (2004b) Accounting for Independent Creativity in the New Cultural Economy. *Media International Australia Incorporating Culture and Policy*. Vol. 112, pp. 150–61.

Shorthose, J. (2005). Nottingham's de facto Cultural Quarter: The Lace Market, Independents and a Convivial Ecology. In *Cities of Quarters: Urban Villages in the Contemporary City*. M. Jayne (ed.). London: Ashgate.

Shorthose, J. (2011) Economic Conscience and Public Discourse. *Capital and Class*. Vol. 35: Issue 1, pp. 107–24.

Shorthose, J. and Maycroft, N. (2011) *Understanding Creative Business: Values, Networks and Innovation*. London: Gower.

Shorthose, J. and Strange, G. (2004) The New Cultural Economy, the Artist and the Social Configuration of Autonomy. *Capital and Class*. Vol. 84, pp. 43–59.

Sinclair, I. (2002) *London Orbital*. London: Penguin.

Sinclair, I. (2003) *Lights Out for the Territory*. London: Penguin.

Smith, S., Ward, B. T. and Finke, B. (eds.). (1995) *The Creative Cognition Approach*. Cambridge, MA: MIT Press.

Solnit, R. (2002) *Wanderlust: A History of Walking*. London: Verso.

Spowers, R. (2003) *Rising Tides: A History of Environmentalism*. London: Canongate Books.

Sternberg, R. J. (ed.). (1999) *Handbook of Creativity*. Cambridge: Cambridge University Press.

Taleb, N. (2007) *Black Swans: The Impact of the Highly Improbable*. London: Penguin.

Taleb, N. (2010) *The Bed of Procrustes: Philosophical and Practical Aphorisms*. Harvard: Harvard University Press.

Tallis, R. (2011) *Aping Mankind: Neuromania, Darwinitis and the Misrepresentation of Humanity*. Durham: Acumen Publishing.

Tusa, J. (2003) *On Creativity: Interviews Exploring the Process*. London: Methuen.

Veblen, T. (1994) *Theory of the Leisure Classes*. New York: Dover Publications.

von Hippel, E. (2006) *Democratizing Innovation*. London: MIT Press.

Wallace, A. R. (1901) *Darwinism: An Exposition of the Theory of Natural Selection, with Some of Its Applications*. London: MacMillan and Co.

Wallas, G. (1972) *The Art of Thought*. In Creativity by P. E. Vernon (ed.). London: Penguin Books.

The Warwick Commission (2015) *Enriching Britain: Culture, Creativity and Growth*. The Report by the Warwick Commission on the Future of Cultural Value: The University of Warwick.

Weber, M. (1975) *Economy and Society: An Outline of Interpretative Society*. G. Roth and C. Wittich (eds.). Berkley: University of California Press.

Young, J. W. (1965) *A Technique for Producing New Ideas*. New York: McGraw Hill.

Zohar, D. and Marshall, I. (1994) *Quantum Society: Mind, Physics and a New Social Vision*. London: Bloomsbury.

Index

For Product Safety Concerns and Information please contact our EU
representative GPSR@taylorandfrancis.com Taylor & Francis Verlag GmbH,
Kaufingerstraße 24, 80331 München, Germany

Printed and bound by CPI Group (UK) Ltd, Croydon, CR0 4YY

01/05/2025

01858385-0002